Democracy in the Making

Recent Titles in
Oxford Studies In Culture And Politics

Clifford Bob and James M. Jasper, General Editors

Fire in the Heart:
How White Activists Embrace Racial Justice
Mark R. Warren

Nonviolent Revolutions
Civil Resistance in the Late 20th Century
Sharon Erickson Nepstad

Ethnic Boundary Making
Institutions, Power, Networks
Andreas Wimmer

Women in War
The Micro-processes of Mobilization in El Salvador
Jocelyn Viterna

DEMOCRACY IN THE MAKING

How Activist Groups Form

Kathleen M. Blee

OXFORD
UNIVERSITY PRESS

OXFORD
UNIVERSITY PRESS

Oxford University Press is a department of the University of Oxford.
It furthers the University's objective of excellence in research, scholarship,
and education by publishing worldwide.

Oxford   New York
Auckland   Cape Town   Dar es Salaam   Hong Kong   Karachi
Kuala Lumpur   Madrid   Melbourne   Mexico City   Nairobi
New Delhi   Shanghai   Taipei   Toronto

With offices in
Argentina   Austria   Brazil   Chile   Czech Republic   France   Greece
Guatemala   Hungary   Italy   Japan   Poland   Portugal   Singapore
South Korea   Switzerland   Thailand   Turkey   Ukraine   Vietnam

Oxford is a registered trade mark of Oxford University Press
in the UK and certain other countries.

Published in the United States of America by
Oxford University Press
198 Madison Avenue, New York, NY 10016

Library of Congress Cataloging-in-Publication Data
Blee, Kathleen M.
Democracy in the making : how activist groups form / Kathleen M. Blee.
    p. cm. — (Oxford studies in culture and politics)
Includes bibliographical references and index.
ISBN 978-0-19-984276-6 (cloth : alk. paper); 978-0-19-022176-8 (paper : alk. paper)
1. Social movements—Pennsylvania—Pittsburgh—History—21st century.
2. Social change—Pennsylvania—Pittsburgh.
3. Democracy—Pennsylvania—Pittsburgh. I. Title.
HM881.B54   2012
322.409748'86—dc23
2011025665

Dedicated to Pam Goldman, Eli Blee-Goldman, and Sophie Blee-Goldman

We are better than we think
And not yet what we want to be
We are alive to imagination
And open to possibility
We will continue
To invent the future
   —"We Are Virginia Tech," from
   Nikki Giovanni's *Bicycles: Love Poems*
   (New York: HarperCollins, 2009), p. 109,
   used with permission

CONTENTS

Acknowledgments   *ix*

1. Making Democracy   *3*
2. Theorizing the Emergence of Activism   *27*
3. Who Belongs?   *52*
4. What's the Problem?   *81*
5. How Should We Treat Each Other?   *109*
6. Lessons   *134*

Appendices   *141*
End Notes   *163*
Bibliography   *189*
Index   *205*

ACKNOWLEDGMENTS

Many people contributed to this project in different ways. This work was supported by the National Science Foundation (NSF) under Grants Nos. 0316436 and 0416500. I am grateful to Patricia White at the NSF for her care in administering these grants. Joane Nagel, then at the NSF and now a colleague and friend, provided a mixture of skepticism and encouragement that improved the project immeasurably.

Earlier versions of this work were presented at the University of Michigan; University of California, Santa Barbara; University of California, Irvine; Harvard University; the School of American Research; University of Southern California; University of Connecticut; and the University of Kansas; presentations were also made at meetings of the International Sociological Association; International Congress of Qualitative Inquiry; the American Sociological Association, Section on Collective Behavior and Social Movements Conference; the Interdisciplinary Network for Group Research; the Section on Comparative and Historical Sociology Conference; and the Pittsburgh Social Movements Forum. Feedback from colleagues and students in all these venues was tremendously important in sharpening the argument of this book.

I am very thankful to John Markoff, Nicole Constable, David S. Meyer, Deborah Gould, Kathleen Bulger Gray, Linda Gordon, and Akiko Hashimoto for their advice at an early stage and to Nina Eliasoph, James Cook, James Jasper, and anonymous reviewers for feedback on the manuscript. A number of graduate and undergraduate students worked on various stages of this project and I am grateful for their advice and insights as well as their careful work: Lisa Huebner Ruchti, Tim Vining, Kim Creasap, Kelsy Burke, Amy McDowell, Anne Richardson, Analena Bruce, Christie Harrison, Kathi Elliott, Amy Gottenthaler, Danielle Kittridge, Emily Long, Cara Margherio, John Nigro, Laura Petruzelli, and particularly Ashley Currier, whose ideas, savvy approach to data collection, theoretical acumen, and friendship have shaped this project from the beginning. I thank Nancy Kasper for her skill and sense of humor in shepherding the project through its administrative aspects.

Activists are the heroes of modern society, turning a critical lens on what *is* and imagining what *can be*. This book highlights the problems and short-comings that can build up in activist groups but shouldn't diminish the courage and fortitude of activists who work every day to change the direction of society. I am deeply indebted to the many activists who permitted this scholarly gaze inside their meetings and events and who generously gave their time to answer questions and be interviewed. It is through their work that a better world is made.

Democracy in the Making

CHAPTER 1

Making Democracy

This book looks at how people come together to change society. In communities across the United States, grassroots activists work tirelessly to end American military intervention abroad, protect laboratory animals, or rid their neighborhoods of guns and violence. Some of their actions occur in the public eye, as solemn street corner vigils, dramatic protests, and emotional press conferences. Others happen behind the scenes, as people encourage friends and neighbors to join them in convincing decision makers to change laws or policies.

Pundits commonly bemoan the general public's lack of interest in politics today. Whether civic engagement is indeed lower now than in the past is debatable, but clearly, few people are involved in politics beyond actually voting. Most even avoid conversations about politics, especially those that might create disagreement or controversy.[1]

The people in this book are exceptions. They spend considerable time talking about political issues and they work hard to change society. Compared to the massive feminist, racial, and anti-war protests of the 1960s and 1970s, their events draw paltry numbers. The groups they form are mostly tiny and short-lived. Yet these activists shape new ways of talking and doing politics, invigorating public dialogue with what Marc Steinberg terms a "moral vision of the world." At its best, Robin D. G. Kelley tells us, such civic activism can "do what great poetry always does: transport us to another place, compel us to relive horrors and, more importantly, enable us to imagine a new society." It provides a means for people to envision what they otherwise would not consider.[2]

Grassroots activism is commonly thought of as ancillary to democratic politics, as making political institutions and elected officials more accountable, and as serving as a conduit into electoral politics. This defines democracy as formal institutions of elections and representative legislatures, with citizen activism as secondary, if beneficial, to democratic life.

There are problems with this definition of democracy. For one, it *overstates* the democratic quality of official state institutions. As activist groups repeatedly document, many practices of democratic governments are contrary to principles of democracy, including widespread use of state secrecy and surveillance of citizens. Equating democracy with governance also *understates* the democratizing effects of grassroots political action. People who join together to work for social change practice democracy differently, but no less than when they act individually to vote or to write to their legislators. Their activism shapes what Étienne Balibar calls a democracy "beneath and beyond the state." Democracy in these instances is a verb, not an adjective. It is the action of people as they deliberate and work together to affect society rather than a form of governance. Activism-as-democracy is not institutional or structural. It is a process, ever being made.[3] Such democratizing practices are the subject of this book.

Some words of caution. Not all grassroots civic activism is democratizing, a reality often overlooked in the rush to herald civic engagement as the safeguard of democracy. Grassroots activism can move toward decidedly undemocratic goals, such as efforts to restrict the political rights of immigrants or prisoners. It can promote nostalgic ideas of the past or fuel fears of racial, national, or gender groups, as did massive movements for white supremacy in the early twentieth century.[4] Indeed, even grassroots efforts that promote democratic goals can pursue these in ways that quash rather than enable democracy. Activists can operate with the very hierarchies of gender, race, sexuality, and social class that they oppose in principle.[5]

This book looks at how emerging activist groups evoke or limit democratic action and imagination. Rather than assuming that the very *presence* of grassroots political action is democratizing, it traces the extent to which democracy is *exercised* in and by activist groups.

ACTIVIST GROUPS

This book is based on an intensive study of more than 60 emerging grassroots activist groups in Pittsburgh between 2003 and 2007. Each came together to pursue social change through non-electoral means. Some were progressive, others conservative, and still others vacillated or defied a clear label. With few exceptions, they were small. Rarely did more than two dozen people attend a meeting, although larger numbers came to protests and rallies.

Only one group had a paid staff person; she worked part-time. The rest relied on members' time and energy.[6] Almost all had tiny budgets, often just what they collected at meetings or rallies. Only a handful had enough money to do financial planning. They met in places that were free and convenient: people's homes, community centers, churches and religious centers, offices of nonprofit organizations, coffeehouses, university buildings, and a peace and justice center. Young adults and college students were the foundation of some groups; in others, it was longtime activists in their 50s and 60s.

These groups tackled a broad range of issues, including the U.S. invasion of Iraq, police brutality, guns, drugs, community violence, gay/lesbian/bisexual/transgender (GLBT) rights, animal protection, and school reform. Most targeted public officials at some point, using phone calls and letters as well as more confrontational means. Some pushed consistently for sweeping social change while others sought incremental improvements or worked for both. The diversity of their politics and members provides a more robust platform for studying grassroots activism than does the more common focus on progressive, youthful, and protest-oriented groups. As Howard Becker cautions, how we understand the social world is "shaped by the collection of cases we have on hand."[7]

Pittsburgh was an ideal place to study emerging grassroots activism—large enough to have many and varied kinds of activism, yet small enough that a single study could span the landscape of local activism. Just as anywhere else, the city's particular characteristics shaped its activism. Still-powerful labor unions provided space and other resources for progressive efforts. A political divide, with the city dominated by the Democratic Party and the state legislature and county government by Republicans, provoked activism on both the left and right of the political spectrum. Pittsburgh's sluggish economy, still reeling from the collapse of the steel industry in the 1980s,[8] kept employment and social issues at the forefront. With its tiny Latino/a and Asian American populations, the city's racial politics were framed almost exclusively in terms of African American and white issues.

Over a three-year period, an effort was made to identify and observe all new grassroots activist groups, along with comparison sets of more established groups. Incipient activism was found by looking for announcements and recruiting notices in newspapers and newsletters; on the bulletin boards of coffeehouses, bookstores, stores, and bars; and in flyers distributed at places where activists congregate, such as demonstrations, alternative music concerts, city parks, and events like Rock Against Racism and gay pride parades.[9] Some groups (29% of those studied) announced themselves to the public through an event, generally a protest, but most (71%) began their public presence by inviting people to a meeting. Many announcements (66%) were framed in terms of opportunity, stressing a unique opening for organizing, such as "we have a chance now to show our opposition." Other announcements (34%) were framed in terms of need, emphasizing the crucial nature of a societal problem, such as "we must confront the corporations." Frames of opportunity tended to be used when groups were launched through a meeting while frames of need were more common when groups began with an event.

Locating an initial set of emerging progressive activist groups was relatively easy as these were highly visible in activist networks. To reach beyond these generally accessible and well-studied forms of activism was more difficult. Repeatedly contacting community and neighborhood leaders and a diverse set of activists (conservative as well as progressive) to ask about new organizing efforts proved successful in locating a wide range of emerging activist groups.

The grassroots efforts in this book lack the formal trappings of rules of operation, settled beliefs, and a collective identity that characterize more established activist organizations, those that scholars refer to as social movement organizations (SMOs). I focus instead on the many tiny and fledging groups from which social movements might emerge. A few of these incipient groups became established SMOs during this study or at some later point. Some may do so in the future. Most collapsed or remained fragile and tiny.[10]

"Tiny and incipient" groups are rarely the subject of scholarship.[11] Scholars tend to prefer SMOs whose importance is clear and which are likely to endure over time. Fledgling groups are risky subjects for study. They are likely to fall apart and disappear. They are unstable, sometimes radically changing focus or direction. As later chapters show, what begins as a peace group can morph into an environmental group with the change of a few members. Moderate peace groups can turn into militant anarchist ones. Once-radical groups can reshape themselves as civic improvement societies. The fluidity of emerging groups makes it difficult to label them, to know what any one is "a case of."[12]

Despite the difficulty they pose to scholars, emerging activist groups are important to study for several reasons. For one, they reveal the difficulties of launching collective activism. The many efforts that fizzle, dissolve, or become something else show how fraught the process of organizing for change can be. So do the false starts, quick reversals, tentative moves, and radical shifts in direction that characterize virtually every grassroots effort.

A second reason to study emerging activism is that people create collective political action differently today than in the past. The labor, Southern patriot, and working-class movements of the last centuries had less need to fashion a sense of commonality among those they organized; they drew on existing ties of occupation, place, and class. In contrast, today's grassroots efforts on behalf of the environment, guns, or animals seek recruits from heterogeneous places; they need to create a sense of commonality, rather than build on it. Their unity requires shared definitions, common beliefs, and agreed-upon ways of acting that are never settled, always provisional, forever being made. However fragile, the unity of activist groups provides a framework of understanding from which they can operate.[13] Watching emerging activism reveals how that framework is made. Supplementing the many studies of where, when, and why collective activism occurs, this study focuses on *how* it happens.[14]

A third reason to study fledgling groups is that, however overlooked, they are part of the landscape of grassroots activism. People's experiences in activism are not just in established organizations with clear agendas and a sense of mission. Activists spend considerable time in groups that are groping for a focus, that can't pull themselves together, that accomplish little. Focusing only on activism that has "made it"—and ignoring what doesn't—truncates what we know. It makes activism seem successful because we study successful activism. This singular focus is a form of skewed sampling, a problem of drawing conclusions from cases that share the characteristic in question. We can't learn what leads people into peace politics, for example, by studying only peace groups. Peace activists might be overwhelmingly well educated, highly social, or suburban. But so might people who are active in all kinds of politics. To know what attracts people specifically to peace politics, we need to compare peace groups with other political groups. The same logic applies here. We can't understand what makes activist groups endure by studying only those that do. We need to look also at those that collapse.[15]

A singular focus on established activism may lead to other erroneous conclusions. For instance, if we look only at organized activism, we might think that organization is a necessary part of activism. Perhaps it is, but we can't know that by studying only activism that is organized. When Gene Burns studied efforts to abolish laws against birth control in the United States, he noted that it was insufficient to examine only successful campaigns. He also needed to look at occasions when people tried to change laws but could not. The study of grassroots activism is similar. We need to know about groups that are not organized to understand those that are.[16]

Most important, fledgling groups present a unique opportunity to understand the relationship between possibility and action. As later chapters show, the talk in new activist groups is experimental, open-ended, and contested. Without a firm set of collective expectations that define "who we are" and "the way things are," fledgling groups weigh their decisions against a broad array of possibilities. Do we believe in conspiracies? Are we willing to fight the police? Should we use graphic imagery on our posters? Allow punk musicians on our event stage? Present ourselves as mainstream Americans? Try to change how schools treat kids or try to change how kids are treated throughout society? Are we in this for the long run? Do we know where we can find more information?[17]

Could we capture this broad sense of possibility by tracing SMOs back in time, rather than start with nascent groups? Unfortunately not. In activist groups, as in other forms of social life, what happens later obscures what happened earlier. Over time, activist groups forge patterns that define who they are, who they should recruit, what agendas to pursue, how they can find information, and in what frames to cast their issues. They settle on ways of interacting with each other: friendly or hostile, conflictual or cooperative, democratic or authoritarian. Even if practices and ideas shift over time, the weight of tradition makes frequent and drastic changes less and less likely. Activist groups quickly take on a character that defines them into the future.

The cultural blueprint set out in the early days of grassroots groups is difficult to reconstruct once the group becomes established. By then, many issues of their early days are gone. As initial questions are settled and dilemmas resolved, activists' recollection of how this happened fades. Ways of acting and thinking become assumed, obscuring the process by which these were established. What was once up for grabs comes to seem fixed, normal, even inevitable. The group *is* African American or mixed race, violent or peaceable, insular or inclusive. The reasons it is this way disappear from individual and collective memory. It is now unquestioned and largely unquestionable.[18]

By looking at the early moments of collective activism we can see directly what later will become opaque. We can watch frames being formed and made meaningful, leaders emerging, dilemmas being confronted, and rules of interaction being etched. Possibilities are evident—competing frames, leaders, and ways of acting—that later are filtered out. Moreover, group dynamics are clearer than they will be later. Since early groups don't yet have a shared framework of ideas, activists talk in more detail about what they think—and why they think so—than they do later when understandings are widely shared and explicit rationales no longer needed.[19]

STUDYING ACTIVIST GROUPS

I collected a vast amount and variety of data to capture a sense of the *process* of activism in Pittsburgh's fledgling grassroots groups. These data are unusually rich by being both longitudinal and comparative. I follow each activist group over time to see how its dynamics change, and by gathering similar information on each group, I compare the process of activism across many groups. These data also provide an extraordinary view of the process of activism that is simultaneously near and distant. By recording the internal dynamics of grassroots groups, they show activism from the inside. And by being comparable across groups, these data reveal broader patterns in activist group dynamics.

Much of the information for this study comes from real-time ethnographic data, including 378 similar semi-structured observations of meetings and other events. These are supplemented with 60 lengthy interviews, several focus groups, and innumerable informal conversations with activists, former activists, people recruited to a grassroots group who declined to join,[20] and those on the fringes of activist groups as well as a vast amount of written, videotaped, and Web material by and about these groups. Other data were collected as well, including information on 1,234 activist events during the 2004 presidential election campaign, 178 funding proposals to a local philanthropic foundation, and biannual one-month inventories of all events and public appearances by activist groups in the city.

The various forms of data provide information on different levels of activism. Group-level data from observations reveal that what activists say—or even what they perceive—is affected by what happens in the group. Individual-level data from interviews and conversations show how activists' ideas, their desires, and their sense of possibilities resemble or differ from those adopted by the group as a whole.[21] Data on the larger political environment provide a context for activist talk and actions.

Observations: Through systematic ethnographic observation, very detailed information was collected on the workings of grassroots groups, providing a lens inside the "black box" of collective activism. These data show how emerging activist groups work and what prevents them from working better.[22]

Grassroots activism is usually depicted in times of great energy. These can be moments of excitement, when recruits are flooding in and plans are under way, or times of crisis and explosive tension.[23] Less documented are the long periods of sagging energy, wearisome discussion, and irritating tedium as activists wait for meetings to start, events to come together, or something to happen, or the times of quiet despair when members slip away and plans unravel. Because grassroots activism is shaped by its low periods as well as its high moments, observations were made at every group event, no matter how routine or seemingly insignificant.

Activism also is commonly described by its visible venues such as press conferences, teach-ins, vigils, confrontations with public officials, rallies, and marches. Such a focus misses important activism that takes place in less visible arenas. Activists don't only confront the police or rally in mass events; they also talk.[24] One frustrated activist echoed this assessment: "organizing isn't throwing an event." These data record the internal as well as the public side of activist groups: meetings, social events, leadership caucuses, planning and strategy sessions, and encounters with other activist groups. With permission, e-mail exchanges among activists on the group's discussion board also were monitored.

In this study, less than one-quarter (22%) of all group occasions were of the type most commonly studied by scholars, such as rallies, press conferences, and vigils. Excluding purely social events, the most common activity for emerging groups (78%) was a meeting (Table 1.1). Public events were more common in established groups, but this may be an artifact of collecting data for established groups from public announcements.

When emerging groups were observed, semi-structured templates were used to collect comparable information on the fine details of everyday social interactions.[25] These templates were designed to capture five broad dimensions of activism.

First, they record the *sequencing* of actions and interactions as they unfold in real time. This preserves the dynamics of action, the decision *making* as well as the decisions *made* by activist groups. Instead of needing to infer a group's strategies from their actions, templates record how a group perceives its alternatives as it formulates strategies.[26] The templates preserve how activists assert and weigh knowledge and how groups frame ideas, showing the contours of action as it is unfolding.

Second, observational templates collect information on *what fails to happen* as well as what does happen. They capture plans that activist groups contemplate but never enact, ideas that fail to materialize, silences that mark the boundaries of what can be considered, and Michel Foucault's "different ways of not saying things," such as topics once talked about but now avoided.[27]

Table 1.1. ACTIVIST EVENTS BY TYPE*

	Emerging groups	Established groups
Meetings	295 (78%)	569 (47%)
Protests/Vigils	58 (15%)	361 (30%)
Educational Forums	18 (5%)	198 (16%)
Other (press conferences, fund-raisers, etc.)	7 (2%)	84 (7%)
Total	378	1212

*Emerging group data are from observations. Established group data are from documents.

Third, these observations include data on *interactions*, the often-neglected intersubjective context of activism. I record not only that activists *do* interact, but *how* they interact, including the content and affective qualities of interactions as indicated in tone, pace, nonverbal cues, intensity, laughter, and irritation as well as words. These subtleties are essential for a full picture of activism that goes beyond events and ideas. To avoid assuming that all members share the group's collective understandings, observations include differences in members' interpretations. By preserving the small details of interaction, the political deliberations that Katherine Walsh identifies as "the social processes of people chatting with one another," these observations capture fractures and tensions that are not disclosed in interviews or recorded in the group's documents.[28]

Fourth, close observation reveals *cultural* dynamics, such as how meanings gain salience or are discarded, and how groups make sense of their environments and themselves as political actors. These are found in the natural language and interpretive categories used in activist groups, as well as their changing interpretations over time. Observation of group dynamics also preserves the role of ordinary members in activism, against the inflated importance of leaders that can emerge if data are derived solely from interviews with leaders and the group documents they produce. In other words, it attends to the ordinary practices of activism.[29]

Finally, observation captures cycles of *reflection*. People do not just act; they reflect on their actions. Humans are knowers, Christian Smith writes, who "not only have experiences, pleasures, pains, and beliefs but are aware that they have them." Human consciousness is the capacity to stand outside "experiences, knowledge, beliefs, and reactions and consider them from different points of view." It enables people to judge their actions, searching for "standards beyond themselves by which they may evaluate themselves."[30] These processes of reflection and evaluation take place on a collective level in activist groups. Observation shows how groups reflect on themselves and their situations and how they reconsider their earlier reflections as their circumstances change.

Interviews: Observations alone do not provide sufficient data because people generally don't talk about what they take for granted.[31] To correct this, lengthy, semi-structured interviews probed activists' experiences and interpretations. Interviews and observations were refined over time in an iterative fashion. Activists were asked to clarify and provide nuance to what observations revealed, and observational templates were then altered to include new issues raised in interviews.

Documents: A vast number of documents produced by activist groups were collected, such as newsletters, flyers, and Internet Web sites. Even larger was the number of documents produced by others about these groups, including textual and video material from mainstream media, alternative media and Web sites such as Indymedia, and other activist groups and support organizations. These documents indicate how grass-roots groups see themselves, how they choose to represent themselves to others, and how they are seen and represented by outsiders.

The data from observations, interviews, and documents are nested, with information on individual activists, interaction among activists, dynamics of the groups in which activists interact, and the external context of these groups. These data provide a rare look at several aspects of fledgling activist groups that are rarely examined by scholars. Rather than the public events and victories of activism that are most often studied, these data reveal the behind-the-scenes and nitty-gritty activities that consume activist groups between their more visible actions. Unlike the more common ethnographic case studies of a single group, this study collects similar, systematic data on a broad array of grassroots groups. In contrast to the many studies of national activist organizations, it examines local groups and extends across the political spectrum, to conservative as well as progressive ones. It focuses on micro-level dynamics of activism, not the well-studied macro-level structures of political opportunity. Finally, this study captures activist dynamics as they emerge and unfold, not retrospectively through documents or activists' accounts.

These data are a lens into the explicit talk and actions of emerging activist groups as well as the deeper, commonsense layers of group life. The talk that *doesn't* take place and the actions that are *not* considered are clues to what activists regard as natural and given, the "*implicit meanings*," in Paul Lichterman's terms, "that activists tend to take for granted" and that circumscribe what activists think they can do.[32] By tacking between these layers—between what is done/said and what is not done/unsaid—it is possible to see what activists collectively regard as possible, authorized, and imaginable.

CATEGORIZING AND NAMING

Activist groups are variously described by their issues (e.g., disability rights), tactics (e.g., nonviolent), or members (e.g., middle class). Yet such labels are misleadingly static, a way of *not* seeing as well as seeing. Just as describing a person, rather than the person's acts or desires, as heterosexual or homosexual obscures how sexual expression may vary over a lifetime;[33] so too, depicting activist groups as anti-war, youthful, or militant implies that such characteristics are essential and durable. The description freezes in time what is actually in flux, treating variable states of activism as fixed attributes.

In reality, activist groups continually modify themselves. They form coalitions and alliances or fracture internally. They reorient from local to national efforts and back again. People drift in and out, turning a group of young professionals into one of economically marginal students or reforming a youth-dominated group into one of middle-aged activists. Boundaries blur as groups dissolve into each other and activists migrate from one to another.

The fluidity of activism is easily overlooked since it is not always evident from the outside. Activist groups can retain the same name and mission statement, even produce identical public materials, while dramatically shifting their issues, membership, or tactics. A Pittsburgh group that organized to oppose animal experiments in university research labs, for example, shifted its energies toward opposing the Iraq War after the members started attending anti-war rallies to distribute flyers about animal rights. From the outside, little seemed to change: its Web site and public materials still focused on animal abuse although there was a subtle shift in the flyers that now decried "the all-too-forgotten loss of animals during times of war." Inside, though, change was dramatic and palpable as members strategized excitedly about the war, rarely bringing up the topic of animals. Labeling an activist group by using only its outward appearance thus risks the error of "misplaced concreteness," equating a model of reality with actual reality. In fact, groups can be much more dynamic than their public appearances suggest.[34]

The names that activist groups adopt show the complexity of labeling. Some select names to define themselves. A young activist said of his group that "the name was a big thing, you know, creating a group in some ways. You're not a group until you have the name that you can refer to yourself by." For others, the process of naming was more casual. A founding member of a protest support group recalled,

> [We decided] we can pool supplies and be more organized and train other people ourselves. So at that meeting [we] more or less came into existence. People said, "we're going to have a group and who's interested and you all put your e-mail address down" and then someone e-mailed the group and said "we're going to have a meeting" and at the meeting we picked a name [and] the group existed.

However names are chosen, they freeze the group in time. Names imply stasis, even when a group is in flux, a phenomenon aptly captured in Andrew Abbott's caution that "the name stayed the same; the thing it denoted did not." Some groups retain their original names (thus, their public identity) even as their attributes change, like the animal rights group that turned to war issues.[35] Others alter their names to reflect shifts in agenda or tactics, like a neighborhood group that shifted from "Death by Heroin" to "People Opposing Drugs" to appear less controversial to funders and recruits.

The mutability of activist groups means that they are not easily compared, since the logic of comparison assumes that cases have a "generically analyzable form."[36] Put another way, comparison requires cases that are unitary and bounded instances of a single underlying phenomenon, like "activist group." But activist groups are neither unitary nor bounded. We cannot simply compare gun control and anti-war groups to see differences in how they recruit members or develop leadership. Groups remake themselves too often to be strictly comparable. Even the underlying phenomenon—what they are a case of—is unclear. Any single group can simultaneously have qualities of an activist group, civic improvement society, electoral pressure group, and social group in shifting proportions.

Similar problems arise when we compare activist groups over time. Longitudinal study assumes a coherent entity that can be traced as a process, the way an apple ripens or a child grows into adulthood. But activist groups are more like a neighborhood ball game. In the course of an afternoon, some children join the game, others leave. Some never return; others grab a snack at home and come back. Still others stay in the game all afternoon. There are some patterns in the shifting set of players. At twilight, for instance, the players will be older and live closer to the field. But there are also idiosyncrasies. Strategies change as players come and go; so does the intensity of the game. Given these fluctuations, it is difficult to say that the team got better over time or that the members played better in darkness than light. For the same reasons, it can be misleading to trace an activist group over time. Any group can be an essentially different entity from one moment to the next, undermining the assumptions of standard analytic models that predict outcomes from origins.[37]

Despite these problems, it is not necessary to abandon the analytic advantages of comparison. Instead of groups, I compare sequences of action and interpretation as defined from the perspective of activist groups themselves. Sequences of action and interpretation are inherently intertwined, but activist groups often define them separately, either lumping together instances of action—as, for example, times in which they are "intensely recruiting" or "in the doldrums" or "on the brink of success"—or grouping instances of shared interpretation, like times when they were "radical" or "open to new ideas" or "rigid."

From the outside, these sequences lack clear start and end points, making it impossible to specify whether events occur early or late. But activist groups treat sequences differently, as having clear beginnings and conclusions such as "when we began to consider a new direction" or "when we stopped fighting with each other." From the perspective of activist groups, then, sequences of action and interpretation are discrete and time-limited, thus meeting the assumption that cases have unity and boundaries. Using definitions generated by activist groups also avoids the problems of retrospection, linking together actions and events in hindsight, and choosing cases based on the characteristic of interest.[38] These sequences provide a robust basis for comparison over time and across groups.

POLITICAL CONTEXT

Context is an important aspect of activism, enabling or disabling the possibilities for action. During the G.W. Bush presidency, for example, progressive activist groups regarded action as necessary but futile. In the same political context, conservative activist groups saw themselves as likely to succeed, but rarely regarded their actions as indispensable.[39]

Much of the salient context of grassroots activism is local. Borrowing Doreen Massey's distinction, activist groups tend to be *place-based* but not necessarily *place-bound*. Their concerns and networks extend broadly, yet they tend to experience even national and international politics in local terms.[40] For example, the 2004 presidential election in which Pennsylvania was considered a "toss-up" and "must-win" state dramatically affected Pittsburgh's activist community. Multiple candidate visits to the city and intense media attention to the wife of Bush's opponent, an influential local philanthropist, forced activist groups to position themselves vis-à-vis electoral politics. They variously used electoral forums to showcase their issues and tried to fend off competition from political parties for donors and recruits.[41]

Most of these activist groups had ties to social movements and activists far outside the city, but on a day-to-day basis, local context was paramount. For many progressive activists (less so for conservative ones), the city supported a local version of what Donatella della Porta and Dieter Rucht term "social movement families" that "share a common world view, have organizational overlaps, and occasionally ally for joint campaigns."[42] Within these families, progressive activists could find like-minded people as recruits and allies; with them they could share ideas, concerns, friendship, places of activism, and culture.[43] Many progressive groups were able to secure funding for their projects from a local foundation.[44] There was also a loose progressive scene in Pittsburgh, constituted through networks and places of interaction such as restaurants, coffeeshops, bookstores, and galleries.[45]

A local social movement family for Pittsburgh's progressive activists was the network around the Center for Progressive Values (CPV),[46] a "resource and organizing center for local peace and justice groups" that dated to 1972 and provided nonprofit tax status, meeting space, and publicity through its widely circulated weekly e-mails and monthly newspaper. It also generated a calendar of progressive events and provided advice from its experienced staff and members. Groups affiliated with the CPV were not formally linked, but their activists bumped into each other at meetings at the CPV office or as they worked in its associated thrift shop or with affiliated projects. CPV events, like its well-attended annual awards dinner and chartered buses to national demonstrations, created a dense network of progressive activists, supported by various institutions and groups like local "Raging Grannies," "Radical Cheerleaders," and independent radio networks, newspapers, and Indymedia.

The conservative groups in this study were less likely to operate through activist networks. In part, this may be an artifact of the study design. Conservative networks in Pittsburgh largely worked through Catholic churches, and I excluded activist groups that were under the auspices of larger organizations like churches or unions that might constrain how activist groups defined themselves and their political direction. Even in the conservative groups in the study, however, activists rarely mentioned other groups as potential allies, referring more often to public officials and media. Nor did they talk about particular venues or scenes—aside from churches—as sites of conservative networking.

THE BIRTH OF ACTIVISM

This book looks at the early moments of activism, but pinpointing the birth of an activist group is not easy. Even activists disagreed about when their group started, hinting at deeper divisions on what constitutes activism. When asked to describe their group's beginning, some activists pointed to personal ties. For them, the group began when people started interacting, even long before it had a common political focus or goal. An anti-drug activist told me, "when we started out, most of the people were just friends. We've expanded since then." For these activists, activism is rooted in interaction and personal ties. In contrast, other activists traced their group to a time when people started learning together. For them, personal ties are merely social; a group of people does not become an activist group until the members start to have common understandings. A protest organizer recalled that "the group itself started based on discussions that we had at the training. The training was organized, you got the group, the group didn't start before the training occurred."

Some activists even resisted the idea that their group had a particular starting point at all. For them, grassroots activism is continuous. Groups don't begin; they simply emerge from previous efforts. Likewise, grassroots groups don't die. They are absorbed into a flow of subsequent activism or enter what Verta Taylor describes as a period of "abeyance" to be revived later.[47] A neighborhood activist captured this sense when he recounted, "I don't see this particular group coming back, but it's a good possibility that another group similar to this will come back." Even when a group never resurfaces, its ideas, connections, political acumen, and enhanced sense of possibility turn up in later efforts. There is one exception: when a group strays from a mission of social change, activists say the group is "dead" even if it continues to meet and stage events. As one young woman put it, "I think it ended up becoming more like a support group (laughs) than an advocacy group. You know, parents sitting around and talk[ing] about what pissed them off."[48]

Differing ideas about a group's birth are not merely disagreements about definitions. Activists' claims are also strategic. When asked to describe its history, different members of one group variously insisted that it was brand-new; had been revived from a previous group that collapsed; was the reemergence of a functioning group that hadn't done much for awhile; and was a faction from a group that split. Why such different answers? Labeling a group as new can be a strategic move to recruit members who want to join groups that are not fully formed. Or it can be a way to distance a group from problems of a former one. Conversely, activists described groups as not-new when they wanted to signal a connection to earlier waves of activism.

The political stakes of defining the starting point of activism are evident in the discussion at an initial meeting of a predominantly African American anti-violence group. At first, the group talked about itself as new, relishing the idea that it could tackle community violence because it had a fresh vision. Soon, however, a different theme appeared, that the group was a reincarnation of an earlier anti-violence effort. As one anti-gang street worker put it, "once again [it] has emerged as a group that the community really feels it needs." Which definition prevailed mattered to the group for more than semantic reasons. Defining its birth set in motion a trajectory of action. If new, the group was free to do anything. If not, it had a legacy, and honoring that legacy would constrain its style and rhetoric.

The last section of this chapter outlines the emergence of three grassroots activist efforts. Two collapsed quickly and have yet to return; one flourished and continues today. Their brief trajectories show the complexities of new grassroots activism explored in subsequent chapters.

NEW DAWN

New Dawn was the brainchild of Yvonne (all names are pseudonyms), a strong-minded but soft-spoken African American woman and longtime activist convinced that she had a new way to stop violence among black youth. To Yvonne, current efforts did little more than preach at kids. Worse, those funded by the government made African Americans dependent on a system that gave free rein to police actions in black neighborhoods. Many just benefited whites, Yvonne told me, like a billboard campaign that featured pictures of murdered black children:

> The powers-that-be came to Joyce [the billboard organizer] and said, "You know what, we'll give you this money and you can put these billboards up. . . . And we know just the person who's going to do it, it's [Company] Billboards." . . . Them billboards is not going to solve one murder and if you go through the history of them, they haven't. But you know that money that went from the City to Joyce to [Company] Billboards, which happens to be [owned by] a white man in a white community, living well. . . . It doesn't solve anything, and it makes our community very gloomy . . . a constant reminder that there is people dead, and the people who murdered them are still out there.

The billboard debacle happened because "no one bothered to go ask the people in the community, 'What do you need—what do you need?'"

Yvonne started New Dawn with a radical aim, to launch a full grassroots movement. She wanted a groundswell of activism among young, poor, black citizens to create changes that would profoundly reshape their lives. To make this happen, they needed a vision of a "New Dawn" and a way to get there. The timing was ideal, Yvonne thought. Pittsburgh's fiscal crisis had closed community centers and swimming pools and slashed social programs. Now was the time to energize poor black kids into action. New Dawn would be a new model of organizing against violence, a bottom-up effort whose direction was not predetermined.

> Instead of trying to get a large group to meet once a week, at say, the library, we will take it street by street and have those people meet on their street and . . . talk about issues.

New Dawn's leadership would be different too. Yvonne recognized that other groups had tried "making a core first and then have them go out and try to dictate what you want the community to do" and they failed. Instead, New Dawn would "go through and by the community . . . to form something that would eventually be the avenue of the voice of the people."

New Dawn had four gatherings, although only Yvonne, her granddaughter, and I attended the final one. In its first three meetings, the fledgling group agreed on several plans. One tied the group to its local environment: it would distribute a flyer in poor neighborhoods and through e-mail to attract young recruits. Recalling an earlier era, when families got together for picnics in the park, its mostly middle-aged members talked nostalgically about how they could bring adults and youth together again on playgrounds, in church, and at the library. Once they had young recruits, one member mused, they would initiate a second plan, to teach youths how to run tours of local stations on the Underground Railroad that had carried antebellum slaves to freedom. When another member expressed a desire to be part of something bigger, the group was swept into a plan to join upcoming protests against the National Rifle Association and the imprisonment of journalist Mumia Abu Jamal.

Given this promising start, New Dawn's activists were caught off guard in its third meeting when Yvonne bluntly declared that it had not "gotten off the ground." Why not? people wondered aloud. They had gathered a solid core of activists and were busily developing plans. But, Yvonne insisted, these activists were not the "right kind" of members. They "want to be in on writing flyers and statements of purpose." Such tactics were a dead end if the group wanted to get past existing ideas and programs favored by the elite. It needed "grassroots people," Yvonne clarified, "the kind who want to work on this in their own communities" and were dedicated to "involving their neighbors and friends in getting this going." Someone from each of Pittsburgh's poor neighborhoods was needed to grow the group.

No one challenged Yvonne's interpretation, but not because she was heavy-handed or forcefully controlled the group. Rather, her message seemed to resonate with other members, at least after their initial shock. In the discussion that followed, members quickly constructed a collective explanation of the problem that Yvonne identified. New Dawn couldn't recruit the right kind of people, they decided, because people in desperate economic shape had no time to participate. Moreover, poor people were rightly suspicious of their neighbors, so it was difficult to build the group from the neighborhood up. Yet these same factors that were so economically oppressive—poverty and isolation—also led to violence. The very conditions that made the present untenable were the ones that would hamper New Dawn from realizing its vision of community life. People left the meeting, floundering and defeated.

Although New Dawn collapsed rapidly, there were moments of great possibility in its short life. By envisioning youth violence as the product of situations that could be reversed by the very youth most involved in violence, New Dawn created new understandings of the problem and its remedy. But it was undermined by its own ambitions. It regarded the people who were needed to sustain its radical vision and develop a new kind of movement—ordinary, non-activists from the neighborhoods—as too poor and isolated to join the group. At the same time, it considered those it could attract—older, long-term activists—as hobbled by immersion in their own ideas of the present. Yvonne's vision was formidable but self-defeating.

Scholars often favor parsimonious explanations. But what happens in new activist groups, even one as short-lived as New Dawn, is not easily explained with simple models of cause and effect. Did New Dawn collapse because its vision outstripped its ability to recruit members? Because it lacked resources? Because Yvonne's voice was too strong? Or perhaps because it was competing in an activist niche already filled with anti-violence groups? Each factor mattered, but none alone doomed the group. Even with these problems, New Dawn's demise could not be predicted. Indeed, the group wrestled with a series of self-definitions—who it was as a group, the problem it wanted to fix, and how members could work with each other—that were handled very differently by two other emerging groups, New Army of Revolution and ALLIES 2007.

NEW ARMY OF REVOLUTION (NAR)

The New Army of Revolution lasted about as long as New Dawn but otherwise was strikingly different. It was the brainchild of Mel, a 30-year-old drummer in a band who saw President Bush's reelection as an opportunity to build a progressive movement in Pittsburgh. During the presidential campaign, Mel was active in MoveOn, the Internet political action committee. After the election, he decided that MoveOn simply "preached to the choir" rather than generating ideas from the grassroots. To launch a new effort, Mel rented space in a community center, posted flyers in his neighborhood and around the university, and encouraged friends and acquaintances to come to an initial meeting.

The first gathering of the New Army of Revolution attracted seven men and one woman, an unusually high proportion of men among activist groups in this study. NAR was an odd combination of ideological openness and structural rigidity, nearly the opposite of New Dawn's focused mission and lack of structure. Mel declared that participants were free to take on any progressive issue, although his examples—Social Security, health care, the war in Iraq, and same-sex marriage—were those for which vibrant local groups were already in place. The unbounded sense of possibilities for the group's mission excited some at the gathering, like the man who declared that it finally gave a space for his ideas. Most, though, were uneasy with NAR's formlessness. Unable to tell what was permissible to bring up for discussion, they were silent. Mel's voice dominated even as he insisted that he would not direct the group.

In contrast to the limitless opportunities to choose goals, the organizational structure that Mel presented was not up for discussion. "New American Revolution" would have a military chain of command with branches termed "garrisons" and headed by "captains." Inexplicably, military metaphors did not extend to meetings. These were to be called "gatherings" to promote informality and personal networking. When someone ventured that its militaristic cast might prevent alliances with local peace groups, Mel dismissed the concern. NAR would have so many members that any group would be happy to work with it:

> If you take the model of an Army and you have a large contingent of soldiers, it would be nice, if you believe in a battle coming up, to lend physical support to other causes. Should [another group] have a rally at CMU [Carnegie Mellon University], we should get behind those guys. It would nice to be able to send a thousand bodies over there and say, "hey we're here to help, what do you need?" It would be nice. That's, of course, in the future that we'll have a lot of bodies.

Mel's tight grip extended into other areas as well. In response to one query, he announced that members could post messages to the Web site but only after he approved the content. Even in the face of such domineering behavior and Mel's lengthy monologues, no one left during the initial two-hour gathering and five of the eight returned for a second meeting, along with eight new people.

If NAR's militarism was a topic of discussion at its first gathering, the subject was clearly off the table by its second meeting. Now the structure was fixed, unquestioned, and unquestionable. Those who didn't like it simply drifted away. New recruits accepted NAR's structure as a given, noting it "sounds strong" and that it suggests a group in which "no one can order you around." Instead of mulling over the group's structure, NAR's discussion again turned to what the group should do. Various possibilities floated through the group, some generating interest but none coalescing into a plan of action. One man raised a potential target for the group, the specter of electoral fraud with the introduction of computerized voting machines, and the group seized on this. But it soon fizzled as other issues were raised. The most sustained talk was about Mel's idea to gather in a neighborhood business district, declare the area "seceded from Corporate America" for an hour, and encourage passersby to enter the "new country" and enjoy "true freedom." After a short time, though, the group dwindled away and no plan was set in motion.

NAR continued to meet and discuss ideas in the same vein until Mel suddenly announced that it had no momentum and not enough people to take any action at all. NAR never met again although Mel continued to maintain its Web site, which still proclaimed a sense of heady possibility:

> We need to rally people to our cause, and help our army of idealistic, peaceful, and caring people grow. We realize that a larger organization can do more good for more people. We will communicate our vision through our website, newsletters, the press, demonstrations, meetings, and online audio programs. We hope to find kindred spirits and motivate them to make this nation a place that can embrace all of its citizens in the ideals of its birth.

Its lack of boundaries made NAR appear open to members' views of what goals they should pursue and how. In practice, though, its unboundedness caused the fledgling group to flounder in its efforts to discuss a political direction. Its approach to structure, however, was quite different. NAR members very quickly operated on the assumption that it would take a militarist form; other ideas for its organization were out of bounds for group discussion.

The New Army of Revolution and New Dawn had much in common, at least in their politics and initial definition. Both had visions that rested on a rejection of similar efforts in the past that lacked connection to grassroots people. Both groups sought ties to other progressives. Both had strong founders who named the group. NAR and New Dawn differed, though, in how they theorized the process of activism. NAR saw the group's *size* as key; for New Dawn, it was the *kinds* of members. They differed as well in whose theorizing counted. For NAR, Mel the founder was the most important source of ideas. In New Dawn, Yvonne saw theorizing as a task for the grassroots members she hoped to recruit. It is tempting to conclude that New Dawn floundered because it lacked structure while NAR collapsed because it couldn't decide on a mission. But that conclusion is too simple, as we see in ALLIES 2007, a group that began with neither structure nor mission but was able to generate both.

ALLIES 2007

Like New Dawn, ALLIES 2007 was formed by several longtime activists to end violence among young African Americans after a series of highly publicized murders of black youth. Its first meeting, announced at a press conference that was covered extensively by local media, brought over 200 people to a packed auditorium in a local community center. The crowd was largely black, with a sprinkling of white politicians, police officers, and community activists. Many were middle-aged, but teens and children were there too. Groups of motorcycle club members—white and black—wore identifying jackets, soliciting funds to provide motorbikes to poor boys to encourage them to venture across the borders of neighborhoods and gangs. Solemn men from the Ministry of Defense of the Nation of Islam ringed back and side walls. While waiting for the meeting to begin, people greeted each other. To strangers, they frequently presented their credentials in violence, introducing themselves as someone who had lost a son to violence or who feared violence at the hand of the community's drug dealers and murderers.

A widely respected local activist opened the meeting by stating that the goal of the group was to "impact the violence" with a comprehensive strategy built on existing anti-violence efforts in the city. The only rule was that "everyone is equal tonight, if you are head of an organization or just a citizen." This rule was put into action immediately: participants who wanted to speak were asked to put their names in a box and each could speak for only three minutes when his or her name was drawn. The result was an emotionally charged and powerful meeting.

As speaker after speaker presented proposals for anti-violence organizing, the crowd began to talk among themselves. These side chats, as much as the formal speeches, began the process of constructing a shared platform of understanding that carried over into subsequent meetings. A large, engaged cluster of middle-aged and older African American women at the back, for example, began as a small group that arrived together. Over the course of the evening, their talk and laughter grew increasingly boisterous (although not disruptive) and more women slipped back to join them. When a street minister talked of going into crack houses to "save souls," one woman loudly whispered to those around her, "Save souls? Shit! Need to give them a job, a place to live," provoking a chorus of agreement.

The women's talk quickly turned to gender, a topic all but absent from the podium. They agreed that women needed to report drug dealers and illegal guns to the police, bemoaning those who goaded boyfriends into dealing drugs to "bring them money for Gucci purses." They applauded enthusiastically when the police chief declared that the police would assist when the community was ready to "take back" its neighborhoods, a statement met with stony silence from many others. When the meeting concluded with a tearful recounting from a woman whose three sons were murdered in two separate incidents, the women's talk became even more animated and their references more concrete. They needed to take back their communities "house by house," the women now said explicitly to each other, promising to stand up to the murderers, drug dealers, and prostitutes who terrorized their neighborhoods. Their anger spilled over from those committing violence to those ignoring it. Drawing attention to the absence of news media at this extraordinary event, they asked: "Where's Channel 11? Channel 2?" "It's a form of genocide," one declared.

Subsequent weekly meetings of ALLIES 2007 were considerably smaller than its massive kick-off event, but the group maintained a solid attendance of 15–30 people each week and quickly developed a detailed set of goals and strategies. Members carefully included new people, introducing everyone at every meeting and frequently interrupting the flow to review the agenda and summarize earlier discussions and decisions to update those who arrived late. No one objected; the group clearly valued new people and ideas. Perhaps as a result, ALLIES 2007 had a constant influx of people, white and black. Speakers affirmed the presence of whites explicitly at each meeting and discussed race in a relaxed, lighthearted manner. When a white man pointed out that schools treat African American kids more harshly than whites for the same behavior, the facilitator for that night joked that he would record this comment and add "a white man said this," sparking general laughter. Laughter was frequent, with attendees poking fun at themselves and the facilitator. A positive spirit prevailed.

Young members were particularly valued in ALLIES 2007 and their input was repeatedly solicited. Most important, new and late-arriving members were permitted to reopen lines of discussion on issues that had been decided earlier, such as how the group could both work with the police against violence and deal with persistent cases of local police misconduct and brutality toward African Americans. There were lively conversations before and after meetings, in which activists continued the night's topic and shared personal experiences.

The ability of ALLIES 2007 to keep its options open was particularly evident in a meeting devoted to sensitive issues of family life. The group began by discussing the need to address the problem of "kids having kids," but quickly veered into new topics and surprising decisions. For instance, when one older man proposed that the group adopt "marriage before having children" as a goal, his idea generated a lively exchange that ended with the decision to support everyone who had children without marriage, including lesbian and gay couples. Conversely, an initial effort to avoid having the group seem too "preachy" was challenged when a middle-aged man argued that young black men too often equate masculinity with the amount of sexual activity they have and the number of children they produce. Insisting passionately that "having children when you are unable to provide for them is an act of violence against our community!" he argued that the group had "crossed the line" by not wanting to sound "judgmental." Others concurred and ALLIES 2007 decided to attack teen pregnancy in the black community with a focus on abstinence and chastity.

ALLIES 2007 began with a broad sense of the issues it wanted to address and a flexible sense of how to do so. By carefully including new members and allowing old issues to be brought back into the group for discussion, it was able to maintain a sense of openness even as it formulated goals and settled on actions.

New Dawn, NAR, and ALLIES 2007 started around the same time, in the same city, and with similar progressive values. Each struggled with defining itself in organizational, ideological, and interpersonal terms in very different ways. New Dawn first grappled with organizational issues, considering who should belong in the group; only after the right members were recruited was it willing to set a political direction or establish ground rules for how people should act toward each other. NAR initially tackled ideological issues; its founder insisted that the shape of the organization would flow from its political direction. ALLIES 2007 took yet another course; it focused intensely on interpersonal dynamics, encouraging people to work together under a broad umbrella and assuming that its political direction and structure would emerge naturally from a larger and well-working group.

To understand the trajectories of these activist groups, it is necessary to attend both to patterns and to deviations from these patterns. Activist groups act in patterned ways that reflect social structural contexts, such as their access to resources and the availability of recruits. They also deviate from those patterns, reminding us that people have agency and can change their circumstances.[49] Such intertwining of patterns and deviations makes it impossible to predict the outcome of any one activist group. ALLIES 2007 began with no organizational structure, like New Dawn. It started with no fixed political plan, like NAR. Yet ALLIES 2007 endured while the other two stumbled.

In the next chapter I present a conceptual framework for studying the varying ways in which the dynamics of activist groups unfold. My goal is not to predict how activist groups will turn out, but rather to tease out the differing paths they take from fairly similar beginnings. Readers who are less interested in the details of this framework can skip ahead to the story of how Pittsburgh's activist groups take shape. Chapter 3 looks at activist groups as they decide who belongs and whom they should bring in to the group. In Chapter 4, I explore the ways activist groups assess the issues to address and, in Chapter 5, the ways they create a sense of how members should act toward each other. A concluding chapter draws lessons from Pittsburgh's activist groups for making democracy through grassroots activism.

CHAPTER 2

Theorizing the Emergence of Activism

One hundred fifty people gathered anxiously in a church basement on a summer night in Pittsburgh. Not all were churchgoers, but they knew the building. Its adjoining school was where they sent their children to avoid the public schools they saw as chaotic and scary. This was Greenview, a neighborhood whose history was easy to read from its appearance. Brick houses, small but solid, attested to a time of relative prosperity for its mostly white, working-class residents, but they also displayed years of neglect in their crumbling steps, peeling paint, and sagging gutters. Fancy lettering etched into building facades advertised the grocers, jewelers, and restaurants from a prior era that now hosted nail salons, check-cashing places, bars, and furniture rental stores.

Greenview's decline began in the 1980s when steel mills closed and thousands of jobs vanished in an instant, throwing the neighborhood into cycles of decline. Incomes plummeted; young people moved away; problems multiplied as the aged, unemployed, drug-and alcohol-dependent, and mentally ill population surged and city services disappeared. Even Greenview's neighborhood center lost its funding and was shuttered. Residents spoke of feeling trapped and scared.

Against this backdrop of despair, the church gathering was remarkable in a neighborhood in which political action generally meant little more than voting a Democratic Party slate. This was not a place where people often challenged authorities. They tended to accept life as it came. But tonight, Greenview residents had gathered together, convinced they could change their fate in some way. There was a handful of men, most wearing T-shirts from local baseball teams. Some women were dressed casually in jeans; others had careful makeup and were wearing dresses. Most were white, but nearly a quarter were African American. Many greeted people they knew, directing them into parking spots, and moving downstairs in groups where they made small talk about schools and athletic teams or shared news about events in their lives.

A few whites and most African Americans asked for directions to the hall, noting they were "not from here." They were from Greenview, but not from "here," this particular set of blocks. Residents used finer gradations of geography and social ties to mark belonging. Those "not from here" didn't know the organizers. They learned about the meeting the same way I did, from the "Heroin Kills" flyers posted in hair salons and bars and on telephone poles.

The meeting began suddenly, with no announcement of a plan or agenda, no introduction to the group or its founders. A line of speakers told of the devastation that heroin had brought to Greenview. Some confessed to addiction, by themselves or family members. Their stories were riveting and horrible; they often ended in tragedy: jail, homelessness, divorce, arrest, death.

That night, there was open possibility in the group, numerous directions in which things might go. Perhaps the group would target adults: one speaker chastised parents who "go to bars and set a bad example" for their children. Or the city: another speaker decried the closing of the Greenview senior center, which gave Narcotics Anonymous nowhere to meet, and criticized police for allowing open drug sales in the grocery parking lot and in front of the high school. The group might become confrontational: a few insisted that direct action was needed to drive drug dealers away.

No one seemed in charge, but a direction eventually emerged. The first speakers simply delivered statements, but later ones built on earlier comments. When one middle-aged man talked of Greenview as "under siege" by drug dealers (implying with a gesture of his head that they came from an adjacent African American neighborhood), he was corrected by a young woman who noted that plenty of drug users and sellers were from Greenview. Neighborhoods need to stand together, she continued, because "heroin isn't a ghetto drug anymore." Others joined in to block a potentially racist direction.

The evening's emotional peak came as Nancy took the stage to tell the story of her son's fatal overdose. She was introduced as the force behind this gathering and, befitting her position, Nancy told a story with the coherence of one often repeated. Her journey from denial to despair swept up the crowd. Many were crying when she finished. Nancy made pointed references to people in the room—"as you remember, Joe" or "wasn't it like that, Norma?"—making it clear that she had invited many who were here tonight. Her story skillfully wove together the threads of discussion. She related her son's death as a tale of individual pain but also as an example of a common tragedy that required immediate action. Surprisingly, though, Nancy ended without saying what should be done. She got things going but insisted that what happened next should be decided by "all of you."

It was more than a year later: fall 2004. What began as a gathering of worried, frustrated residents now had a name (Greenview Against Drugs, GAD), officers, and a bank account. But at this meeting there were only 16 people, all white. They clustered together in a tiny Veterans of Foreign Wars hall, behind a gas station, difficult to find for anyone not familiar with this section of the neighborhood. Its sole entry snaked through a private tavern, across a room still set up for the funeral held earlier in the day. As they chatted about relatives and friends, it was obvious that everyone occupied the same tight social circle. There was no discussion that night about drugs or how GAD should work. All of that was settled. GAD's sole aim now was to recruit people to attend what was termed a "reality tour." Set up in a bleak section next to the city jail, the reality tour ushered dozens of visitors every month through a set of successive tableaus in which a teenager is pressured to take drugs, arrested, convicted, jailed, and finally dies from an overdose. The performance was artful and emotional, ending in a funeral scene with a teen lying in a casket and surrounded by sobbing parents and friends and a confrontational talk by actual inmates at the jail. In GAD, all talk was about preparing for the next reality tour. Earlier possibilities for combating the neighborhood's drug problem were off the table. No personal stories were related, no emotions expressed. No one was looking for new members, only actors for the pre-scripted show.

What happened? How did a group that began with a wide horizon of possibility decide on such a narrow goal? The answer can't be found by talking to its activists. They say they only dimly remember its beginnings. When pressed, they insist that there simply is no explanation. It just happened.

The argument of this book is that what happened in Greenview is the product of two related dynamics. Activist groups quickly develop routine ways of operating that shape what they will do and will consider doing far into the future; this happens in ways that are difficult for current members to perceive or change. And they operate from a collective sense of what is possible that tends to contract over time.

This chapter introduces a conceptual framework to explain these dynamics. The goal is not to predict the direction that any particular group will take. Activists make different choices even when in similar situations. Some narrow their visions, like Greenview's activists, while others take on a broad mandate. Rather, this book traces varying trajectories of grassroots activism and identifies how patterns of action form and shift over time.

The conceptual framework of this study borrows ideas from four quite distinct research literatures. Studies of workplace task teams, largely from organizational psychology, suggest the ways that group-level factors matter. Cultural sociology highlights the importance of cultural interpretation and meaning-making to group action. Path-dependency theories, mostly found in studies of built environments and nation-state development, show how sequencing shapes the possibilities of action and interpretation. Theories of agency and time provide a way to locate turning points in the sequences of action and interpretation.

To begin, this chapter introduces ideas of group-level factors, culture, sequencing, and turning points. It then shows how these concepts can illuminate otherwise obscure aspects of activist group trajectories, like those in the Greenview anti-drug group. The chapter concludes by applying these concepts in an extended case study of an animal rights group.

GROUP-LEVEL FACTORS

An extensive scholarship shows that people with a common task to complete, such as work groups or teams set up in laboratory experiments, take on characteristics beyond those of individual members. For example, task teams develop "collective intelligence" (CI), a body of shared understandings beyond the specific knowledge, experience, or ability of individual members. CI gives teams a broad foundation for action. It allows members to rely on each other as repositories of memory, providing a stable expectation of the effects of actions based on the past experiences of other members. Task teams similarly exhibit "group potency," a shared belief in their group's efficacy, which gives members an impetus to take action since they expect that their acts will be influential.[1]

Like task teams, activist groups develop group-level characteristics. What happens in grassroots activism is not a simple product of the motives, acts, beliefs, or goals of individual activists. Although activist groups serve as platforms for individual activism, they are also consequential "in their own right." When GAD morphed from potential social agitators to staid producers of a reality tour, its trajectory could be neither predicted nor explained by the motives or desires of any individual member. GAD, like task teams and other social groups, developed supra-individual properties that shaped its trajectory over time. If GAD initially stretched its members' perceptions of political possibility, beyond the imagination of any single member, it also developed collective blind spots that later made these alternatives unthinkable.

CULTURE

In task team research, culture is generally understood as a consensus of values or norms that molds and constrains action. Task teams characterized by cultures of cooperation, for instance, work differently from those rooted in an ethos of risk-taking, minimal effort, or avid competition. In this understanding, culture shapes action in a relatively static fashion.

I turn to recent cultural sociology for a more dynamic sense of culture, as the process whereby meanings are generated in social life. In this definition, culture is not external to social action; rather, culture *is* meaningful social action. Culture is how social life works.[2] This sense of culture is useful for the study of activist groups that, as Melucci observes, operate in a "field of meanings constructed by social relations." Melucci's insight is twofold. First, it underscores that collective action is laden with multiple meanings. A simple anti-war message, for example, might draw out the political implications of militarism in a democratic society, make a claim about morality in warfare, express a socially normative idea about peace, and employ discursive understandings to distinguish between war and conflict. Meaning-making is ubiquitous across the activities of grassroots groups as well, as they weigh strategic decisions, decide what are appropriate emotional exchanges, and evaluate their results to learn whether they are successful. Second, Melucci's statement shows how meaning is embedded in the dynamics of social interaction. Activists make meanings as they interact with other people. Meaning-making is not external to social life; it is a social product. Since culture is embedded in social action, it is always contested and being remade. Culture is not consensual or fixed, nor does it stand outside and channel group action. Activist groups push for shared definitions and meanings, but these are never finally accomplished and always emergent.[3]

Culture is central to activism because activist groups are more than vehicles through which people assert political claims in public life and gain political advantage. They also are venues in which people work collectively to understand their world, decide what is just or unjust, and express their values. Culture is not peripheral to, or even just one aspect of, grassroots activism; it is the core. As Doug McAdam writes, activism is a "collaborative cultural project." Activism is not undertaken as a cost-benefit calculus, nor is it a "brute fact" whose meaning speaks for itself. Rather, activism is a process in which actions and meanings are deeply intertwined.[4] An activist group's culture is what Gary Alan Fine describes as an *idioculture:*

> a system of knowledge, beliefs, behaviors, and customs shared by members of
> an interacting group to which members can refer and which they can employ as

the basis of further interaction. Members recognize that they share experiences, and these experiences can be referred to with the expectation that they will be understood by others, and will become tools by which to construct a social reality.[5]

Cultural processes are particularly important in horizons of possibility. Even as they seek to envision the world in new ways, activists act within culturally meaningful boundaries of perceived possibilities. Boundaries thus enable as well as circumscribe the action of activist groups.[6]

SEQUENCE

What activist groups do, and consider doing, changes over time in sequences that are path-dependent, a concept more commonly used to describe changes in large-scale structures like nation-states or built environments.[7] The geographer Allan Pred conceptualizes such sequences as the intertwining of paths and projects. Human actions are *paths* that move through social institutions or *projects*. As people travel through society, they are continually confronted with new influences, information, and feelings that lead them toward certain actions. In the shadow of a nuclear power plant, residents consider options for developing their community that are different from the choices they would have considered otherwise. They still make choices, but these are constrained by the earlier decisions (paths) made by those who constructed the nuclear plant (project).[8]

Paths create projects. Social institutions are the result of intentional human action. The nuclear plant did not simply appear; it came about through earlier actions. As Pred explains, in a paraphrase of Karl Marx's famous dictum, "people do not produce history and places under conditions of their own choosing, but in the context of already existing, directly encountered social and spatial structures."[9]

As the accrual of social action, social institutions are provisional, temporary, and ever changing, reshaped by unfolding human action. In turn, human action is bounded by the institutional framework in which action is taken, a framework itself created by earlier action. Action thus generates its own boundaries, a point that Pred illustrates in a description of one person's actions:

Once a person makes a commitment to partake in any project at a given time and site it becomes impossible for her: (i) to do something else simultaneously elsewhere; (ii) to join any other spatially separate project which starts at another time but temporally overlaps with some portion of the project in question; or (iii) to join another project that presents no simultaneity conflicts but which is out of "reach" because of travel-time requirements.[10]

By stressing the interplay between events and social institutions, theories of path dependency link micro and macro levels of social life. People produce their societies, but they do so within preexisting and human-created structures. Structure and action are iterative.[11] When a nuclear power plant is built in a community (an action path by builders and politicians), wealthier citizens leave the area (their action path), lowering the community's tax base and political clout (institutional projects), thus making it more difficult for the remaining citizens to fight off future environmental hazards (constraints on their future actions).

Properties of Path-Dependent Sequences

Path-dependent sequences have several distinct properties. William Sewell puts the first attribute succinctly: "what happened at an earlier point in time will affect the possible outcomes of a sequence of events occurring at a later point in time."[12] In other words, events tend to cascade over time as actions shape options for later action.

Consider the comparative study of Ventura and Santa Barbara, California, by Harvey Moloch and his colleagues. Both cities are seats of county government, rich in history, and blessed (or cursed) with oil reserves. They share a similar climate, oceanside locations with long beaches, and a diversity of fauna and flora. Their populations are similar in size and socioeconomic status. Despite their similarities, the cities took quite distinct paths of development. Santa Barbara became a center of information and technological innovation with a vibrant public life and high-end consumer goods and services. Ventura became a dreary industrial seaport with a meager public life and little land-use planning.

Events cascaded to produce each city as a distinctive place. In Ventura, local decisions about how to manage oil production spurred a series of negative developments. Unsightly oil tankers marred the city's oceanfront and stymied any possibility for upscale housing or recreational development on its waterfront. For Santa Barbara, the result was markedly different. There, citizen groups forced oil tax revenues to be used to make the waterfront more attractive. A scenic waterfront proved a lure to educational institutions and upscale businesses, which then attracted affluent residents who spurred the development of more amenities. Such cascading actions, in the language of structuration theory, were the result of "co-occurrences," as social practices built up some things and undermined others.[13]

A second property of path-dependent sequences is that options for action are increasingly constrained but always contingent. Once taken, particular paths of action are progressively more likely to continue, as actions of the past makes some future decisions more likely than others. Yet, no action is inevitable.[14] New events and unexpected decisions can, and often do, alter trajectories. Douglass North captures this synergy of choice and constraint:

> At every step along the way there [are choices]—political and economic—that provide . . . real alternatives. Path dependence is a way to narrow conceptually the choice set and link decision-making through time. It is not a story of inevitability in which the past neatly predicts the future.[15]

Their durability and dynamism is the third property of path-dependent sequences. Durability is the result of cascading sequences: what came before shapes what happens next.[16] Ventura and Santa Barbara gained different characteristics because each step of development built on previous ones. Dynamism exists because sequences are built on events that are unfolding and always different. If the waterfronts of Ventura and Santa Barbara are different from each other, each is also different from itself over time. Moloch and his colleagues describe this simultaneous durability and dynamism as a "*rolling inertia* [that] allows for continuous flux within a stable mode of operation."[17]

In path-dependent sequences, timing matters. This fourth property is described by Charles Tilly's observation that "*when* things happen within a sequence affects *how* they happen."[18] Early events in a sequence, even small events, can be enormously consequential. Military challenges to civilian rule when states are being formed can change the direction of state formation; later, such challenges may have little long-term impact. The life of a 20-year-old sentenced to prison will be changed forever by barriers to education and entry-level employment, whereas a prison term for someone at the age of 60 carries fewer consequences. Wanda J. Orlikowski's metaphor of scaffolding describes the salience of early events. Although scaffolds are temporary and fragile, they create the stability that permits an enduring and robust structure to be built. Even when scaffolds are discarded, their impression lingers in the structure that remains.[19]

A fifth property of path-dependent sequences is that history matters profoundly. Events of the past create an imprint that can endure for a long time. The effects of antebellum slavery are evident today in racial disparities in wealth. Violent conflicts leave scars on societies that last for generations. The past lingers through what Becker terms "congealed social agreements" that structure social life long after such agreements are made—for example, the way Wal-Mart's decision to locate a store in a community reshapes the terrain of local businesses for decades.[20]

In path-dependent sequences, action is always contingent. This has three implications for causation. Path-dependent sequences do not have simple relationships of cause and effect, so similar initial conditions don't necessarily result in similar end points. Oil production didn't make Ventura's problems inevitable. Nor did the actions of Santa Barbara's residents necessarily result in its scenic character. Second, chains of cause and effect can occur throughout a pathway, set into motion by unfolding structures and the sequential choices of social actors. Thus, causal factors are not found only at the beginning of a sequence.[21] Finally, in path-dependent sequences, there is not a primary, single, or even small number of causes since a multiplicity of factors propels action along a pathway. An ultimate determination of which factors are causes and which are effects is impossible. As Harvey Moloch and his colleagues note, "variable independence and dependence are lost in each other [as] . . . path-dependent sequences of action structures emerge together." Given the complexity of cause and effect, the task is to understand unfolding processes, not to predict their realization or final "accomplishment." This task requires thick description of sequences over time.[22]

Path Dependency in Activist Groups

Activist groups exhibit the five properties of path-dependent sequences.[23] First, cascading sequences of actions are common in activist groups. A bleak financial picture shrinks the number of events a group can stage, causing members to drift away, so the group has more and more difficulty in finding new funding. A group recruits members similar to those it already has, progressively increasing its homogeneity, which further increases as those who are dissimilar start to leave. Activists recruit through personal networks of people who tend to have similar politics, creating a self-reinforcing process that can narrow a group's vision.[24]

Paths of action create projects that make future action paths more or less likely. In a group that breaks store windows as a tactic of protest, those opposed to illegal actions will drop away and new members who favor such tactics may join. Because of the illegal behavior, the police will intensify surveillance of the group, further reshaping its membership as activists grow more careful about whom they recruit. Donors who oppose property destruction may stop giving money; perhaps new donors will appear. Media sources that support the group's actions now seem more relevant and those that oppose or ignore them seem less important; this change in information flow further reshapes the group's understandings of what is possible.[25] With this cascade of events, for the group to shift away from illegal actions becomes more unlikely, more difficult, and more costly.

Second, activist groups also act in ways that are constrained but sometimes unexpected, another property of path-dependent sequences.[26] In activist groups, as elsewhere in social life, once a choice is made, it's easier to take everything that comes with that choice than to make more decisions. For example, a group that agrees to make decisions by consensus ceases to consider actions that are not likely to win unified assent. Even constrained actions can take varying directions. The decision to sponsor an educational forum can predispose an activist group either to value its most articulate members who can address the forum or to emphasize the need for a larger budget to pay for speakers.

If, in Paul Pierson's terms, "cumulative commitments on the existing path . . . make change difficult,"[27] what activist groups do isn't fully constrained. Their actions aren't simply a product of changing situations.[28] Rather, members of activist groups act on their circumstances through intentional, innovative, and coordinated actions. In other words, they exert *collective* agency.[29] By recognizing the influence of both human agency and structural constraints on action, models of path dependency acknowledge unpredictability; they don't brush it aside apologetically. Thinking of action as a constrained but contingent sequence is a way to avoid over-emphasizing patterns and losing human action, or focusing entirely on the vagaries of action and neglecting the influence of social structure.[30]

Third, grassroots activism is simultaneously dynamic and durable, exhibiting the third property of path dependency. An activist group can vary considerably in its composition but display surprising consistency in the way it operates. Patterns of strong leadership or routine information sharing can persist even as the entire membership changes.[31]

Fourth, timing matters in grassroots activism. The early actions that activist groups take can be very influential for a long time, even beyond the presence or memories of those particular actors.

Finally, historical imprints linger in grassroots activism, the fifth property of path dependency. A founder's vision can shape a group indefinitely. Interpersonal tensions can etch an interactional pattern reproduced in successive waves of recruits. A decision to rotate leadership can have ramifications that endure long after its origin is forgotten.[32]

Whether a group will become violent, rigid, or enthusiastic is not predictable from its starting point—it is the product of distinct paths of action in which subtle and small factors matter. Whether a single member is present at one meeting can abruptly redirect the trajectory of an activist group. So can an offhand decision to march a block farther than originally intended in a demonstration, or failure to pursue an alliance with another group that had been considered earlier. Path dependency captures the impact of such incidental action better than do simple models of cause and effect. It draws attention to the dynamic and contingent nature of activist groups in which any particular configuration of members, ideas, and actions is likely to be temporary and alternative trajectories of action are possible at every point.[33]

TURNING POINTS

Although path dependency emphasizes human action, agency tends to diminish in large-scale structural processes over long periods of time, such as how choices for action constricted in the development of Ventura and Santa Barbara. This isn't as true of the small-scale cultural processes in activist groups.[34] Early actions limit the range of what members consider, but activist groups also exhibit moments of dramatic new envisioning when they are open to fresh possibilities. In studying activism, we need to pay attention both to trajectories of action and to the *turning points* at which these trajectories change.[35] Attention to the turning points of trajectories preserves the centrality of human agency in activism. As Andrew Abbott puts it, turning points are moments in which "action might make particularly consequential bridges."[36]

In macro-historical accounts, turning points generally are identified by tracing events backward in time to locate major alterations in direction.[37] For example, we now consider the 1911 fire at the Triangle Shirtwaist Factory in New York to be a turning point in U.S. labor law, creating public sympathy for protection for industrial laborers. Yet the effect of the fire was not obvious until well after it occurred, when protective labor legislation was enacted and violators were prosecuted. Similarly, the uprising of gay men in New York in the wake of a police raid in 1969, now termed the Stonewall Riots, came to be regarded as a turning point in sexual politics only after a substantial GLBT movement emerged. Whether the 2008 election of President Obama was a watershed in U.S. race relations or a blip on a longer trajectory of incremental change is not predictable at the moment. "What makes a turning point a turning point rather than a minor ripple,"

Abbott reminds us, "is the passage of sufficient time 'on the new course' such that it becomes clear that direction has indeed been changed."[38]

Like macro-historical changes, turning points in micro-action and interpretation are most obvious in retrospect, when new directions are established. Whether a fiery battle between new recruits and veteran activists will alter the direction of an activist group or just fray relationships can only be known for sure in the long run. However, it is possible to find hints of new directions in activist groups without waiting to see what develops over time. One way to do so is by observing shifts in their shared logic, the deep frameworks upon which social actors draw to understand the world in a meaningful way. Such shifts are evident in changes in how activists assess evidence, establish criteria on which they make decisions, and give meanings to their actions. Shifts in these logics signal turning points in sequences.[39]

A second and often easier way to observe turning points in sequences is by observing how actors shift their orientations in time. Here, I draw on Mustafa Emirbayer and Ann Mische's argument that intentional action (agency) not only takes place *over* time, but also *in* time. In their theory, agency is (often simultaneously) oriented to the past, as habitual ways of acting are selected and used in new settings; this provides continuity and stability in social life. It is oriented to the present, as actors evaluate possible actions in light of current realities. And it is oriented to the future, as actors project goals distant in time.[40]

Drawing on George Herbert Mead's idea that social life is emergent and requires "a continual refocusing of past and future," Emirbayer and Mische describe actors who select and switch the orientations of their actions in time. Agency is apparent, they argue, as actors "recompose" their orientations to the past, present, and future in changing contexts. At these points, actors make choices based on their considerations of the conditions they face: "Choices are imagined, evaluated, and contingently reconstructed by actors in ongoing dialogue with unfolding situations." Actors "reconstruct their view of the past in an attempt to understand the causal conditioning of the emergent present, while using this understanding to control and shape their responses in the arising future."[41]

Using Emirbayer and Mische's theory, I look for turning points in activist groups by observing how actions are reoriented *in* time as well as *over* time. Emirbayer and Mische's perspective is a theory of individuals, but it can be extended to collective actors like activist groups.[42] Grassroots groups orient toward the future as they imagine new ways the world can be organized.[43] They orient toward the present when they become preoccupied with matters of immediate concern. And they orient to the past as they discern lessons from what happened before as a guide for what to do now. This latter action, the reshaping of habitual action for new situations, is described by James Jasper as "ways of getting from here to there" that involve "experimental efforts to transmute existing traditions into new creations by problematizing elements that have been taken for granted."[44]

Focusing on the orientations of activist groups in time has benefits beyond discerning turning points. It provides a better vantage on the role of agency in collective action than does the more common focus on decision making because it includes examination of how groups imagine and interpret themselves and the world, as well as how they act. As a group plans a protest rally, it remembers police reactions to protestors from their *past* experiences. The group imagines *future* contingencies, speculating about what might happen if police closed the subways during the rally. It is situated in the *present* as activists deliberate how to respond to the denial of a rally permit. The shifting and multiple ways in which groups are oriented in time reveal subtle aspects of activist group dynamics. They also obviate the implicit definition of a normal time against which turning points stand out as a crisis or deviation.[45]

In activist groups, agency can be exerted even in habitual and routine forms of action, including those that seem unreflective or inevitable. How activist groups can act with deliberateness in mundane ways is illustrated in Charles Kurzman's description of Iranian revolutionary movements that energetically worked to "maintain practices as they are" by policing the "boundaries of the routine, handling disruptions, and making some changes to prevent others." Attending to how action is oriented in time provides a lens not only into agency in times of great change and energy but also in the more common "normal periods" of activist group life.[46]

INTEGRATING GROUP, CULTURE, SEQUENCE, AND TURNING POINTS

The scholarship on groups, culture, sequencing, and turning points informs the two propositions developed in this book:

1. Over Time, Activist Groups Operate in Path Trajectories with Turning Points

How activist groups decide what to do is a path-dependent process. So are their shared interpretations. Options tend to narrow when prior actions and understandings solidify as the taken-for-granted character of the group, much like the development of Ventura and Santa Barbara was circumscribed by sets of decisions that shaped the characters of these communities.

Trajectories are not fixed; they can shift at turning points along a sequence. In activist groups, turning points are those extraordinary times when people consider "options that were previously dismissed as unthinkable" or "moments of madness" that propel new actions. They are breaks in what Christian Smith describes as "'habitus'-like" practices, or "subconscious, unintentional, and institutional" routines.[47] At turning points, groups adopt new interpretations and see new kinds of actions as possible. A group long accustomed to seeing its mission as local school reform, for instance, suddenly widens its scope to consider broad issues of economic justice. In the process, activists collectively begin to see themselves in a different light, imagining alliances with groups with which they formerly saw little in common. They now regard themselves as capable of actions like boycotts and street blockades that earlier could not be considered. In the language of hermeneutics, turning points involve both first-order and second-order interpretations. Actors reinterpret their habitual, commonsense actions and understandings (first-order), as when the school reform group takes on economic justice issues, but they also interpret their new interpretations (second-order), as when that school reform group discusses its newfound ideas and the implications for what it should do next.[48]

Becker uses Diane Vaughan's study of divorce as an example of how to identify trajectories in social life. Instead of asking how divorcing couples differ from those who stay together, Vaughan asks how each step in the couple's relationship—like childbirth or infidelity—creates conditions for a subsequent step. In Vaughan's process-oriented account, Becker notes, no step is inevitable. Even when one partner was unfaithful, there is more than one possible ending for a couple because people react differently to similar situations. Vaughan traces the trajectories that led to divorce, showing *how* a couple moved toward divorce without suggesting that this was inevitable.[49]

Process-based accounts or trajectory models are useful in the study of activism because they show how grassroots groups actually make decisions and build shared ideas. They reveal the intricacies of how these take place in "numerous small ways,"[50] responding to Emirbayer and Mische's call for "studies of the communicative processes of challenge, experimentation, and debate by which actors formulate new temporally constructed understandings of their own abilities to engage in individual and collective change."[51] Trajectories highlight the *process of acting* rather than actions and the *dynamics of interpreting* rather than interpretations. They open the possibility that activist groups can travel along different paths from a similar origin to a similar destination, information that is lost in causal models that measure only beginning and end points.

2. Small, Even Incidental Actions can be Important in the Trajectories of Activist Groups, Especially When They Occur Early

In path-dependent sequences, large consequences can follow from even tiny events at the right moment. Although studies of collective activism often focus on what Tilly calls "big structures, large processes, huge comparisons," small factors, including those of happenstance and idiosyncrasy, also can matter a great deal.[52]

The lesson here is that what happens in an activist group may be explicable only by understanding events from a remote past. It is tempting to explain why a particular group acts or thinks in a particular way by using proximate causes—its current size or ideological proclivities—but activist groups also act in the shadow of their pasts, however distant, forgotten, or shaped by the tendency that Kwame Anthony Appiah observes: "once we have a stake in a practice, we shall be tempted to invent a past that supports it."[53]

These two propositions highlight the role of sequence and temporality in what activist groups do and what they talk about. Path dependency shows the sequencing of interpretation and action in group life. The lingering effects of early actions and interpretations show the temporality of what activist groups consider possible and what acts they decide to undertake.

The empirical chapters that follow use these propositions to illuminate how Pittsburgh's emerging grassroots groups form and the range of alternatives from which they choose their actions and interpretations. As the chapters show, fledgling activism takes shape in fits and starts. In some groups, path-dependent sequences begin early and quickly become self-reinforcing. In others, group dynamics remain unformed much longer. In many groups, some sequences take on a predictable form while others do not. For instance, a group might set off on a path-dependent sense of its political focus while remaining quite in flux in terms of its membership.

The remainder of this chapter illustrates the logic of analysis with an extended case study of a single sequence, a protest campaign by the Animal Liberation League (ALL).

CASE STUDY OF TRAJECTORIES AND TURNING POINTS

ALL's campaign began when they decided to force restaurants to stop selling the appetizer foie gras on the grounds that geese are harmed in its production. It ended when Pennsylvania passed an "eco-terrorism" bill that ALL interpreted as outlawing its protests. Three distinct sub-sequences define this campaign. The sub-sequences overlapped in time but had different chains of causes and effects.[54] Sequence A commenced with ALL's decision to campaign against foie gras, a move accompanied by a radical shift in the group's sense of itself. Sequence B began as ALL shifted tactics, with a new definition of what it faced in the campaign. Sequence C was marked by a shift in the group's emotional and affective nature as ALL reconsidered the nature of its allies and enemies.

Sequence A. Deciding on the issue: When ALL launched its campaign, it was regularly attracting 15 to 20 people to meetings and working on a variety of issues. It was protesting at an upscale shop that sold animal fur, distributing free vegetarian food to customers at fast food hamburger places (an action it termed "feed ins"), demonstrating at a shopping center against wool production, lobbying against required animal dissections in science classes, distributing flyers about research funded by a pet food company, and fund-raising at grocery stores. Despite this full plate of activities, no one objected to the idea of adding yet another campaign. To the contrary, the meeting brimmed with feelings of excitement and confidence.

The campaign against foie gras was a turning point for ALL, but the shift was not visible from the outside. To ALL's supporters and audiences, protesting foie gras looked like any other campaign, a series of actions aimed at fomenting public outcry against animal cruelty. ALL's pamphlets and flyers featured graphic pictures showing how farmers expanded the livers of geese before slaughter by forcing food down their throats. The juxtaposition of brutal humans and innocent geese, designed to evoke sympathy for animals and disgust at their human abusers, was not much different from ALL's earlier campaigns against fur (lovable baby seals), meat-eating (doe-eyed cows), and wool production (cuddly lambs). From the outside, the foie gras campaign seemed an example of habitual action, a repetition of ALL's well-trodden path of activism.

From the inside, however, it was clear that the meaning of the action had changed. When a member first mentioned the idea of attacking foie gras, she didn't frame it as another instance of animal abuse, as might be expected. Rather, she urged the group to protest foie gras because it had become a visible demand of the larger animal rights movement and thus crucial to demonstrate the movement's strength. That ALL should consider its actions within a larger context of a movement for animal rights was startling; it almost never mentioned animal rights activities outside the immediate Pittsburgh area. Indeed, ALL's sense of itself was firmly built on its place in local progressive politics: it judged itself only by comparison to other progressive groups in the city. These local groups were the reference point by which ALL assessed how it was doing, how large it should be, and what it should do next.

Although novel, the idea that it was part of a larger movement of animal rights sparked immediate interest in the members of ALL. People were clearly energized and the meeting buzzed with ideas. Instead of talking about details of the abuse of geese, a habitual motif at the launch of other campaigns, ALL discussed how to position itself to become part of a larger movement to change how society treats animals. Foie gras quickly took on a unique status, not just another campaign but a springboard to new possibilities. It opened the door for ALL to think of itself in a new way.

ALL's changing sense of itself was apparent almost immediately. As members worked out the details of their attack on foie gras, they measured themselves against a new and less familiar standard. Their goal was not to protect geese or build a progressive Pittsburgh but to fit into a potentially vast movement for social change. In the language of time horizons, ALL was switching toward a future orientation. Its horizon of possibilities was no longer local and fixed; it was now fluid and expansive.

ALL's new stance was evident in its increasingly frenzied pace. In contrast to its prior leisurely speed when campaigns were discussed thoroughly before being adopted, ALL launched its foie gras effort in a frantic rush with members voicing impatience that it had not happened faster. There was no evident deadline for stopping foie gras, but activists griped that they had lost precious time by waiting until after Thanksgiving so that members could protest at grocery stores that sold turkeys and enjoy a vegan holiday potluck for "all who showed up to demonstrate." As one young man put it, summarizing the frustrations of many, "We are *finally* going to be starting our campaign against restaurants that use foie gras soon—[but] most likely after Thanksgiving is over."

The foie gras campaign broke other patterns as well. In the past, the number of people ALL could muster for any event was, almost by definition, enough. The group simply adjusted its sense of the right scale of an event to the number of people who came. A protest was successful, members decided at one point, if there were enough people there to distribute literature, hold the banner, and get signatures on a petition. Five would do, for a group consisting of fewer than two dozen (in present time). With foie gras, however, standards changed. Efforts became measured against what was possible (in future time) for a major movement. By this standard, ALL was sorely lacking. Its meetings became characterized by worries that the group didn't have "enough people" and needed more. It needed a "big crowd" to attract the media and show that it was part of something big. Such rising standards had a demoralizing effect. Members who insisted that the campaign was going "extremely well," even that they were making Pittsburgh a center of international opposition to foie gras, were increasingly drowned out by those who saw the campaign as "stalled" in contrast to what needed to happen.

Sequence A began with a decision that seemed minor and incidental at the time, to add another cause to ALL's extensive set of campaigns against animal abuse. Yet this small action provoked a set of cascading decisions that fundamentally altered ALL's sense of its actions within the larger political environment. As ALL increasingly assessed itself as responsible to a broad movement on behalf of animals, the membership size and pace of events with which it had operated no longer seemed viable. The group had turned a corner that reoriented it to what it regarded as possible and reasonable to do.

Sequence B. Changing tactics: Although the foie gras campaign ushered in a new sense of itself as a group, ALL initially stayed with familiar tactics. Letter writing had worked before, so members wrote to five pricey restaurants and demanded that foie gras be removed from their menus. So confident were they that this would succeed that ALL spent a meeting composing the wording for thank you notes to restaurants that made "the intelligent and compassionate decision" to withdraw foie gras. It came as a major shock when not a single restaurant replied.

The group faced a dilemma. Should it wait for answers? Send another letter? Find a different tactic? Forget restaurants and target foie gras distributors or producers? Abandon the campaign altogether? After much discussion, members decided to stay the course, sending another round of letters. These warned that if a restaurant didn't schedule a meeting with ALL within a week, they would be the target of public protest.

It is revealing to take a close look at the dynamics in ALL as it initiated a new round of letters. Although ALL was relying on a well-worn tactic, its horizons of possibility had shifted considerably. Letter writing was not simply chosen automatically or out of habit; rather, a range of other tactics was considered and rejected in favor of more letters. In this case, what seemed to be a repetitive, habitual action was instead an intentional and deliberative act by a group weighing its options in light of an unfolding situation. Repeated actions need not indicate the dead weight of tradition.

ALL's decision to write more letters was propelled by its new theory of political action. This was evident in its debates over issues that had long been off the table in the group. An example is a worried discussion of when "groups like ours" needed to concede defeat that slid into an energized debate over which groups it was most like, followed by speculative talk about which groups it could aspire to be like. What started as a despairing account of the costs of escalating conflict with restaurants thus became an exciting scrutiny of its capacity for action, now and in the future. Talking about whether they could sustain a lengthy campaign led members into an animated set of predictions about what could happen under various scenarios of actions and responses.

To ALL's dismay, no restaurant replied to its second letter. In earlier campaigns, such an impasse would lead the group to abandon the campaign. But members no longer saw this as an option. Since they were part of a larger movement, they didn't have the right to simply stop. The only possibilities now were to continue to wait, write yet another series of letters, or begin a protest. They decided to protest.

At the same time, ALL exhibited a shift in its theory of the connection between resources and action. Up to that time, the group rarely worried about the details of its planned actions. If it decided to protest at a shopping center, for example, one or two people would "take charge" and the group as a whole would do no further planning. The scale and nature of the event was simply whatever those in charge could arrange. If two people showed up and could stay an hour, that became the event. If they brought flyers, they were distributed; if not, there was nothing to hand out and no one fretted over whether there should be. (In this respect, ALL differed considerably from other Pittsburgh groups, most of which spent a great deal of time deliberating over the particulars of their events and campaigns, even allowing logistics to swamp all other items of business.)

Different from their earlier patterns, the members of ALL worried that they wouldn't have the money or people to pull off the foie gras campaign. Some even criticized the protests—not enough people, bad choice of time, few posters. Such rebukes—heretofore unheard of in ALL—began as sideline muttering among friends but quickly leaked into open displays of friction in meetings. ALL shifted to a new theory of resources and action: now it would only plan events after it had assembled the resources needed to stage them. It would no longer agree to a protest and then look for a way to carry it off.

The resource issue breached ALL's implicit ban on criticizing events, allowing other conflicts to emerge. Eyeing tactics being used in other cities, some members insisted that they should stage day-long protests at each restaurant. Others argued that it would be more effective to protest for a shorter time every week. And still others complained that the campaign was being rushed or that going to several protests a week was too burdensome. Another conflict erupted over who was an appropriate protestor. Before that point, protests were made up of ALL members and anyone they could bring along. Now, some members pushed to attract additional protestors from the public at large by advertising protests on a new Web site, although, ironically, the site had nearly the opposite effect. By insisting that an announcement on the Web site was a prerequisite for staging a protest, ALL became hostage to technical problems. Protests were planned, then canceled as the Web site crashed. Instead of stimulating protest activity, ALL's decision to recruit protestors from the public caused its protests to stall.

In Sequence B, ALL confronted the difficulties of pursuing its new agenda for a broad animal rights movement with its familiar set of tactics and decided to switch to a more protest-oriented approach. This set the group on a new path of actions and deliberations as members began to fret over whether protests would be sufficient and whether ALL was capable of sustaining these.

Sequence C. Altering the mood: The final shift in ALL's sequence was its abrupt affective change. From its beginning, ALL was remarkable among Pittsburgh's activist groups for its lack of emotionality. Meetings were largely devoted to exchanging information. Even in situations in which emotions ran high in other groups, such as after confrontations with police or their targets, ALL's discussions showed little passion. When someone described what happened at a protest, his or her report was rarely met with cheers, moans, or even expressions of support or incredulity. Indeed, across all my field notes on ALL, there are few accounts of highly charged emotional moments. One of these rare occasions was when its longtime leader expressed frustration that things were not getting done fast enough. Even then, no one reacted. ALL's lack of emotionality is particularly striking because it adeptly used emotional appeals to garner sympathy for animals with photos of innocent, abused animals meant to elicit pity, disgust, and empathy from their audiences.

The first hint of a change in its affective nature appeared when ALL discussed which restaurant to target first. In the past, such decisions were always made on practical grounds, like whether a location was on a bus route that would make it easy for protestors to participate. In the foie gras campaign, however, different considerations emerged. Although every restaurant failed to respond to their ultimatum, ALL decided to target the one whose manager was "terribly rude" when asked about the menu. Oddly, this incident had been mentioned earlier when ALL was reviewing the week's events, but had elicited no reaction. Now, it became the core of ALL's strategy. For the first time, members seemed fully energized and passionate. They decried the manager's attitude as "unbelievable" and agreed that such rudeness demanded a dramatic response. In the words of one activist, "this means war."

Emotion now assumed a new place in ALL: it was a basis for decision making. In earlier campaigns, ALL assumed that people would change once exposed to the awful realities of animal abuse. After being properly educated, trophy fisherman would catch and release their fish, buyers would adopt fake fur, and consumers would substitute tofu for cheese or meat in their diets. Its animated discussion of the "rude" restaurant owner, however, led ALL in a new tactical direction. Members now saw two different audiences. One profited from animal abuse and deserved to be condemned. The other merely consumed animal products and could be converted to ALL's position.

ALL's changing emotional trajectory is evident in its choice of tactics. A meeting to plan the first protest against foie gras, on Valentine's Day, boiled with members' anger and the desire to attack recalcitrant (profiting) owners of restaurants. At the same time, they cautioned each other to be mild-mannered and conciliatory toward the (consuming) restaurant patrons. Protesters were to "look presentable to attract the attention of the people going into the restaurant," a message that most took to mean they should mimic the expensive attire of those who eat at high-priced restaurants. In a similar vein, the flyers meant for patrons were far less abrasive than the letters they sent to restaurant owners such as "Have a Heart. Stop Selling Foie Gras!" written in red over a large heart. The underlying theory was clear: patrons could be their allies.[55]

However mild, the Valentine's Day protest produced a tense confrontation with restaurant owners who were described by members of ALL as "angry" and "unreasonable." One activist claimed that the owners were "clearly rattled by us being there, as evidenced by the fact that they kept popping out and looking at us about every 10 minutes," a behavior that convinced the group that it was making progress. Less expected and far more demoralizing was the reaction of customers. Even when greeted politely, those entering the restaurant were "extremely closed-minded and either outright ignored us or made negative comments." ALL's newfound openness to discussing emotions made it possible to attend to nuances that would not have registered in its deliberations earlier. If restaurant patrons were close-minded, they were to be considered ALL's foes, no better than the owners. No longer would ALL try to convert them; they were "beyond the compassion of their hearts." Only pressure tactics made sense in this new context:

The staff at BV [restaurant] are even worse, and the owner . . . is the worst of all . . . trust me, these people are not going to be swayed by compassion . . . nevertheless, we are going forward with a full-scale comprehensive campaign . . . our strategy being to become one big major annoyance to them until they don't want to deal with us anymore since they're probably not going to stop out of the goodness of their hearts. They are going to be a major challenge for us, but we would not have taken on this campaign if we didn't intend to win it.[56]

ALL's new tactic, in members' words to be a "big major annoyance," consisted of a series of angry verbal exchanges with customers and staff in a fast-paced series of protests at the restaurant that stretched its financial and human resources to the limit and threatened to swamp all other projects. When another month passed without concessions, ALL began to confront the possibility that the owners wouldn't give in. But members didn't see switching tactics as an option. Even if protests weren't doing much, they reasoned in one meeting, they should be continued so it would be clear that ALL wouldn't give up easily. The struggle had become as important as winning. Protest was now the habitual path of action.

The path of protest became untenable when, without mentioning ALL, the target restaurant simply stopped serving foie gras. After an excited discussion, ALL proclaimed victory and announced that its protests had been effective. The lesson, members concluded, was that protests needed to be both confrontational and frequent. No longer would they consider persuasion as a possible tactic; all discussion now included an expectation of conflict. ALL even chose Susie's, a relatively new and upscale restaurant, as its next target because its location, an area with much foot traffic, would produce witnesses to the confrontation. This was a particularly odd scenario since ALL's only prior experience with Susie's, a meeting with the chef, had been, everyone agreed, "successful" and one that "we should be happy about." Yet, in selecting tactics, ALL's new set of assumptions outweighed its actual experience with Susie's. Memories of the positive meeting with Susie's chef seemed to evaporate; its staff and owner were now talked about as beyond hope and its customers as "stuck up."

If the earlier ALL had been careful not to offend, now it seized on offense as a tactic. One example was a Mother's Day protest in which it set out to disgust customers during their meals by creating large displays of the gruesome methods ("torture" in ALL's terms) used to feed geese. Customers now were regarded as part of the problem and therefore fair game for such assaults, even though the notion that consumer demand caused restaurants to serve foie gras was an interpretation that ALL had dismissed earlier when voiced by restaurant owners.

Protests at Susie's were tense from the beginning. ALL claimed that someone was taking members' pictures, trying to steal their signs, and even crushing a poster. Within a week, the restaurant's window was broken and a statue in its front yard destroyed, although ALL consistently insisted that it was not responsible. ALL meetings became increasingly somber. People talked openly of the restaurant owner and staff as the "enemy" who likely "vandalized themselves" to make ALL look bad and who needed to be "hurt." Subtle distinctions disappeared; discussion was phrased in stark terms of "us" and "them." As its activists grew angrier, ALL stepped up its efforts until it was staging protests almost daily. The group now had a sense of urgency; it had to do more and more, faster and faster. Activists could no longer be satisfied with removing foie gras from restaurant menus. They also had to go after caterers and ordinary people who served it at receptions and fund-raising events.

ALL's changing theory of political action precluded a number of previously viable options for removing foie gras from menus, such as negotiation and public pressure. It also created a problem for the group itself. If restaurant owners lacked good will and responded only to pressure, how could ALL ensure that they wouldn't put foie gras back on the menu as soon as ALL stopped protesting? The only solution that members could imagine was to monitor every restaurant forever, although "backtracking" to check on those that had agreed to ban foie gras would interfere with targeting new restaurants. This dilemma took a toll on the group. Members grumbled that ALL was losing ground and confided that they felt boxed into an endless and ultimately futile campaign.

As the group seemed stuck in a self-reinforcing cycle, it had a turning point. Opening a line of discussion that had been closed since the failed effort to recruit through the Web site, a few members raised the question of finding more members to deal with the mounting workload. Although they were not able to design a plan to get these members, the very idea that things could be different freed the group to envision other alternatives. Eliminating foie gras was once again positioned as just a step toward another goal, now framed as stopping commercial animal farming altogether.

In Sequence C, the decision to embrace the cause of foie gras set ALL on a new emotional path. It opened the door to making emotions a central aspect of the group's decision making. At the same time, this new path constrained the range of tactical possibilities that were earlier apparent in ALL's discussions. Negotiation and persuasion, in particular, were no longer regarded as viable options.

Implications: In its attack on foie gras, ALL recomposed its time orientations at several points. Its progression of tactics from persuasion to protest was oriented to the *past*, drawing on the group's earlier experiences to shape similar actions that were, at times, inscribed with new meanings. The group's declarations of war or ideas about changing how all animals were treated in this society oriented it to the *future*, with distant objectives and a sense of the group's capacity to reach them. How ALL assessed itself was firmly rooted in the *present*, as activists weighed alternative courses of action compared to those of other progressive groups. In some decisions, events, and sub-sequences, ALL operated simultaneously with several time orientations; in others, its time orientations changed sequentially. Even in this single campaign, ALL demonstrated agency as it switched from past to present, or future to past, rather than be mired in one time orientation.

The example of ALL also shows that activist groups do not recompose their time orientations in a predictable way. I coded the dominant time orientation in 11 ALL meetings or events. Table 2.1 shows the shifts over time, as ALL initially was oriented to the future, shifted to the present, then to the past, and so on.

ALL didn't just start oriented to the present (or future) and then develop a sense of the past. Nor did it move from the past to the present or future. Rather, ALL recomposed itself differently depending on a complex mixture of changing realities, its unfolding interpretations of its context, its theories of political action, and its sense of collective competence and efficacy.

Activist groups do not react in any simple manner to external structural conditions or even to their perceptions of those conditions. As the case of ALL shows, they formulate and reformulate their reactions—along with their strategies, tactics, and sense of themselves as political actors—over time. Even when ALL took actions it had done before, like letter writing or protesting, it didn't do so in a robotic fashion. Rather, it selectively focused on aspects of the current situation that it regarded as similar to situations in the past and that made these meaningful in the present. As ALL embarked on each new path of action, it operated from a different range of options it saw as viable. Occasionally, a path of diminishing options ruptured, leading ALL to consider a wider range of possibilities. In activist groups, the collapse of workable options can trigger a turning point; so can small shifts in action and interpretation that rupture an existing path and create new openings. More often, however, groups stick with a path that diminishes their sense of possibility over time. The exact paths that activist groups will follow is not predictable, but that their actions and interpretations will take the form of paths is foreseeable.

What happened with ALL, even in this brief sequence of events, is not fully captured by looking only at its resources, political opportunities, and

---

Table 2.1. CHANGES IN TIME ORIENTATION IN ANIMAL LIBERATION LEAGUE (ALL) MEETINGS OVER TIME

---

future

present—hope for now, against past mistakes

present

past/habitual actions

future

past and present

present—evaluating the past

future

present

past/habitual actions

present

---

strategies, or how its members rationally calculated benefits. It also involved the dynamics of the group. In the chapters that follow, I explore these dynamics across a number of emerging activist groups. In Chapter 3, I look at how activist groups define themselves *organizationally* as they decide who is part of the group. Chapter 4 explores how activist groups define themselves *ideologically* as they consider what political issue to address. In Chapter 5, I focus on how activist groups define themselves *interpersonally* as they set standards for how members should treat each other. These tasks of self-definition—membership, political issues, and personal interactions—are not the only ones that fledgling groups face. They even may not always be the most consequential. Yet these are tasks that every group confronts in its early days. They provide a lens for seeing how emerging groups shape their character and provide a platform for their subsequent actions and interpretations.[57]

CHAPTER 3

Who Belongs?

When 37 people showed up at the second meeting of Ecology Now (EN), the organizers were thrilled. The room was filled with excited talk as people generated ideas at a rapid pace; many suggestions were met with shouts, applause, funny rejoinders. This was quite a change from its sparsely attended meeting a week earlier. Then, talk was subdued and modest, little beyond encouraging recycling and "influencing public opinion" about President Bush's destructive environmental policies. Tonight, the mood was strikingly different. In the grip of a "collective effervescence,"[1] EN imagined a much more expansive agenda. It could "create a large citizen-based movement" to "fight for the environment" and drive Bush from office. It could take on "big issues" like logging and urban sprawl, not just easy ones like recycling. Talk swiftly turned to plans for action. A few people volunteered to contact other environmental groups about collaborating locally. Others promised to check what was happening in nearby states. Everything seemed in place for a synergy that would transform the buzz of collective energy into concrete projects that would solidify and further energize the group.

As the second meeting wrapped up, the tone suddenly changed. A young man casually mentioned that EN needed more members to make all this activity possible. At that point, one of the organizers seized the floor. "This needs to be a community-based movement," she admonished the man, "not a narrow effort among friends." She pointed to two of the evening's most active participants and declared that they "obviously look like environmentalists," an apparent reference to their dreadlocked hair and tie-dyed shirts. "If we don't start recruiting in a different way," she insisted, "the movement will start looking like a Phish concert." Her comments had a devastating effect on the group's enthusiasm. How could it be "community based?" Who could it recruit, if not members' friends and people like them? No answers were forthcoming, and the mostly young white crowd shuffled out in a sober mood.

The founder of Black Antiwar Pittsburgh (BAP), a group mobilizing African Americans against the U.S. military presence in Iraq, had a similar reaction. By most measures, BAP was thriving. Many people came to its events, and other activists cited it as a model of grassroots organizing. Surprisingly, however, its founder seemed depressed about the group's future, even about a vigil that drew more than 100 people:

> The turning point was for us the fact that we didn't think that there were more than 10 people who we hadn't seen in an anti-war demonstration before. So while you [might] say "wow," we were not happy. . . . We know that we're missing our objective of mobilizing the black community, that we have not really effectively pulled them—black people—to this as we wanted to.

The crowd was large, but its members were not the kinds of people the organizers wanted to attract. It was not the group it wanted to be.

Christian Smith writes that our "suppositional assumptions and beliefs" are not built on "an indubitable, universal foundation of knowledge" but rather they resemble rafts that "float freely in the shifting seas of culture and history." As activist groups shape a sense of themselves, they become similar to the passengers on these rafts. They become "communities of believers," in Smith's terms, who can't see past their rafts to the vast sea and so think that their raft is "all that exists and is true."[2] This chapter looks at how activist groups become "communities of believers." It explores how their actions and interpretations take a path-dependent form, what happens at turning points along these paths, and how small and incidental factors have lingering effects. And it examines the ways that activist groups establish shared and meaningful assumptions about who they are that come to seem self-evidently true, as well as the consequences of these assumptions for what groups do and consider possible.[3]

Defining who they are is a fundamental accomplishment of activist groups.[4] It is key to a group's sense of itself, as people who are like-minded or diverse, dedicated activists or a collection of the mildly interested. It creates what I term a group's *organizational* character. *Who we are*, in organizational terms, is a platform on which activist groups produce a unified voice, standards of leadership and authority, rules and procedures, political agendas, and strategies.[5] It is also the foundation of distinctions and inequities, since those who best fit the group's self-definition gain power to make claims and exert influence within the group. One group defines itself as a collection of experienced activists, so it values members' prior knowledge; novice activists have little standing to shape its direction. Another sees itself as a voice for ordinary people, so it favors and empowers new activists.

Self-definition is both accomplished and malleable.[6] Even a group's provisional sense of itself has a stickiness that influences its actions and interpretations. REBORN, a queer rights group, struggled through several stressful meetings to debate who it was. After trying on several self-definitions, it decided its members were "radical queers" who were "sick and tired of the mainstream." Once that was decided, REBORN was set on an organizational path that meant anyone who wanted to join needed to accept that label. "What about those currently in the group?" someone asked. After a brief discussion, the group concluded that everyone had to fit this definition to remain. Even its founding members were not exempt from the group's narrowing sense of who should be part of REBORN.[7] When REBORN declared itself as "radical queers," two people walked out and never returned. Those who remained were determined to find other radical queers to join the group. These two sets of actions—the exit of those who didn't fit and the recruitment of those who did—reinforced the group's self-definition. So did its explicit instructions to new people that the group was one of radical queers. Never again would it consider bringing in people who supported a queer agenda but did not define themselves as radical. That option was closed.

Self-definitions set other boundaries around action that further shore up a group's sense of who belongs. After its declaration, REBORN simply ignored ideas that did not conform to its image as radical queers, a striking example of cascading actions. When a young man suggested that the group work with other GLBT groups on the annual Pride Fest, for example, no one responded. After a moment of silence, members resumed planning their own separate actions for Pride Fest. There was no explicit statement that one couldn't be a radical queer and take part in the activities of more mainstream gays—but there didn't need to be. The message was clear. A similar episode occurred at the next meeting, when a new recruit suggested that REBORN work with another local gay rights group. She too faced a wall of silence. When she persisted, complaining that she didn't understand what was going on, another member took her aside to say that they couldn't work with the other group because it was tied to the Republican Party and at odds with their radical aims. No longer was its political direction debated; it was simply off the table.

Self-definitions are temporal. Establishing *who we are* sets guidelines for what *we should be,* even though present and future definitions need not be identical. A group may see itself as one of experienced activists now but aim for a broader membership later. Desired future members can affect activist groups, even long before the group identifies or recruits them. A school reform group didn't schedule meetings on weekends to avoid interfering with members' "family time," although no one in the group then had such a conflict. It hoped to attract people with young children, though, so it wanted a schedule that would work for those who should be members. These activists thought making accommodations would help their recruitment.

Self-definitions also are spatial. *Who we are* can be situated in the local or be more expansive, based on current or desired members. A group advocating Middle East peace regarded itself as an international group after an extensive discussion of other possibilities. Although its current members were all U.S. citizens, they didn't want this to be the case. They wanted deep connections with people outside the country. So, de facto, the group was international. Other groups wrestled with more local spatial definitions. Were they residents of southwestern Pennsylvania? Pittsburghers? Residents of the city's politically progressive East End? And did these spatial labels identify who they were as members, or also who they represented?

Some activist groups define themselves by imagined external standards. A civil rights group initially labeled itself as "reasonable," in contrast to other (unnamed) groups who were not. But soon, some members doubted this self-definition. One older man questioned why they thought of themselves as reasonable; could it be simply that they just thought alike? Another man jumped in to note that disadvantaged people might see being "reasonable" as simply acquiescing to the status quo. With this, the idea of assessing themselves through the vantage point of an abstract "disadvantaged" person caught on. Returning to Christian Smith's idea, outside criteria gave activists a vantage point to judge how they were doing.[8]

By taking account of how others might see them, activist groups engage in a collective form of reflexivity. Individual self-reflection consists of an awareness of experience and an awareness that we are experiencing. Collective self-reflection, by analogy, occurs when a social group *"knows that it is a knower,"* to borrow Smith's words, observing itself (individually or collectively) from an external point of reference. For activist groups, the outside point can be located in a variety of salient audiences, including potential recruits, public officials, other activist groups, national organizations, or simply the general public.[9]

As activist groups define themselves—as poor people, citizens, faith communities, mothers, marginalized persons, and so forth—their definitions are self-reinforcing, setting out paths of sequential action that are both dynamic and durable. Self-definitions influence the horizons of possibility for actions and interpretations. Whether they see themselves as—or aspire to be—rabble-rousers or suburbanites, young or middle-aged, families or individuals shapes what groups consider and what they do.

This chapter explores dynamics of action in new activist groups as they define themselves organizationally on three dimensions: belonging, membership, and recruitment. It concludes with an extended comparison of two groups, illustrating the paths and turning points in their trajectories of self-definition.

BELONGING

In fledgling activist groups, questions of *who belongs* typically arise quickly and as a matter of great urgency, lest the group fizzle away before getting started. Groups set on this path of action from their very earliest meetings as founders and initial members discuss whether to reach out to seasoned activists or look for members with fresher ideas. In private, early participants and prospective members also assess their own fit in the group. Just outside an anti-war group meeting, a group of middle-aged women talked worriedly about whether the group was "too male" for them. Similarly, at an early meeting of an immigrant rights group, a U.S.-born man decided that he didn't belong because he had no personal experience with immigration issues.

Belonging can have a broad meaning in new activist groups. At an initial gathering of an anti-drug group, people offered their credentials to show they belonged. Some mentioned personal tragedies with illegal drugs; others made clear that they were community leaders who knew about the problem. Initially, neither form of belonging seemed favored; people just belonged. But as the group took shape, belonging began to have finer gradations. People with personal connections to drugs were still welcome, but those who *most* belonged were those with "more practical" ways to help the group meet its goals, like ties to local politicians. As a later chapter will show, groups make a similar distinction between personal and practical forms of belonging as they assign levels of credibility to their members.

Nira Yuval-Davis tells us that there is a "politics of belonging."[10] A sense of *who belongs* (and therefore *who doesn't belong*) is forged in the same dynamics of talk and actions that then shape the composition of the group. As the membership becomes younger, more oriented to religious faith, or tied to sexual identities, the sense of *who belongs* shifts accordingly.

Even as it takes form and affects actions, the sense of belonging is always unfolding. The changing agendas of a group can divert its paths of belonging. After intensely recruiting at local universities, an animal rights activist argued that her group "needed older people [since] they were being treated like they were just little college kids and nothing serious." Too, a group's changing membership can alter its sense of belonging. In a tiny group—like these fledgling Pittsburgh ones that averaged fewer than 13 members per meeting—the addition or exit of a member or two can have large effects. If the women who congregated outside the anti-war meeting had decided to enter, their decision would have made the anti-war group a mixed-sex one, and future recruits would not have to wonder whether women belong. If the U.S.-born man had stayed in the immigration group, it would have been a group in which both immigrants and their supporters belong.

How belonging unfolds in cascading sequences of action and interpretation was evident in Race Equality (RE), a civil rights group that initially defined itself as African American. Its early claim to represent "the community" was tied to actions like distributing flyers to "never let people forget" about racial injustice. After a while, however, RE's members became convinced that only large rallies and protest marches would change racial practices and that only a multiracial group could mount such large actions. Its original sense of belonging became unworkable with this theory of action. Talk of who belonged, earlier restricted to those who had experienced racial injustice (so, only racial minorities), expanded to include those "not afraid to [pass out] flyer[s]" in African American neighborhoods, a definition that opened the group to some (but not all) whites. However, this didn't work. The category of those "not afraid to flyer" was too vague to identify who should be brought in, so only a few people were approached to join and none actually did. What might have been a turning point in RE's self-definition, that is, expanding who belonged, fizzled out. The group began a downward spiral. Members complained of being "burned out" and "wearing out" and attendance at meetings and events dwindled. For the first time, members were openly disgruntled. As one put it, "downtown [local government] is wearing us out." Within a few weeks, RE stopped meeting altogether.

Belonging and Action

How the meaning of belonging shapes action and vice versa is evident in the history of Eliminating Police Violence Together (EPVT), a group fighting police assaults on civilians. As early participants in EPVT deliberated who belonged to the group, or, as they sometimes phrased it, "who the group belonged to," a variety of possibilities emerged. Maybe those who were personally victimized by the police. Or victims and their family members. Maybe all African Americans, since they were all potential victims of police violence. Or just African American men. Or African Americans from poor neighborhoods. Perhaps everyone with an interest in racial justice was an appropriate member. Sentiment was mixed. Some pushed for broad inclusion. Others wanted to exclude activists from anti-war and anti-death-penalty groups that, despite their focus on violence, never spoke out against violence by the police.

The debate over belonging continued for several weeks, spilling from meetings into informal discussions among EPVT's activists. Eventually, they reached a solution. The group would work "in alliance" with whoever supported its goals, but two kinds of people would not be considered for the group: police officers and those from "potentially violent" racial justice groups. Police didn't belong because they supported each other, even in violence against the black community and thus couldn't be trusted. Members of racial justice groups that used violent tactics didn't belong because they didn't renounce violence. The decision seemed straightforward, but questions lingered. Did a racial justice group that had had a physical brawl with Ku Klux Klan members count as a violent group? What about militant black nationalists? Members of the Nation of Islam? Or anti-gang street workers who were formerly gang members themselves?

Deliberations about belonging often continue over time, but even provisional definitions are consequential. When EPVT decided that it belonged to police victims, it no longer sought support from white progressives and tried to make more contacts in the city's most economically bereft neighborhoods. Its racial balance shifted as a few African Americans, but no whites, joined. Authority slid away from white members and toward African Americans, even those without personal ties to victims. White members began to speak less often and more tentatively while the ideas of African Americans were taken more seriously and were more likely to be accepted. The dynamic was self-reinforcing. Soon, it was assumed that all spokespersons at events would be African American victims; in response, the concerns of these members gained further credibility.

Issues that seem settled don't necessarily remain so. Months after the shift toward African Americans, a white member of EPVT made the seemingly innocuous proposal to connect with young African Americans by sponsoring an essay contest for high school students. This spurred new tensions over racial belonging, in the form of a debate over the prize for contest winners. Several African American members argued for cash prizes, invoking their knowledge of the black community to assert that this is what the teens would want. A white activist challenged them, invoking a more general knowledge of activism to assert that EPVT would suffer "bad PR" (public relations) if the winners used their prize money to "get into trouble," and insisting that EPVT should award coupons from local merchants.

Another challenge to EPVT's definition of belonging flared when a member proposed that they "take on" the case of a woman abused by her police officer husband. Initially, the group considered this within the context of their strategy and mission: was it consistent to extend their understanding of police violence to include domestic violence committed by a police officer? Soon, however, the discussion meandered into thorny questions of belonging. Clearly, the police don't belong in EPVT; they are adversaries. But might the families of police officers belong, if they too are victims of the police? Or only if the families are African American, like other victims of police violence? Their existing guidelines for belonging weren't sufficient and the group seemed stuck. After a frustrating debate in which no solution appeared, the group sidestepped the problem by cobbling together a new principle of belonging, one that was oddly rooted in the bureaucratic logic they deplored in official investigations of police violence. They decided they could only be involved in violence that happened in Pittsburgh's Allegheny County and, since this victim lived outside the county, they couldn't help. A turning point was possible in this sequence that could have expanded the group's sense of itself, but it was thwarted.

The circuitous ways in which paths of belonging take shape are evident in Stop Gun Violence (SGV). SGV was initially convened by Salu, a longtime local activist, who saw the impending National Rifle Association (NRA) national convention in Pittsburgh as a chance to build a local movement against gun violence. Its first meeting, on an icy day in January, drew eight people, mostly white and all middle class. They came from local faith and anti-violence groups, pulled in by personal appeals from Salu. From the very beginning, SGV focused on generating protests at the NRA convention, then just four months away. Only when someone suggested that it mount a second protest in a low-income African American neighborhood ravaged by gun violence to attract a "different" kind of member did SGV step back and confront the question of who belonged. An interracial movement would be valuable, everyone quickly agreed, but could racial minority communities be brought into SGV so quickly? The discussion stumbled on, awkward and convoluted. Since SGV lacked a "minority presence," some argued, it did not have the credibility to "take up the cause" of how gun violence is ruining minority communities. But neither could it ignore those communities without reinforcing its image as a white middle-class group. The mood picked up when Judy, one of the most experienced activists there, made an impassioned declaration that the "immediate goals" were to recruit minorities to attend meetings and involve leaders from minority communities in the fight. When no one disagreed, Judy suggested that they try to recruit an African American member of the anti-police violence group EPVT.

For a moment, it seemed that SGV would diversify its membership. Judy had set out a rationale and a plan to do so. And other members seemed willing to go along. Yet, almost at once, this path was blocked. While careful to agree with Judy's assessment that it needed a more diverse membership, Salu spoke up to undercut the implication for action. There was no need for SGV to recruit more minorities, Salu insisted. He had already extended many such invitations and only the bad weather had kept them away so far. The rest of the group seized on Salu's point, anxious to resolve a difficult situation and move back to the comfortable ground of the largely white and middle-class groups with which they were more familiar. If the weather prevented racial minority members from attending (but not white members, the unspoken corollary), SGV didn't need to do anything to diversify itself. It would just happen as the weather improved. As the discursive ground shifted, other members joined in. Citing her earlier experience in grassroots politics, one woman insisted that it took time to create a minority presence in a group, so the absence of minority members was not pressing. No one was willing to contradict her: the topic of the group's lack of poor and racial minority members had been silenced.

SGV's initial path toward a diverse sense of belonging was diverted by Salu's intervention. So, do founders have a special influence on group dynamics? Not necessarily. In the same meeting, Salu repeatedly insisted that SGV should become a coalition of groups, not an organization of members. But this argument was ignored and, chastened, Salu gave in. A similar fate met his effort to build SGV into a permanent entity. The rest of the group quickly rejected the idea as both premature and likely to undermine the NRA protest. Salu never raised it again.

Salu was able to create a turning point away from a path toward racial diversity because doing so allowed SGV to skirt a difficult problem, not because he had undue influence as the group's founder. If racial minorities would eventually come to the group (as Salu claimed), but slowly (as the woman member insisted), SGV need not spend time crafting a recruitment plan or criticizing itself for having an all-white membership. Members could stop talking about race yet feel confident that they were on track for becoming a racially diverse group.

Since SGV no longer allowed open discussion of race, it could produce only an odd resolution: racial minority activists should produce their own anti-gun events, which would provide "local dynamism" for a broad community effort against the NRA. How this would happen was never elaborated. The idea that SGV itself would stage actions in poor black neighborhoods was foreclosed. It would never again be raised in an SGV meeting. Later, there was scattered, vague talk about the need for more racial diversity, but the specifics were now off the table completely. Who belonged had become firmly, but invisibly, racialized. Two implicit principles now defined SGV's action: it is difficult for mostly white social movements to diversify racially; and activist groups should keep their events within their racial base.

Disputes over Belonging

When activist groups talk about belonging, members can operate with implicit but conflicting logics that quickly become contentious. SECURE, a group working on national security issues, exploded after a meeting attended by a reporter. Some insisted that everyone had a reason to worry about national security and therefore everyone belonged. Others insisted that ordinary citizens belonged, but members of the media did not. Switches in a group's logic, like those that define belonging, can reveal turning points in paths of action. The decision to allow media in a meeting would pull SECURE toward a style in which private talk would be shaped by how the group would appear in the media, so expressions of uncertainty and conflict would likely be submerged, according greater power to the currently central members, and so forth. The decision to exclude the media kept it off that path.

Among fledgling activist groups, the most common logics used to define belonging are those of expediency and mission. Expediency logics define belonging as similarity. People belong who are similar to those already in the group: their friends, relatives, neighbors, colleagues, and like-minded activists. Such people are easy—expedient—to fold into the group because they resemble the current "us." An environmental group used this logic when it looked for members who would fit the group's casual, friendly atmosphere, despite its public insistence that anyone who agreed with its goals would fit in.[11]

In contrast, mission logics define belonging by contribution. People belong when they can add to the group's mission and goals. Such people might be difficult to bring into the group since they can be very different from the current members. But they provide something that is lacking in the current group. When its founder said that Black Antiwar Pittsburgh was failing, even as it attracted large numbers to its events, she used a mission logic, arguing that it didn't have the *right* members to accomplish its aims. Mission logics are evident as well in the groups that define belonging by particular skills or resources. A health reform group described itself as one of "professionals and students," despite having no student members, because it regarded students as having "the time to travel to DC" for demonstrations, which current members lacked. A civil rights group decided that retirees belonged for the same reason. Some groups defined belonging to include those who might attract favorable attention, like an AIDS advocacy group that wanted members of a faith community "to show that this is a moral concern." Others wanted those with particular attributes; an example is a group pushing for global debt relief that sought male recruits on the assumption that women, who made up most of its early participants, "all relate to one another in a certain way" and would be less successful in meetings with high-level (presumably male) officials. GAD, the anti-drug group profiled in the last chapter, worked to establish the kinds of people who belonged in its group—those who knew a drug abuser, had "conviction," were empathetic and willing to "stand up" for what's right. Although a concrete definition was difficult for them to put into words, everyone seemed to understand what kind of person this was: someone enmeshed in neighborhood life but who could rise above its problems. By these measures, an elementary school principal fit, as did members of Narcotics Anonymous and a deputy jailer. The local city councilman and a close friend of one of the members did not.

A women's peace group, Women against War (WAW), defined belonging in a different but also a categorical way. As they chatted informally before a meeting, members discovered that they were mostly nurses or health professionals. With this knowledge, they started to frame who belonged. That they were health workers, they agreed, was no accident. Being for peace was an extension of a general orientation to care for others. It was a small leap to conclude, as one woman summarized the discussion, that the peace movement was "based on caring." People who demonstrated caring by their choice of profession were those who belonged.

Expediency and mission logics can be used simultaneously, but it is revealing to see when groups switch their emphases from one to another. When expediency logics are used, it seems logical to recruit the most accessible people, and those people become valued; a mission logic empowers a different set of people. And these logics cascade. Each tilts a group's future in a certain way, making it more and more one of artists, neighborhood leaders, mothers, longtime activists, or political moderates. As groups switch between logics, they open new lines of interpretation and action that were otherwise off the table. A group of mostly poor people considers whether having professional members would give it more political power and how that would change the feel of the group. A group dedicated to educational reform thinks about reaching out to neighborhood activists and what effect that would have on its mission. Logics of belonging, like other logics of action, are largely invisible but highly effectual.

Distinctions of Belonging

Pittsburgh had several groups that focused on the same issue—the Iraq War, peace, queer/GLBT rights, violence, racial equity, and animal rights—so activist groups needed to define belonging in a way that was specific to their *group*, not only to their *issue*. They did so by contrasting themselves with other activist groups rather than emphasizing commonalities within their group, much as belonging to the white race is a matter of not being nonwhite. The politics of belonging, Yuval-Davis reminds us, is not only about attachment but also about being able to decide whether others, including those you meet in the future, stand "inside or outside the imaginary boundary line . . . of belonging, whether they are 'us' or 'them.'"[12]

Emerging activist groups commonly used three types of distinctions to define belonging: tactical, emotional, and social. The most common distinction was *tactical*.[13] Those who shared an interest in confrontation or letter writing belonged; others did not. A same-sex marriage group declared that its members would never hold signs in public, a tactic they variously described as "degrading," "not respectable," and not "distinguish[ing] us from all groups who are protesting something." A civil liberties group, desperate to attract young people, debated during several meetings whether it could imagine itself using the aggressive practices that seemed attractive to youth in other groups.

Tactical distinctions can become a matter of great concern, as shown in the fallout from a large anti-war rally. An anti-war protestor tore away a sign held by a pro-war heckler, only to be chastised on the spot by another protestor who yelled that such actions could bring in the police and give them all a bad name in the press. For weeks, Pittsburgh's various anti-war groups debated these actions. Those who favored confrontational tactics declared that the protestor who intervened didn't have the guts to belong to a group like theirs. Those who opposed such tactics insisted that people who assault others didn't belong. As one said, summarizing a long meeting, "those who engage in civil disobedience are responsible for their actions." Someone in another group said it more plainly: "We respect them, but we are separate from them. They are not us."

A second way that groups distinguished belonging was by *emotion*. An anti-war group positioned itself in contrast to the uninspired "feel" of one group's vigils and the "undignified" rallies of another.[14] The kinds of people it wanted, by implication, were inspired and dignified. A young woman distinguished her group from those with similar politics that were more internally contentious:

> A lot of young protest groups are really volatile and they come and they go and they have enormous disagreements and they spend a lot of time self-defining and usually they're defined in opposition to something. Pittsburgh Antiwar Network, on the other hand, has things that I always disagree over but we're a fairly stable group.

Third, groups distinguished themselves by *social* categories that define belonging and mark its boundaries. Their names—Black Antiwar Pittsburgh, Antiwar Campus Now, Queer Organizing Network—declare belonging as African American, college students, or GLBT persons in addition to people fighting for peace, against war, or for progressive causes. They also define who is less welcome.

Pittsburgh's activist groups, especially progressive ones, have overlapping memberships, so distinctions of belonging can be very risky. Among the activists I interviewed, 66% belonged to another group. It is not surprising, therefore, that New American Revolution (NAR) found it tricky to distinguish itself from MoveOn; nearly one-third of its members had earlier worked with MoveOn. To discuss MoveOn's deficiencies could create a political space for NAR but also might destroy it. Indeed, as NAR's organizer listed examples of what MoveOn did wrong, people looked down or glanced at each other with discomfort. Shifting focus, he tried other ways to distinguish NAR: it was different from Republicans; unlike "people who don't care;" even, oddly, dissimilar from groups that focused on informing members about current issues since it also embraced people "who don't want information." But none of these gained traction and the discussion became progressively more disjointed and ultimately fizzled out.[15]

Even when distinctions are easier to construct, using social categories to define belonging can be explosive. A gay rights group nearly did not survive its initial meeting because of such a dispute:

> After the meeting, Marvin expressed his indignation at John's assumption that everyone at the meeting was in a [gay/lesbian] partnership because that "excluded a lot of people from participating" and said he came to the meeting simply because he was horrified that such an injustice has not been corrected yet, not because he had a personal investment in getting marriage rights. (Author's field notes)

A conservative group found itself embroiled in a similar dispute about categories of members. As it tried to develop a way to prioritize which issues to tackle first:

> One man offered advice about how to establish a rating system, if the group would take advice from "old geezers." He poked fun at the group's targeting of youth and said he was hurt that he couldn't rise to a leadership position in the group because of his age. (Author's field notes)

By identifying himself as an "old geezer," he made visible the group's operating premise that younger members were more valuable and opened the question of whether older or younger members most belonged, a matter that formerly had been silenced.[16]

When people do not fit an expected category, subtle questioning may be used to establish whether they belong. In an animal rights group, it was young, urban participants with modest incomes who were assumed to belong. Newcomers who fit that profile were absorbed without comment. The arrival of a middle-aged suburban woman, however, provoked friendly but pointed questions. Did she have children in college? Had she been involved in other politics? How did she find out about them? In other words, these probing questions were an attempt to determine whether she belonged.

Matters of belonging are contentious and dynamic in emerging activist groups. They rest on interpretive foundations that shift over time as a result of actions and evolving sets of meaning but take form in paths that forge the group's subsequent actions and interpretations.

MEMBERSHIP

Activist groups regard membership and belonging differently. To be an authentic member is to have the right to shape the group's direction as well as some obligation to do so.[17] But defining membership is not always easy, as an anti-war activist notes:

> In a lot of groups, it seems like there is no outward recognition of members or non-members, so it's sort of in the gray area what makes a member a member.

In activist groups, the distinction between member and non-member can be vague. Ron Aminzade and Doug McAdam argue that even established social movements include many who are not members in any organizational sense and are "only superficially and sporadically engaged by the struggle."[18] Even long-term participants, like Chuck, struggle about what membership means:

> Well, I paid dues, so maybe you could call me a member. That's a question of semantics, I mean, what is a member of the No War Committee? People drift in and out; I have done that. I'm a little more involved at the moment, so I am fine with the word participant. That's what I do—I participate.

Membership is not fuzzy simply because activist groups fail to define it. Indeed, these ambiguities can be deliberate, as groups seek to avoid narrowing their options. Participants in Stop the Killing (StK), a fledgling anti-violence group, pressed for clarity on what the group would be into the future. A lasting presence? A short-term group that would plan to end? A coalition of existing groups? They wanted to know whether it would be a small or large time commitment, whether it would complement or conflict with their existing activism, whether it would take their energy for a short while or for years.[19] After much discussion, StK simply decided not to decide. It was just "planting the seeds" for whatever would happen. Freed of a definition, StK did not rule out anything in advance. Anyone could join, any action could be considered.

Other groups define membership in a fuzzy way to cast a wide net for members. One advertised that people could "try out" the group without committing themselves to the obligations of full membership. Another announced that people could define themselves as "volunteers," "members," or "activists" depending on their commitment and could change this at any time. Still another had two levels of membership: those who "carry on tasks" and a larger group who were "members in name only," including those who were enrolled by someone else, such as several who simply "had received their membership as a gift from a friend" and never intended to join. Only those who had shown interest in taking on tasks were expected to participate.

Albert O. Hirschman's famous claim that people can choose to remain loyal, exercise voice, or exit resonates in activist groups in which people easily slip away.[20] A broad definition of membership can link people more closely to a group, encouraging the options of loyalty and voice rather than exit. A women's peace group pondered those who signed up for its e-mails but did not attend meetings. Were they members? Could one be a member of a group without expressing intent? Yes, they decided, those who received e-mails were members because membership meant political agreement, not participation.[21] When a recent arrival questioned whether she could vote in an anti-violence group, the immediate response was, "If you're here, you're a member." Another group embraced the rule that "if you show up to a certain number of meetings, or whatever, you're a member."

Groups generally assume that people want to be members and will be happy to be asked. As this is not always the case, the strategy of broad membership can backfire. When I talked to those who came to a few meetings then stopped, several said that they felt pressed to join before they were ready. Seeing no option to participate casually, they backed off. Even someone who stayed, becoming a committed activist, said that she felt uneasy at first:

> I had just gone to see what it was about, and my going, to everyone there, seemed like I wanted to join. But I was really just trying to see what things were about. I don't think I voiced that sufficiently. . . . They really wanted everyone to stay and be there consistently.

Quick offers of membership can cause friction among current members. One man remembered his frustration as his anti-war group debated a controversial issue without a clear sense of who could vote:

> We were voting on whether I should have [former Senator] Carol Moseley Braun come or not. . . . There was someone there, that was the only meeting she was at. And she was, like, "Can I vote?" And it was like, "Yeah, you can." And then that decided the outcome. It was decided by one vote, her vote.

With exit always a possibility, it can be difficult for activist groups to make demands on their members. Any obligations, even attendance, can be fraught. An anti-violence group listed its founder as a member long after he stopped coming to meetings and events. Among themselves, people mentioned that he had quit. Yet the group continued to treat him as an important member. Members mailed him minutes of each meeting—which dutifully noted his absence—and made note in discussions that they would have to "catch him up" when he returned. This changed only when he responded with some anger and insisted that they drop him from membership.

For activists, membership can be a gradual process. Many sample different groups before committing themselves to membership. They talk of sliding into membership over time. An animal rights activist said "[I] started to think of myself more as a member 'cause I was going regularly." In her interview, another woman found it difficult to decide whether to call herself a member of a school reform group, ultimately deciding that she was a member "because I've gone to meetings and . . . because I signed up somewhere to be a member." Another, asked how she started thinking about herself as a member of her group, responded:

I don't know. . . . I never did. I just showed up. I did stuff. . . . Probably around February I started to think of myself more as a member as I'd go every Sunday.

Some activists never see themselves as members of their groups, even if they are very active. As one young woman told me, "I see myself as kind of standing on the outside. . . . I see myself in a different capacity—I don't know what that is yet." But for others, even a tentative approach can turn into an immediate connection:

I went the first time to just see what their agenda was and everything that was involved. And then after the first meeting I thought, well, these people have their heart in the right place and they have an awful lot to do and I very much believe in their cause so there's no reason for me not to help them out in some capacity. I had no idea what the capacity would be at that time.

Membership and Action

An activist told me about one of the first meetings he attended of an anti-war group:

[I was] pretty uncomfortable only because we really didn't know each other yet and probably didn't know most of the people's names. But yet it [the group's goal] was something that we really needed to resolve because it was going to be one action as a group and it was going to reflect on all of us since we were all members of the group. So we really needed to resolve what we were going to do.

Activist groups generally expect their members to support common actions, but this is not always possible in practice. REBORN, the radical queer group, considered how to respond to Reverend Phelps, a virulent homophobic and anti-abortion preacher visiting Pittsburgh. One woman declared that the group must protest the event, since she "couldn't stand seeing anti-abortion and anti-gay supporters there with signs, while no one confronted them about their homophobia." Others objected, like a woman (who insisted she spoke for many) who feared being beaten up as a "small group in a homophobic majority." The meeting fragmented into a variety of claims and counterclaims. Some argued against the protest, saying it would give Phelps more publicity, while others asserted that protesting would make the public take them more seriously. Ultimately, the group could not come to a resolution. Members were left to picket as individuals if they wanted.

Tensions arose in an animal rights group whose founder set out what members were expected to do:

[She] strictly said that there need to be more members at the protests. She addressed the need to collect more money by asking for sidewalk donations. The members were silent. They shamefully looked down and avoided eye contact with her. Two members then volunteered to go to this weekend's protest. Two volunteered to collect sidewalk donations. Others were silent the entire meeting. (Author's field notes)

In their interviews, activists often talk about membership in deeply personal ways, with an emotional resonance that is markedly different from the dry talk of member rights and obligations that occurs during meetings. Activists describe membership as emotional attachment to other members and to the group itself—what Yuval-Davis discusses as feeling "at home" and feeling entitled to this feeling.[22] Membership is connectedness to a community of like-minded activists. An older man insisted that he was not a member of an anti-war group, despite his long and intensive involvement, because "it's not like [how I'm a] member of my family." In contrast, an anti-violence activist said that she started thinking of herself as a member of that group "from the outset":

[Although other members] were not my blood children, I felt very connected to these people. I felt like they could have been my son, my brother. . . . Some people [think] "I would [have] never thought that could be me." [But] I always thought that could be me—that's the difference.

A middle-aged woman who was active in several groups maintained that she was a member of only one: "That is the group that I am the most tied to emotionally. . . . It was the first group that I got passionate about."

Like belonging, membership is a construct that activist groups use as a foundational assumption. It guides their actions but is also shaped by what they do and how they interpret their actions and themselves.

RECRUITING

Activist groups generally start with a burst of enthusiasm for recruiting, although how many people they want to attract is vague. A civil rights group, for example, talked of unlimited possibilities for growth, confident that its message would attract "thousands." In their early days, activist groups struggle to develop an operational sense of size, that is, a shared sense of how many people make a rally or demonstration worthwhile and how many members are required to make decisions at a meeting. Such initial operational definitions can be fairly imprecise, like a peace group's conclusion that "without a decent turnout" it could not "democratically discuss issues and come to decisions . . . fairly" or, AID/S, a group fighting for AIDS funding, that set out to recruit "a lot" of members, after an animated discussion of how a "good group" requires many people to have momentum even after its founders leave.

Over time, groups generally create a shared sense of how many members are sufficient to hold meetings or make decisions although the exact number can vary, as in a peace group that avoided important issues during the summer when it had only a "floating membership." Almost always, these understandings are implicit, although one anti-violence activist recalled making a more explicit formulation at an early meeting of Stop the Killing:

> We had I think 150 people at High House. I said, standing at the microphone, "this will not last." I said that, not to be negative, but I have been out here forty years or so. We will come down to about eight, ten, fifteen people and that's where we are, okay. . . . I am very happy if we have like about fifteen to twenty people at the table.

Even such seemingly simple decisions, like whether to recruit a lot of members, are based on collective political theorizing about the nature of activism, momentum, and continuity. Under similar conditions, one activist group decides that recruitment is vital for sustaining activism over time while another theorizes that collective activism simply attracts members automatically, so little effort is needed. In turn, these understandings shape the groups' horizons of possible action. When AID/S began to equate a "good" meeting with a well-attended one, the group created an impasse for itself because it couldn't persevere through the ups and downs of attendance that are typical of activist groups. Whenever attendance was low, it simply dissolved the meeting. A similar result happened in a conservative group, CONSERVE, whose exuberant predictions of members flooding into the group were dashed by meager turnouts. Members became disgruntled and attendance dropped even more.

Activist groups generally operate with an upbeat sense of themselves and their future even under difficult circumstances. A declining membership tends to curb their sense of possibility only when the group is about to disappear. At a scheduled meeting of an African American community empowerment group, RISE, only one member showed up. After waiting in vain for more to arrive, its leader, Lucinda, became frustrated and declared that the group would never get off the ground. She stopped trying to recruit and the group never met again. But the path to extinction is not inevitable—the same situation in the animal rights group ALL had a different ending. When no member appeared at a meeting at which crucial decisions about impending events needed to be made, ALL's leader, Heather, was undaunted, insisting that she "didn't want to factor in" why others were missing and proceeded through the agenda. She talked about each issue at length to a member of the research team who was present, made a decision, and recorded it in minutes that she later circulated by e-mail. Heather's actions would be seen in some groups as a violation of democratic decision making; in ALL it simply reinforced her centrality. At the following, better-attended meeting, no one challenged Heather's decisions or the principle that one person could make decisions for the group. Instead, members worked out how to implement the choices she had made.

Groups are emotionally buoyed when the number of people at a meeting or event is larger than expected or larger than in the past. Yet the opposite is not true. When the turnout is smaller than expected, activist groups often make a pronounced effort to keep the mood positive by explaining away the turnout as due to holidays, student exams, family obligations, or inclement weather.[23] This is true even when central members are missing. In most, the topic of low or declining attendance is only broached, and then tentatively, when it reaches a cataclysmic point, a turning point at which groups may have to confront the possibility that they are dissolving. Otherwise, problematic attendance easily becomes a silenced topic.

On the eve of its first public protest, picketing the lecture of a Pentagon spokeswoman, Pittsburgh Antiwar Network (PAN) weighed what to do next if the protest was as successful as it thought it might be. Once people come and are allowed to voice their "outrage" about the war, they reasoned, they will want to "get involved again," so PAN needed to show how they could do so. "Let's sponsor an action right away with Military Families Speak Out (a group of families of soldiers in Iraq and veterans opposed to the war)," someone suggested. The widespread enthusiasm for this idea was cut short, however, when John, a founding member, interrupted to point out how few people had joined so far. Like a balloon bursting, the tenor of the meeting changed abruptly. The buoyant mood of a moment before was replaced by expressions of concern. Why were there so few people at today's meeting? What about those at the last meeting who promised to draft a flyer for the protest? Where had they gone? One member rose to leave, apologizing that he had a lot of work to do. John countered, "we *all* have a lot of work to do," trying to build a sense of solidarity. But two more members rose to leave and John made only a weak effort to stop them.

Working to Recruit

Activist groups talk expansively about recruiting, but their actual efforts are quite limited. Every new activist group, at one time or another, developed a plan to recruit new members, yet few plans were implemented and these were largely perfunctory. Some asked members to bring friends, with no sustained effort to make sure that happened. One changed its meeting location to a restaurant to draw in more people, but it didn't announce itself to customers or invite nearby patrons to join the meeting, so the group didn't garner a single new member. Many activists claimed that dynamic, energetic groups naturally attract people, so they put their energies into events. One member of an anti-war group, frustrated at its dwindling size, decided to go door-to-door to recruit new members. Other members praised her initiative but dismissed it as futile. Recruitment, they declared, was an endless uphill battle.

Even as activist groups talk about recruiting, they adjust their expectations of how many members they need to make recruiting less important. One striking example is No War Committee (NWC) in the month before a large march on the anniversary of the U.S. invasion of Iraq. The march involved complicated logistics: sound systems, police permits, coordinating with other groups to recruit speakers and attendees, and publicity. At one tense meeting, NWC's leader first tried to scare members into working more by listing what remained to be done for the rapidly approaching event. When that failed to produce more volunteers, he announced that people had too many outside commitments and they might as well give up. Even in this urgent situation, no one suggested that they try to enlist other people. Although members earlier had talked extensively about recruiting, none of these ideas were raised now. Even in the face of a failed march, the group only considered ways to motivate existing members to work longer and harder, not how to entice new people to join.

Recruiting also slipped off the agenda of ALL during a particularly intensive sequence of actions to protest university research on animals. Dedicated to staging many events at once, the group's members were taxed to manage them all: film showings, protests, letter-writing sessions, and literature tables where they handed out brochures and flyers. Despite Heather's efforts to buoy enthusiasm by reminding members that they "really make a difference," the strain on the group was evident. Members' energy continued to flag. Tasks promised by certain members, like creating a Web site, never materialized. Attendance at meetings slid until only a small handful of people appeared at each one. At the same time that recruits were more urgently needed, ALL's interest in recruiting seemed to decline further.

After one meeting in a coffeehouse, a man approached Heather to inquire about the group. She gave him only the group's name before walking away. Asked later why she hadn't invited him to a future meeting, Heather seemed puzzled: "It really hadn't crossed my mind." Another woman approached as they were distributing flyers to say that she was interested in investigating animal labs at the university. She was told it was impossible to close the labs and was brushed away. No further effort was made to enlist her in ALL's work. That ALL might benefit from bringing in new people was no longer considered.

After an initial flurry, recruiting quickly stops in most activist groups, although they may continue to talk about it. For instance, an international issues group that began with lofty goals and a large following saw its attendance drop precipitously after its third meeting. Yet no one made any effort to attract new members. The group simply scaled down its goals. The existing members presumed the group was to be what it became. In some groups, even the mention of recruiting can become awkward. In the East Side Progressive Coalition (ESPC), as the group discussed which neighborhoods to target in distributing its flyers announcing an upcoming event, one member interrupted to express her frustration; she complained that issues of race and racism, originally central to the group, were now ignored. An uncomfortable silence ensued. The implication was clear, if unspoken: ESPC recruited from poor African American neighborhoods for people to attend their events but not to join the group. Without any discussion, the members soon resumed planning the event. Such feeble or nonexistent recruitment efforts mean that the tendency of activist groups to become more homogenous over time is due more to attrition and retention than to patterns of joining. Those who are similar to current members—in ideas or other factors—stay; those who differ, leave.[24]

Newcomers

Despite the minimal effort that most activist groups put into recruiting, new people occasionally show up at meetings. Their appearance is usually regarded by current members as more disruptive than welcome. At a meeting of a civil liberties group, volunteers were solicited for a number of tasks related to its upcoming protest. A new young woman spoke up that she would "love to do so" but hadn't "done anything like that before" and would need "some guidance." The immediate response, from a longtime member, was that she should not volunteer because "we're looking for more experienced or activist members." No one objected and she left the meeting without an assignment, never returning. Similarly, when a new member arrived at a racial justice group eager to join in, his zeal was quickly extinguished in a conflict with other members about a party they were planning. His concerns were the group's plans to have alcohol and marijuana available around teenagers. "I don't think it's the best idea in the world to incorporate underage drinking and pot smoking at an event that we are labeling a '[group] event,'" he argued. The group responded angrily, denying that these would attract the police and that he was simply "ruining their plans."

Not only do activist groups allow little opportunity for newcomers to participate, but they often quash their ideas, even while appearing to welcome them. No War Committee (NWC) frequently talked about wanting new members with fresh ideas, and when four new people arrived at the same meeting—in a group that had attracted 23.7 people on average (over 45 meetings)—the newcomers had the potential to change the group. Why didn't this happen? The meeting began on an emotionally volatile note. People were on edge, just back from a demonstration in which the police had used dogs and taser guns and had arrested several members. The situation was complicated since the demonstration had been officially sponsored by an anarchist direct-action group, which NWC regarded as irresponsibly provocative. In an informal talk before the meeting, some blamed the anarchists for causing the police reaction, but no one voiced this in the meeting. Instead, members expressed "outrage" over the "unjust and unnecessary" police response. Their only disagreements were whether federal and military authorities had pressured local police to respond so "cruelly" and whether the media had minimized the police overreaction to control public perceptions about the wars in Iraq and Afghanistan.

As the conversation turned to police use of tasers, all conflict ceased. Members described their experiences of police brutality and gave emotional testimonials about the recent tasering. The story of a young woman who was tasered after having been subdued under the firm grip of a police officer was proffered as evidence that the police had "become more militant." As the anger peaked, one member offered to draft a "statement of solidarity" with the anarchists and all those arrested, injured, or tasered so it could be signed at the meeting. Any disagreements with the anarchists were now shelved.

In the midst of this explosion of anger, someone suddenly turned to the four new members and asked them to talk about what brought them to the meeting. To the surprise of many, two made comments that violated the group's sense of itself. One man declared himself against the war in Iraq but believed that war might sometimes be justified, contrary to the broad anti-war sentiment of most members. Another expressed doubts about whether the police action at the demonstration was really wrong, citing earlier demonstrations in which protestors had blocked access to a military recruiting station.

Despite these comments, the group remained engaged with the new arrivals, eager to bring them into the group's collective sense of opposition to war and the military. One longtime member explained why it was important to oppose all war. Another said that military recruiters had closed the station before protestors arrived and that the protestors were careful not to impede access. Several joined in to praise the protestor's actions, noting that military recruiters used unscrupulous methods to recruit young people. A young man related a long story about a military recruiter who assaulted him, saying that he had "no idea" what it was like in Iraq, and then threw him to the ground.

When one of the new arrivals revealed that he was a probation officer, the tone changed. One member put it bluntly: "I thought I smelled a cop when you walked in here." From that point, the group ceased its dialogue with them. Although only one identified himself as a probation officer, all now were assumed to be unacceptable recruits. This became exceedingly awkward late in the meeting when the group was casting about for a volunteer to read a script at a local concert asking for funds and one of the new arrivals volunteered. After exchanging glances, the existing members simply ignored her offer and turned to a longtime member, asking her to do it. Although she balked, noting that the concert was scheduled for late in the evening and she had young children, other members continued to press her until she accepted. No one referred to the new arrival's offer and no one explained why it wasn't appropriate for her to speak. In fact, members ceased to direct any comments or even glances toward the new arrivals. They did not fit the group's sense of what members should be like.

CASE COMPARISON

To understand how organizational issues of belonging, membership, and recruitment define groups over time, I compare two groups that started as a single entity: the Civil Liberties Defense Committee (CLDC) and the End the War and Occupation Committee (EWOC). CLDC splintered from EWOC to pursue new goals after the latter was successful in passing an anti-war resolution in the Pittsburgh City Council. In addition to overlapping members, the groups recruited from the same pool of the city's most visible progressive activists. CLDC attracted between 2 and 10 people to its meetings (the mode, or most common number, was 4) and EWOC's attendance ranged from 6 to

38 people (with a mode of 18). Despite commonalities, important differences emerged over time in the groups' definitions and expectations of members.

CLDC began with an expansive definition of how people could participate in the group. Borrowing from the success of EWOC, CLDC established as its goals convincing the Pittsburgh City Council to pass a resolution against the federal legislation known as the Patriot Act and raising public awareness about the potential harms of the act's restrictions on civil liberties. These goals became the basis on which CLDC created a multi-layered recruitment strategy. Members were those who attended meetings regularly, assumed responsibilities, and participated in decision making. Equally or more important to the goal of passing a city council resolution were advisors (those with political contacts), supporters (including members of other progressive groups who would help out, but not be centrally involved), and volunteers (those working for the same goal, but not expected to attend meetings regularly or participate in decision making), although all these people were to be coordinated and directed by CLDC members. These distinctions became more clearly delineated over time. For example, members came to assume that advisors, supporters, and volunteers would not become members in the future; indeed, it was understood that they would participate in these ways *in lieu of* being members.

Although meant to maximize the goal of passing a city resolution, CLDC's recruiting strategy was limiting. The time-urgency of its goal placed a premium on contacting council members and circulating petitions, thus necessitating a focus on enlisting advisors, supporters, and volunteers rather than members. The resulting lack of new members facilitated the formation of a core group that worked together intensively and developed a collaborative sense of responsibility, making additional recruitment seem less urgent.

The turning point for CLDC came when it found city council members less enthusiastic about passing a resolution against the Patriot Act than they had been for an anti-war resolution. Realizing the improbability of a "quick-win" with the council resolution, CLDC was forced to shift to a long-term goal, so a membership strategy designed for a short-term campaign became problematic. As members left the group, there was no mechanism to replace them. Attendance at meetings shrank to the point that CLDC considered disbanding. Yet the prospect of defeat proved to be its second turning point, confronting the group with the need to discuss its recruitment efforts openly. Rather than dissolve, CLDC decided to recruit from the general public by advertising in a local paper. Although this brought in only a few new people, most of whom did not remain, the decision to try to revitalize the group created a momentum that was not even disrupted by the subsequent departure of the main leader. CLDC shifted its meetings to a coffeehouse to have an environment that was more welcoming to new members, discussed how to establish new goals after the city council vote, and identified new categories of potential supporters such as librarians. Its efforts to recruit new members, however, were not successful since CLDC continued to devote its time to convincing the city council to pass a resolution against the Patriot Act rather than reaching out to potential members. When the Pittsburgh City Council passed such a resolution, CLDC vowed to continue its effort in other localities, but only one member tried to create a similar campaign in an adjoining community.

Despite overlaps in personnel and ideology with CLDC, EWOC developed a different sense of membership. Compared with the variety of levels of involvement in CLDC, the meaning of participation in EWOC was unidimensional: membership meant discussing and approving plans. EWOC had no categories of non-member supporters or advisors. Moreover, from its beginning, EWOC operated with a strong leader, Jim. Initial members knew each other from an earlier anti-war protest, and Jim's leadership in this event gave him immediate authority, although unacknowledged and not formalized. Jim controlled the agendas and dynamics of meetings, channeling the discussion and structuring members' permissible range of decision making and talk. Meetings began with updates of war news and then shifted to discussion of tactics, division of tasks, and reports on work accomplished. Jim admonished members for speaking out of turn, engaging in side conversations, or deviating from the agenda. Rarely was the group itself a topic of discussion and generally only when Jim perceived members as overstepping their authority. When a member who had been charged with securing the endorsements of faith groups for an upcoming march announced that he had invited a high-ranking Catholic Church official to speak, for example, Jim chided him for acting on behalf of the group without explicit permission. The boundaries of member action were not simply logistical. When a member proposed that the group consider addressing the treatment of Iraqi women, Jim refused to enlarge the group's discussion to accommodate this issue.

At two potential turning points, EWOC might have expanded its sense of membership, such as the roles and levels of responsibility that members would be allowed to assume by the leader. The first opening occurred when several members broke the usual flow of the meeting by raising questions about the "overarching framework" (the theme and slogans) of a planned march. Members generally only talked about how to implement plans brought by Jim, but now a number of them jumped in, debating whether the march should call for withdrawing U.S. troops from Iraq immediately or accommodate "fence-sitters" by calling for United Nation (UN) replacement troops ("UN in, US out"). The change in dynamics was startling: members talked directly to each other, not waiting to be acknowledged by Jim. The feeling was heady, spiraling into a heated debate over how they should inform marchers about the direct actions planned by another group at a university site connected to Iraqi war contracts. As the discussion of the march wound down and members turned to the next item on the agenda, however, Jim again seized control. Instead of the energetic talk that had characterized discussion of the march, with people speaking over each other and at great length, laughing, and shouting, the meeting returned to the old businesslike style. Members now raised their hands to get Jim's permission to speak and kept their comments short and to the point. Soon, participants started grumbling among themselves that they did little at meetings except sit through endless committee reports. The brief glimpse they had had that meetings could be different had vanished from possibility.

The second possible turning point occurred as EWOC reflected on a recent protest and rally and decided that the details of planning had taken too much of members' time and energy, a discussion that left unsettled what members should be doing. After a few tentative comments about other ways to involve members, however, this line of discussion fizzled. Meeting time continued to be consumed by assigning tasks; broader questions about the role of members receded into the background. Despite its considerable decline in attendance over time, for example, EWOC never discussed how members might recruit others. In contrast to the widespread responsibilities that CLDC members assumed, members of EWOC expected to make decisions only within a limited range. Certainly, they did not see it as their duty to ponder the vitality or future of the group. As a consequence, EWOC's goals became more limited and circumscribed as the group shrank.

CLDC and EWOC were originally a single group, but, as they separated, their understandings of membership sharply diverged. In CLDC, being a member became just one of several ways of participating in the group; for EWOC, there was no other way and what membership meant was sharply delineated by its leader. Differences in structure and leadership style tugged the groups in different directions, but their sense of membership was also the result of the particular dynamics and actions of their members. Moreover, although EWOC and CLDC defined membership very differently, both definitions ultimately limited their efforts to recruit and to sustain the respective groups over time. With its attention riveted on the City Council resolution, CLDC considered gaining additional members less pressing than finding advisors and supporters. In EWOC, the meaning of membership did not include responsibility for the group's future—that was the province of its leader—so members didn't regard recruitment as an appropriate topic for broad discussion. CLDC's path was disrupted when it couldn't get a council resolution passed, creating an opportunity to reevaluate its strategy of membership. In EWOC, there were several times in which the group could have moved toward a broader sense of membership, but it did not.

CONCLUSION

From the earliest days of each group's organization, grassroots activists struggle to define who fits into the group by assessing questions of belonging, membership, and recruiting. Through these issues, a group comes to see itself in various ways, as reserved or combative, dignified or enraged, young or old. These definitions operate as cascading actions and interpretations that tend to reinforce a homogenous sense of who—and *what kind* of person—fits a group's evolving sense of self. Although never completely fixed and sometimes amorphous, such dynamics stamp the group with an organizational character that has lingering effects.

The examples in this chapter highlight two ways to see turning points as they are happening. One way is by observing shifts in logic. As they wrestle with the question of belonging, activist groups move between logics of mission and expediency. Using a mission logic, they assess how people fit the group's goals. Using an expediency logic, they assess whether new people are similar to current participants. As they switch between them, new possibilities open. Groups that emphasize similarity start to consider who might help them make progress toward their goals. Those that emphasize goals discuss who would be compatible with current participants.

The second way to see turning points is to observe how activist groups are oriented in time. As they talk about membership, activist groups evaluate themselves in the context of immediate concerns (present), draw lessons about who should be in the group based on earlier situations (past), and imagine themselves differently with the addition of new members (future). As they switch from one orientation to another, they alter their current paths and move in new directions. But that doesn't always happen.

When activist groups define sequences of action and interpretation, they do so in ways that are meaningful and consequential for them. These do not necessarily coincide with how an outside observer might define such sequences. For example, most grassroots groups saw themselves as recruiting for a long time with unclear and unspecified beginning and ending points. To an outside observer, however, it doesn't appear that groups did very much to recruit and that they quickly ceased even these minimal efforts.

This chapter has implications for the democratizing potential of grassroots activism. When a group's sense of itself is set very early and then woven into the cultural fabric of the group through self-reinforcing sequences of actions and interpretation, it can be difficult for later members to rectify problems, steer the group in a new direction, or even raise topics that have been shelved. EWOC and CLDC couldn't create a viable means of recruiting because the issue of membership had been resolved earlier. It had become their normal way of operating. Their democratic impulses were hindered by the cultural framework they had adopted. That such frameworks are both invisible and constituted in the distant past make them particularly resistant to democratic challenge.

CHAPTER 4

What's the Problem?

Marriage Now (MN), an effort to secure same-sex marriage rights in Pennsylvania, was launched with notices in local gay and arts papers. Five people met at a café, each eager to begin work. The issue seemed clear enough in the notice, but conflict about how to define the problem arose almost at once. Should the group campaign to allow all same-sex persons to marry? Or only *responsible* couples? MN's founder was unable to contain the discussion from spilling into a more delicate issue: If same-sex marriage were permitted, might GLBT people with little commitment to each other marry? Was the problem only the lack of recognition of gay marriage or also the libertine lifestyle that some gays embraced? Tensions ballooned and the fledgling group sank into an awkward silence.

Women against War (WAW) became embroiled in an argument after initially settling on the Iraq War as the problem it would address. During a fairly routine discussion of tactics, a thorny question arose: Should WAW criticize war in general, or also those who fought in wars? One woman argued that the military was the problem since soldiers "know what they're getting into." Another countered that soldiers "didn't know they were signing up to fight in a war" and they needed support, not criticism, from peace groups. The debate grew heated as members marshaled different kinds of evidence. Those who saw the problem as war, not soldiers, offered personal stories of teenagers they knew, however remotely, who were hounded by military recruiters in their schools or enlisted because they perceived few alternatives. Others saw the problem as militarism, using hypothetical examples of teenaged boys who entered the military to display their new-found masculinity.

GAYVOTE came together in a neighborhood bar with the agenda of ousting U.S. Senator Rick Santorum as "bad for queers, Pennsylvanians, and Americans." Initially, its young and mostly white members saw the problem narrowly, as the danger posed by a homophobic and powerful politician. Those it recruited, although similarly young and white, saw the issue differently. These new members wanted to tackle bigger problems, like "assimilation," "corporatization," and "classism" in the queer community and the "oppression" that squelches "expression." They weren't content with simply making change at the ballot box.

This chapter explores how activist groups define the problem they will work on. Although they generally begin with a focus, grassroots groups often reformulate this almost from the beginning. A gathering called to end the war in Iraq might decide that the real problem was the culture of militarism, or U.S. dependence on Middle Eastern oil. A group begun to redress racial inequities might come to see the problem as under-representation of racial minorities in elected office or as inequitable funding for public schools. As activist groups define a problem, they engage in collective theorizing. They wrestle with fundamental issues of political life, such as how society is organized and how it can be changed. They also reflect on themselves as political actors.

There is considerable research on how activist groups frame issues for an audience, but scholars have paid much less attention to how groups create a shared understanding of what they believe and value. We know, as Jeffrey Alexander puts it, that activist groups "learn the art of translating their particular injustices into the more universal language of civil justice." But we don't know how they come to understand "their particular injustices" in the first place.[1]

Defining a problem for themselves and framing issues for external audiences are very different processes. Framing is largely instrumental, involving, Alexander says, "not specifications of broader moral concerns but strategies for mobilizing masses." In contrast, when activist groups define a problem internally they evoke moral concerns, such as whether there are essential human rights, what constitutes fairness or justice, by what right can people intervene to change society, and, to paraphrase Gayatri Spivak's famous question, for whom can they speak?[2] As activist groups work toward what team researchers call "cognitive integration," they revise and reinterpret problems as the group shifts, different members assert their ideas, and situations change. How groups define a problem, even provisionally, shapes how they act and how they see themselves and the social world. Defining the problem, in other words, is an aspect of how activist groups create an *ideological* character.[3]

Activist groups define a problem through reflective political talk that is otherwise generally absent in public life. Grassroots activism thus is both an arena for collective action and a space for collective political thoughtfulness. Nina Eliasoph and Paul Lichterman note that "how people can *talk* about their own action is, itself, a crucial part of action. People can't change anything until they consider it a problem." Grassroots politics is a vehicle for such talk, as captured in Pam Oliver and Hank Johnston's description:

> People think a lot in social movements, along with the related activities of reasoning, judging arguments, evaluating evidence, testing predictions, recognizing connections, and developing new knowledge. . . . It is essential to appreciate the intellectual aspects of ideology (what Heberle calls the debate of ideas over the centuries) as well as their function in motivating action.[4]

As activist groups define their problem, they undertake each of these activities: reasoning, judging, evaluating, testing, recognizing, and developing knowledge. And, as this chapter will show, they grapple with multi-layered political questions: Is the problem the war in Iraq, or does U.S. imperialism always generate conflicts, of which Iraq is just the latest? So, would ending the conflict in Iraq solve the problem, or only deflect conflict to a new region? Is violence against women an isolated matter or only one example of male domination? So, can violence against women be stopped without attacking its roots?

The dynamics of shaping a shared political ideology are complex and often surprising. Activist groups do not simply adopt the ideas of their founders. Neither do they just aggregate ideas brought by members. Rather, they forge a meaningful sense of politics in the process of working and talking together. They make an ideological character for themselves in the mundane processes of deciding. It is in *how* they decide, as much as *what* they decide, that their political character emerges. Eliasoph and Lichterman's general point about group life is applicable here: "People always make meanings in specific social settings—large or small, face-to-face or virtual—and they make those meanings in relation to each other as they perceive each other."[5] In the small details of how activists argue, ponder, and debate, we can observe the making of collective political ideology.

Emerging activist groups typically work through four issues in defining the problem they will address. The chapter begins with two ontological issues: how activist groups work on a problem's scope and moral status. The chapter then shifts to two epistemological issues: how activist groups consider what they know and how they can learn more. In each of these issues, activist groups develop trajectories of action and interpretation that make some possibilities more robust and push others to the side. In each trajectory, however, there are moments of renewed possibility, or turning points, in which actors reorient the paths of their groups. The chapter concludes with an extended comparison of two groups as they defined the problem they would address.

WHAT IS THE SCOPE OF THE PROBLEM?

Founders usually set an initial scope for the problem an activist group should address. This can be broad, like global imperialism or liberalism. Or it can be narrow, like poor school lunches or drug-related deaths in a specific neighborhood. Yet, as activist groups talk about the problem, they rarely retain the scope with which they started. Generally (although not always), a group's scope narrows, as in a group that organized to combat global imperialism but quickly reduced its scope to U.S. policy on the Middle East. But some groups expand their political scope, as did one brought together to stop a gun control law that redefined its problem to include other conservative issues like abortion, or a group started to deal with school lunches that decided its problem would be societal neglect of children.

Shifts in scope happen gradually, almost imperceptibly, as activist groups mull over what they can do. It is not simply that groups start with a broad sense of a problem and then narrow it into a feasible set of actions. Nor that they begin with a limited sense of the problem's scope and broaden it as they become more confident of their ability to act. Rather, actions and scope are defined iteratively over time.

A forming sense of the possibility of action crafts a notion of appropriate scope of the problem and further redefines a group's possible actions. These changes can be subtle and difficult for members to detect or recall afterward. A problem whose scope is amenable to action *by this group at this time* is likely to gain traction; wider or narrower definitions of the problem just fade away. Within a few meetings, AID/S moved from "the worldwide AIDS pandemic" to "U.S. government intransigence." The latter focus allowed the group to undertake actions that were widely popular among its members, such as "bird-dogging," a tactic of repeatedly confronting local politicians who didn't support AIDS relief. In contrast, groups that cannot define a suitable scope for action get caught in a negative self-reinforcing cycle, as did a conservative group described in the author's field notes:

> [It] still doesn't know what it wants to do, yet refuses to engage with any proposals until they are concrete. So CONSERVE has nothing to discuss. Waiting for something to happen.

Grassroots groups do not first develop collective political understandings and then formulate actions that reflect these beliefs. Rather, they build shared beliefs as they consider what it is possible for them to do.[6]

How political ideas and actions become intertwined is evident in ALLIES 2007, the anti-violence group. In its first few meetings, ALLIES 2007 talked extensively about the problem of violence, mulling over its many manifestations: gang, drug, police, economic, and interpersonal violence. After a couple of meetings, however, this broad array of possibilities disappeared, replaced by a small set of problems tightly bound to the actions the group imagined as possible. Members who wanted to enlist former gang members to fight violence reduced the problem to gangs. Those who saw the possibility of gaining more social services for communities—but who didn't think they could ease tension among gangs—narrowed the problem to poverty. The group's actions and interpretations were iterative; the scope of the problem rested on what it saw itself as capable of doing.

Defining scope is an exercise of political imagination. It leads activists to imagine possibilities for changing the world—not abstractly, but in terms of their own actions. How the self-reinforcing cycle of scope and action is propelled into the future is nicely captured in an activist's conclusion to an anti-war strategy session: "We need to create a movement that captures our imagination, that lets people plug in and be creative." Collective political imagination is more than speculation or thinking about the future. It is a way that activist groups define the reach and limits of what's possible. And it shapes what they will do to understand and reach such possibilities. "How things are imagined," Marcel Stoetzler and Nira Yuval-Davis tell us, is "fundamental to *why, whether* and *what* we are ready to experience, perceive and know in the first place."

> Imaginings build on and are informed by cognitive processes as much as the latter depend on and are shaped by the imagination. Whatever meaning we attribute to experiences or specific sense data is as much an imaginary as it is an intellectual interpretation of sensual perceptions. Furthermore, what we expect, are ready to perceive and admit as (valid) experience depends on the particular mental setting that lies within the faculty of the imagination—which in this sense both constructs and is constructed by experience.[7]

In some moments, political imagination evident in the internal meetings and talk of activist groups is expansive, as they embrace new ways to think about—and do—politics.[8] More often, and especially over time, groups operate with political horizons that are narrower, restricting the actions and goals they consider possible. Indeed, when activist groups engage a political imagination in internal discussion, they usually do so in fairly limited ways. Talk of a distant future, when broached, is cloaked in humor or sarcasm, minimized as little more than off-handed, unrealistic, even childish fantasies: "when the revolution comes," or "we'll see the day when women get respect," or "I'd like to be around when schools take kids seriously."

This is in stark contrast to the external talk of activist groups, which is less fettered by questions of action. In public, grassroots groups routinely display an expansive political imagination as they describe alternative ways that society could be organized or the many things they could do to change society. The bifurcation between the internal and external talk in a single group can be quite startling. In the publications it produced for the public, for instance, an environmental group routinely called for a complete change in how people relate to every aspect of the natural world. In its private meetings, in contrast, its political horizon extended only as far as the need for recycling.

The synergy between scope and action in the internal dynamics of activist groups has another consequence. Because their political imagination narrows so quickly, activist groups can find it hard to shift gears when a set of actions becomes unfeasible because they have lost track of the underlying problem. When the anti-violence group ALLIES 2007 settled on gang violence as its problem, it was unable to shift directions when it noticed that increasing the number of street anti-gang workers had little effect on levels of violence. Its ability to focus on earlier, broader ideas about violence had simply disappeared. Similarly, an environmental group, organized originally to fight for cleaner air, decided that automobile emissions were the problem. When it was unable to increase local use of hybrid cars, it floundered. In this case, however, as most members drifted away, the group, facing dissolution, decided to reorient itself and was able to shift to a new focus: industrial pollution.[9]

A new group excitedly pondered how to make gay rights more visible. At first, many ideas seemed possible, but its enthusiasm ruptured when one man complained that such demands "always get thrown back in our face" by Christian fundamentalists. His challenge brought the group to a discussion of the scope of the problem. Was it, as a founder insisted, simply that gays didn't have the same rights as heterosexuals? Or was there a deeper issue here: as another member put it, were right-wing Christians going after everyone they don't like, so homophobia is just part of a larger crusade? The talk turned contentious, as other members insisted that harassment and discrimination were experienced by many groups. One woman cited Eartha Kitt's statement during a gay pride march on Washington, that she had marched with "the blacks, the women, and now the gays; if we all got together, we'd be a majority." But the founder and other members continued to object vehemently to broadening the agenda beyond gay issues. After someone told a story to illustrate troubles of people with disabilities, one of the dissenting members turned to another and in a very audible aside, bluntly commented, "What the fuck is that guy saying about getting rights for a woman and her retarded son? What does that have to do with anything?" She was greeted with hostile stares, but the attention gave her the floor to speak. Others might be denied their rights, she insisted, but not for the same reason as are gay persons. Gays face a unique problem—homophobia—and the group needed to stick with that focus so it could agree on what to do. Although many in the room remained unconvinced, her appeal to action seemed to settle the issue. The scope would be anti-gay discrimination, not broader issues of family rights or Christian fundamentalism. What for a moment were alternate possibilities for action were never again mentioned.

As activist groups settle on the scope of their problem, other and broader possibilities have difficulty finding a hearing. Although PAN, the anti-war group, identified its problem as U.S. military intervention in Iraq and Afghanistan, a few members continued to challenge this scope, posing the problem as war in general, or imperialism. Such arguments were quickly dismissed by others on the grounds that they made it hard to act. The need to take action was a shared understanding; anything that jeopardized action was off the table. Soon, as dissenting members drifted away or gave up, the group's focus became self-reinforcing. One evening it seemed that the cycle might be broken—and a turning point might emerge—when PAN discussed how it might distribute flyers at an Amnesty International event. Out of the blue, a younger woman insisted that the time was ripe for it to broaden and work for "an end to perpetual war and the culture of militarism that sustains it." In the past, similar pleas had been rejected out of hand. Now, however, people jumped in with new ideas of how they could do this, drawing comparisons with other groups whose rallies and events they had attended. The discussion spiraled in a variety of directions, as members imagined taking on problems of racism, living wages, and social justice. Just as it appeared that PAN might widen its sense of the problem, however, one man definitively evoked the group's ideological character, declaring that it *was* an anti-war group. Those who wanted a broader scope were silenced.

It takes work for a group to remain the same. What appears static from the outside can conceal a great deal of activity inside a group. One that began broadly as a "citizen-based movement through education" quickly narrowed its scope to environmental degradation. Yet for a number of meetings, other issues were raised ranging from Latin American counter-insurgency training at the School of the Americas to abusive animal experimentation, the need for a "sensible" drug policy, abortion rights, and the rights of families of comatose patients. Even as it seemed to consider other possibilities, however, the group remained firmly focused on environmental issues. Ultimately, its sense of scope was made explicit and the group settled on a plan. Only environmental topics could be discussed at meetings; other issues could be raised as matters of information. Members could take up these issues (or not) as individuals or by affiliating with other groups, but they would not be matters for the group's action.

Talking about Scope

Issues of scope appear in a variety of forms in new activist groups, including in talk about strategy, tactics, or ideology. Using the methodology pioneered by Sophie Duchesne and Florence Haegel to unlock subtle dimensions of group processes,[10] I look in close detail at one sequence of talk in the anti-war group No War Committee to show how a sense of scope is formed as groups ponder the options for action. Italicized excerpts from author's field notes are interspersed with quotations from members.

A member insists that they start talking about imperialism and colonialism, not just war. Initially, the suggestion is angrily dismissed, declared out of bounds for discussion. They need to take action. That is the reason that they should not change:

"No, we shouldn't talk about imperialism and colonialism. Our focus should remain the same: war. That is settled. We need to use our time to work out the details of our upcoming march and rally."

There is a visible pause as members anticipate an objection. Despite his claim, their focus has never been so explicitly stated. No objection is voiced. The discussion moves to details of planning the march and rally:

"We should think of a theme that will resonate with the people of western Pennsylvania. We could do a funeral march. That will be visible and dramatic for the media and other people. We can have coffins and flags, a silent march with solemn drums, and end up at the military recruiting station."

More members jump in and elaborate ways to create flag-draped coffins. A subtle shift occurs. Earlier, broad ideas are reintroduced. They are now presented as consistent with its agreed-upon direction:

"Let's let different local groups do the flags that [lie] across the coffin. So the Palestinian group can do a Palestine flag . . . and one can be for New Orleans, representing how it was hurt by the cuts in the budget for the war."

Without acknowledging that its scope is being debated, those who want the group to remain the same now advocate a specific form of vigil:

"We should do a [peace] vigil, with a veteran or a family member of a soldier as a speaker. . . . Our theme should be a funeral march. We should have speakers only at the first part of the rally, then we'll have a concert at the end because you tend to lose people then. . . . Let's have a program committee to set up the times of the march."

The debate changes tone as some members insist that the plan is problematic for both political and personal reasons:

"The funeral march idea is too depressing a theme."

"We need to invigorate our movement."

"The funeral march doesn't work for me."

Abruptly, the dynamics shift. No longer does the chair recognize people to speak one by one. Now people talk over each other, speaking when they like. Some grumble about the breakdown of the meeting, others refer to it as a "brainstorming session." When things settle down, the debate over scope continues—now tucked into an argument over the logistics of the march, with one side contending:

"'Bring them home alive' or 'NOW—bring them home' should be our themes, just like in the past. We should do street theater with coffins of soldiers. We want to show that the anti-war movement is strong and growing."

And the other pushing for expansion by insisting,

"We need better outreach to other groups that support us. We didn't do that enough last year. We need to ask groups to help, not just to endorse us or give us money. Isn't anyone else here interested in expanding to a larger focus on the role of the U.S. in imperialism, rather than just staying focused on planning events? Shouldn't we consider the issue of Israel/Palestine? Globalization? Attacking the causes of war?"

A member states, forcefully and as fact that

"Our mission statement is broad enough. We need to stay focused on the war in Iraq. Staying focused on Iraq brings people onto the streets, so we should stay focused on this, our mass mobilization."

This last statement effectively ended the debate by leaving no room for objection, a situation that Paul Ricouer terms discursive "violence."[11] Although some members continued to disagree and take exception to the logistics of the march and rally, their ideas were ignored. The group moved ahead with planning. Months later, this sequence was brought up at a meeting as evidence that things were decided and could not be revisited. The group had embarked on a firm path.

As activist groups shape a sense of the problem they will tackle, they also build a sense of themselves as collective political actors. The result can be an expansive political imagination that pulls members into new ways of thinking about how to change the world. At least as often, however, activist groups operate within a declining range of alternatives and an ever-narrowing scope of the problem.

WHAT IS THE MORAL STATUS OF THE PROBLEM?

As activist groups identify a problem, they also assess its moral status. Along with what it is *possible* to do, they consider what it is *right* to do. Put another way, activists do not simply assess opportunities and then seize them. Rather, they use ethical (as well as strategic) criteria to select among the opportunities they perceive.[12] And these criteria change over time.

Faith-based groups talk explicitly about the moral principles that guide their work, as did a Christian peace group in this study. But secular activist groups—the majority of those studied here—generally invoke moral claims indirectly, and often awkwardly, in their internal talk. This is true even for groups that use direct moral claims in their public appeals and whose activists privately cite moral standards as guiding their actions. When asked why they so rarely express such commitments in group discussions, activists generally respond that it is "divisive" to bring morality into politics. They regard politics as a social process, a product of discussion and compromise, and morality as outside the social, an external standard of judgment. As Susan Neiman comments, "Western secular culture has no clear place for moral language and its use makes many profoundly uncomfortable."[13]

In secular fledgling groups, explicit mention of moral concerns is generally understood as inappropriate. When a woman said that she couldn't go along with the proposal for an illegal protest march because it went against her (moral) beliefs, other members jumped in and declared such reasoning irrelevant; they insisted that her comment be ignored. Theirs was more than a reaction to a novel standard of judgment; other new criteria did not provoke such complete dismissal. Rather, they wanted morality talk off the table for group discussion, even if it shaped the actions of individual members. Similarly, when a woman in a group advocating "queer rights" wouldn't agree to the confrontational vigil that was taking shape—not because she saw such actions as futile or counterproductive, but because she regarded them as "wrong, not respectable"—her comment was studiously ignored.

Although activist groups rarely talk openly about morality, they frequently evoke moral principles indirectly as they decide how to act. Philosopher Kwame Anthony Appiah says that moral perception "is a way of seeing, and seeing is always seeing *as* and seeing *that*." As an example, he cites a story of a Polish peasant woman in World War II who saved a Jewish girl from being hurled into a well by insisting to a group of villagers that "she's not a dog." The peasant woman's moral argument was not expressed in abstract theologies, but in modes of categorization: *"She's not a dog."*[14] The moral arguments that pervade activist group talk, although far less dramatic, have a similar form. Like the comment "she is not a dog," activist groups make moral claims by how they categorize problems, considering why action is needed, why it matters, and what actions are right to do.[15]

Consider the discussion of a protest at the Shrine Circus by with animal rights group. At the meeting, one member repeatedly shouted out, "I hate that circus," intending, she said later, to create energy for the protest. Her exclamations were met with loud affirmations by the others and inspired a sequence of talk in which people shared what they disliked about the circus, ranging from a childhood fear of clowns to their current sense that circus animals were mistreated. As the momentum built, however, one woman abruptly interrupted her own tale about attending a Shrine Circus with the thought, "isn't that the one that gives money to hospitals?" A competing, and more sympathetic, view of the circus broke the spiral of negative storytelling and the normally boisterous group fell silent. Members shot glances at each other and whispered in worried tones. The moral category of the Shrine Circus was no longer clear. Was its essence that it abused animals or that it raised money for injured and disabled children? Quickly though, such questions ceased and the group returned to planning its protest, reaffirming the circus as a hateful institution. A possible counter-interpretation (and a potential turning point)—that there was moral ambiguity to the circus—was never again mentioned. Yet several members, obviously uncomfortable, failed to show up at the circus protest and soon left the group.

Some groups vacillate among varying possible moral judgments. An anti-war group wanted to express its anger over prisoners abused in U.S. military custody. But when a member suggested that they "build momentum from [public] outrage" by dramatizing a torture scene at a public square to seize "the moral high ground," they were in a quandary. Several insisted that the event was itself "wrong," that they would never participate in such an action. Others were silent, but pointedly stopped paying attention and engaged in side conversations, both unusual for this group. Another group discussed how to act toward people who voted for President

Bush. Although accurate in the minds of most group members, was it right or wrong to treat Bush supporters as "stupid," "ignorant," or as people whose "brains are still evolving," they asked each other? Would it be "right" to act instead as if Bush advocates were simply "misled?"

Moral Paths

The moral character of activist groups is established early. Even if the formative process is forgotten by later activists, activist groups quickly develop a collective moral sensibility that makes some options for action likely and moves others off the table. Consider DebtFree, a group formed to pressure the U.S. government to forgive the debt burdens of the world's poorest countries. Its first meeting attracted nine white women enlisted by its organizer, Sue. Of the initial attendees, some knew each other, but most did not. Sue began by announcing that they would attract members from a broad array of local "religious organizations, congregations, social action groups, and student groups." In fact, she had already moved in that direction by affiliating with the Center for Progressive Values (CPV), the resource and organizing center. Despite Sue's aspirations, however, such an expansive sense of possibility narrowed considerably.

The way this happened shows how small acts can reverberate to provoke large effects. As people settled into chairs for the first meeting, Sue prompted them simply to "introduce themselves." The first person to do so gave her name and also her religious affiliation. Following her lead, all other attendees then identified themselves by their faiths, as Quakers, Jews, Unitarian Universalists, and Lutherans. Such labels were not the only possible ones, given the secular focus of the group. In fact, several attendees later revealed that they worked in immigrant services or international programs, affiliations that would have been at least as reasonable to announce in a group working on global debt policy.

This small act, that members identified themselves by their faiths, had major consequences. As DebtFree shifted to consider how to find people to write letters and call their legislators to protest the U.S. policy on debt, members didn't follow Sue's initial idea of focusing on students and social action groups. Instead, they seemed to think that only people in faith congregations were possible to recruit. Other alternatives were never mentioned again, even months later when the group had dwindled to a couple of members and it was desperate for new people. (Students, at least, would have been feasible recruits, as a similar but unrelated group soon started up on a college campus.)

The path toward identifying as a faith group took another step as DebtFree discussed where it would meet. Even though its members had connections to a variety of alternative venues, including the CPV, DebtFree considered only church buildings as meeting places. When it selected a Lutheran Church, the group encouraged the pastor to join and immediately deferred to her in its decision making. Moreover, within a few meetings, the group took yet a further move to define itself as a faith community, by asking the pastor to lead it in prayer whenever feelings of anger or frustration broke out among members. The path toward a religious, and Christian, sense of itself was self-reinforcing. As it moved further in this direction, more church members were attracted to the group and non-religious and non-Christian members drifted away.

Faith issues also shaped how DebtFree expressed its rationales for action, that is, its moral understandings. When it considered how to convince people to support third-world nations—in spite of the Bush administration's insistence that aid monies supported immoral activities like abortion and birth control—members almost exclusively considered frameworks of Christian action. Some of the talk among members was light-hearted, like joking comments that they should wear Christian "collars and crosses" to assert religious authority. As one stated, "They should know we're from churches!" But other talk was more serious. How, the group pondered, could it win over Catholics and Baptists who were sexually conservative and opposed abortion? Should members approach Episcopalians or would they be unlikely to be interested, given the denomination's internal turmoil over the issue of gay clergy? DebtFree's moral logics were not only meant for external effect, to convince its audiences. Moral logics also structured how the group considered its options internally. Members could imagine working to persuade politicians of their cause, but they deemed any talk of exerting political pressure as inappropriately secular and too political for what, they reminded each other, was a faith community working on a "moral concern." The small, almost incidental act— how the first person had introduced herself—had large ramifications.

Activist groups, even those that shy away from the language of morality in their public statements, use moral criteria to shape their problem. Their moral interpretations aren't always explicit and don't remain explicit over time, but they form a blueprint for what the group will consider morally appropriate to do or talk about into the future.

WHAT DO WE KNOW?

To define a problem, new activist groups must assess what they know about it. Faced by a deluge of information from members, outside activists, and media sources, they decide what knowledge is relevant and what gaps they need to fill.[16] The groups in this study typically do so by switching between classifying problems as *representative* or *unique* and looking for information accordingly. They analyze representative problems by comparing incidents to similar problems, a process nicely described in Carol Heimer's discussion of the care of critically ill babies. Medical personnel, Heimer found, regard these infants as cases of a larger category of babies (premature, born to drug-dependent mothers, and so forth), so how a particular baby might differ from others in the category is less relevant than its similarities. In contrast, the parents of ill infants eschew comparison with other sick babies and instead look at their infants as unique, focusing on how their particular baby changes over time.[17]

How activist groups classify a problem matters for what they do. When they regard a problem as unique, they value specific information; for problems they deem representative, they value broader information. Either direction takes them on a path of information seeking that is self-reinforcing. How activist groups alternate between seeing problems as representative and unique, and the consequence of doing so, can be seen by looking at sequences of action and interpretation in two groups. The first is Stop the Killing (StK), a group fighting black-on-black violence, which I trace in a sequence that lasted over a series of meetings. The second is an anti-war group for which I focus on a single meeting several years after the U.S. invasion of Iraq.

Knowing about a Representative Case

The information exchanges of StK were unusually structured and explicit, compared to those of other emerging groups. Most activist groups schedule times in their agendas to share information for the first few meetings, but few continue to do so. At every meeting of StK, however, there was time set aside to report new incidents of violence in the community and to update members on earlier ones. Its members also traded information in animated conversations in the hallway and on the steps leading into the community center where they met, in whispered asides during meetings, and as they lingered afterward to, as one woman put it, "catch up on the news" and "fill in the gaps."

Although StK's members often spoke at great length about the current state of black-on-black violence in the community, they did so in a surprisingly cursory way, even when they had intimate familiarity with the incident.[18] Similar to Heimer's medical formulation, members of StK were more interested in violent incidents as representative cases of a broader problem than as unique occurrences. For instance, when one woman stood up to recount news on a homicide of someone in her family, she emphasized that it should be seen as "just another murder in which a young person died." Brushing aside questions about the specifics of what happened, she challenged the others: "How many of us here," she asked, "know someone who has been murdered?" There was little hesitation; almost everyone there raised a hand. She continued, "how many know someone who is a *murderer*?" After some hesitation, many raised their hands. To her, violent incidents were examples of a general category. The only relevant factor was race, to establish it as a case of black-on-black violence.

Stop the Killing continued to classify incidents of black-on-black violence as representative cases even as its definition of violence ballooned from an initial focus on murders, drive-by shootings, attacks on intended victims, and incidental injury to uninvolved bystanders to a later concern also with home invasions, death threats against court witnesses and jurors, weapons smuggled into schools, and even the "stop snitching" (to the police) campaign. Regardless of the type of violence, specifics of incidents were rarely mentioned, and there was no need to ask. Violence from drug dealing, gang conflict, or general poverty and misery were all the same: a dreary accumulation of cases of black-on-black assault, understandable within and by virtue of this category.

By classifying incidents as cases of a larger pattern of violence, StK opened some options for action and foreclosed others. It made action more pressing, as the sheer number of incidents underscored the "epidemic" they faced. At the same time, seeing all incidents as cases of a broad category made it difficult to design a response. What did it mean to fight against "violence" as opposed to, say, drug-related violence, domestic violence, or gang-related violence? In the diffuse category of violence, only the most general solutions seemed relevant, although these did not always lend themselves to clear directions for action.

There was one striking time that StK saw an incident of violence as unique, in a discussion of a catastrophic fire started by two young boys that killed five African American children while their mothers were at a neighborhood bar. A series of dramatic events, including the eventual arrest of both mothers, kept the story at the forefront of the media and in the discussions of StK for months. Initially, StK talked of the fire as just another case of black-on-black violence. Over time, however, its talk shifted to its unique characteristics. Why did the mothers leave the children alone? What would happen to the mothers? How would the two surviving children be affected by their siblings' deaths and their mothers' arrests? Such questions made the group press to know more details. What was it about the mothers that would lead them to abandon their children this way? Was teen pregnancy to blame? And where were the fathers while this was happening? Should they take some responsibility for the tragedy since they were not around? Here, StK had an opportunity to tailor its actions to the specific factors of this violence, but with the vast array of possibilities—parenting, sex education, black manhood, child care—it could not decide what to tackle; and, worried that members could not agree, it simply urged them to donate money and household goods for the surviving children.

How activist groups classify problems shapes what they want to know about them. For representative problems, particularities and inconsistencies in individual cases are less important than knowing about the general category. For a unique problem, they want to know about its specificities, as in the second example of an anti-war group.

Knowing about a Unique Case

The efforts of the Pittsburgh Antiwar Network (PAN) to hinder military recruiting of African American and poor white kids included vigils, hunger strikes, marches, demonstrations, and acts of civil disobedience such as a blockade of a military recruitment station. The police responded with arrests and regular harassment of protesters. In one meeting, members told about Lisa, an older white woman and core member of PAN, who had been arrested and bitten by a police dog. The way they talked about what happened to Lisa illustrates how logics of comparison are tied to a sense of possible action, shown in the italicized author's field notes below.

PAN members first saw the incident involving Lisa as part of a general pattern, which permitted them to speak definitively without having specific knowledge about the incident:

Two members speak alternately, competing to position themselves as the main expert on unnecessary arrests of protesters. Each acknowledges that he had not been at the event in question, but seeks to establish his credibility by making a series of claims. These are announced in ever-louder tones, showing outrage.

Each speaker referred to Lisa's incident, but the claims they made were based on the underlying, unspecified category, not on the particular characteristics of the event. Four claims were made:

The police did not give an order for the protestors to disperse, "which they never do."

Federal authorities and the military are responsible because they "probably pressured local police" to respond swiftly and cruelly because they are trying to control public perceptions about the war.

If the protestors had been drunken passersbys leaving the stadium after a game and urinating in public, the police wouldn't have bothered them at all.

We know, from earlier activist experiences, that the police can be terribly brutal to protesters.

The speakers asserted expertise in, and evidence of, these *kinds* of cases rather than knowledge of this specific event. They described the incident with Lisa as *a case of* police brutality, so all necessary knowledge was already available.

> *As confirmation, each relates the story of an earlier event in which police tasered a protester as evidence that, as one concludes, the Pittsburgh police have "become more militant."*

Categories can change even as activist groups retain the same logic of comparison. In the same meeting, Lisa's incident also was discussed as a case of overzealous protestors.

> *Several other members jump into the discussion. Some ask questions about the details of the protest event. Were protestors violating the law by blocking access to the recruiting station? One cited a friend who had witnessed previous counter-recruitment protests in which protestors broke the law.*

Another category also appeared, that Lisa's situation was a case of misconduct by military recruiters.

> *The conversation shifts to the tactics of military recruiters. Members relate stories of shady tactics by recruiters. Some recount incidents of recruiters in schools.*
>
> *One says military recruiters offered to falsify his mental health record to let him enlist.*
>
> *Another tells of four military recruiters who assaulted him last fall at a protest when he was dressed as a torture victim in black robe and hood, throwing him to the ground, and announcing that he had "no idea" what it was like in Iraq.*

Later, the group shifted to consider the specifics of Lisa's event. Even this discussion, however, was shaped by an assumption that Lisa's incident was a case of something broader. Members talked with knowledge of how these kinds of cases are handled.

> *One member comments that protesters will face reprisals from the judge and police if they make noise about their arrests.*

This statement, though, opened the door to a shift, a turning point, in the group's logic. One of the members with firsthand information about Lisa's incident intervened to say that this event was not like the others. Noting that the judge did not respond in the predicted way, she argued that the event was unique, one with unusual characteristics like the judge's sympathy for protestors.

> *Another member, who had herself been arrested in this protest, intervenes to correct him. She insists that the judge's comments were not meant to be intimidating; indeed, that this judge, himself earlier on active duty in the military, told one protester that he "appreciated what you are doing by exercising your rights" and hoped [the protester] appreciated the low bail amount he was setting.*

This was a turning point in the group. With an opening to talk about Lisa's event in a different, non-categorical way, members—including Lisa—saw themselves as needing new knowledge, and people with details of the incident now spoke up.

> *Lisa talks about her emotional distress and declares that so many people are upset about her attack that "the pendulum has swung" in the anti-war movement's direction.*
>
> *Others jump in to urge that they find the name and badge number of the officer with the dog. They speculate that she had been arrested because the police feared that she would sue after the dog bit her so they tried to preempt the lawsuit by arresting her.*
>
> *Several ask whether those arrested were still in "emotional and physical distress."*
>
> *Many questions about the specifics of the protest and the arrests. A member (who was not arrested) reiterated that the protest was orderly, even though they did not have a legal permit. But they didn't block traffic in the street or on the sidewalk. The police didn't issue a request for the protestors to disperse, but what caused the situation to escalate was when a young man posting a sign on the door to the recruiting station pushed away a Fox News cameraperson's camera. It was unclear if the young man damaged the camera or touched the cameraperson, but the police intervened when the cameraperson asked the police to arrest the young man.*

There were implications for its actions depending on how PAN categorized Lisa's arrest. When members regarded it as a case of a general problem, they applied standard solutions to the varying categories to which it seemed to fit, a process that generally led to affirming their existing strategies and tactics. As a new case of an old problem, in other words, it seemed to require no new information, no envisioning of new possibilities. Moreover, such categorization allowed the group to overlook details that were inconsistent and focus on those that were familiar. When PAN classified the arrest as a unique episode, though, the group considered a different and less familiar array of actions. Members suggested that they encourage those who were "unjustly" arrested to file lawsuits or at least to write narratives about what they had witnessed. They also talked about the possibility of creating a "statement of solidarity" with all those arrested and about mobilizing a broad alliance of every peace group in the city to sign it; after some discussion, they implemented the solidarity statement tactic.

Gathering information about a problem is not a straightforward task in activist groups. It requires members to consider how to interpret information and how to gear their actions to an evolving sense of what they know.

SHOULD WE KNOW MORE AND HOW SHOULD WE LEARN?

When I talked to founders of activist groups, they often mentioned that they wanted to create a space in which people could learn together, not unlike Paul Lichterman's idea of a "forum" with "critically reflective discussion [where . . .] members converse and learn together as an end in itself."[19]Almost without exception, grassroots activists said they wanted their groups to be like this.

It is striking, therefore, that few emerging grassroots groups actually took time for such "critically reflective discussion." Indeed, they rarely gave more than perfunctory attention to collective learning, at least after the first couple of meetings. Even those who saw part of their mission as educating themselves on political issues tended not to do so for long. Among the 60-plus groups in this study, only one continued to include "news of the day" in its agenda over time; a couple of others sent occasional informational e-mails to their members. Some openly worried that they lacked enough knowledge to act, like a civil liberties group that wanted more information about the attitudes of Arab Americans, Muslims, and recent immigrants, but even these groups rarely tried to acquire the missing data. A new conservative group Liberty Now (LN) struggled to define its mission, weighing whether it should fight hate crimes legislation, oppose gun control, or take on some other issue. Eventually, it bogged down over a member's provocative inquiry: "Who determines what's conservative?" Was it favoring lower taxes and less bureaucracy, members wondered aloud, or working to preserve freedom and liberties? Did conservative groups do grassroots organizing, or did only liberals do that? None of them knew for sure, participants concluded, and left the meeting without considering how to find out.

In most groups, collective learning dies away with no acknowledgment. An anti-war group came to a shared understanding early on that the United States entered Iraq to secure oil supplies; from that point forward, all new information was simply slotted into the group's interpretive template. The disinclination to self-educate remains, even in the wake of very dramatic news. An animal rights group spent little time trying to learn about a state anti-terrorism bill even though they feared that it would curtail their ability to stage public protests. Even when groups perceive themselves as making mistakes, they are not likely to try to learn from these mistakes. In a study of the disastrous launch of the *Challenger* spaceship, Diane Vaughan found a workplace culture in the space command in which mistakes were routinely attributed to tactical errors or lack of follow-up, but not to a lack of information.[20] Activist groups similarly see their errors as those of judgment rather than as gaps in knowledge. Very quickly, they come to view knowledge as what they provide to the public, not what they could gain in the group. This pattern is generally interrupted only when the group shifts to a new problem focus, although not always even then.

Phasing Out Collective Learning

How does learning disappear in activist groups? Activists say that immediate needs, like planning events, simply swallow up the time and energy necessary to learn together. A civil liberties activist told me that they had "news time" at first, but it "got lost" in the rush of arranging logistics for their many protests and press conferences. But less visible factors also push against collective learning. Lichterman found that as their members develop more shared interests and identities, citizen groups regard discussion and new information as less necessary.[21] This is the case in grassroots groups too; cultural factors diminish collective learning.

Some grassroots groups actively suppressed shared learning to avoid internal conflict. This was especially true when members regarded their political agreement as fragile or shallow. An anti-war group frequently talked about its need to learn about quickly changing events and praised another group in which such learning was routine. At the end of a frustrating meeting, however, the group decided that, while desirable, collective learning was unworkable because it would create "open debate" and provoke "factionalism" among members. Similarly, a conservative group started with elaborate plans for internal education, including films and discussions, but quickly shelved these ideas as likely to cause friction. When a member raised the topic again, asking directly why members didn't talk about current events any more, the atmosphere in the room became uncomfortable. Talking about why they didn't talk was out of bounds and her interjection was dismissed as divisive. Current events were discussed only at strategy sessions, another member instructed her.

Collective learning also declines, although less abruptly, when activist groups decide to make learning irrelevant. An anti-drug group initially engaged in extensive self-education at its meetings, learning about illegal drugs and sharing ideas about how it could learn more. Within a few months, these learning attempts were abandoned as the group decided to model itself on another group, deciding simply to rely on what that group had already learned.

The most common way that new activist groups phase out collective learning is by designating, often implicitly, the task of learning and knowing to one or a few members. These "cognitively central"[22] members are charged with being informed, thus absolving others of the need to be so. Cognitively central members may not be the group's official, or even unofficial, leaders in a broad sense; often they are not. They do not necessarily guide the group's strategy or lead the group toward a definition of its mission or goals, nor are they the most authoritative members or the ones to whom other members turn to resolve conflicts or finalize plans. But cognitively central members are assumed to have unique access to information whose value or accuracy is rarely questioned.

The first meeting of a queer advocacy group, QUERE—described as a "re-organizational meeting" to acknowledge an earlier group with the same name but different members—became embroiled in a conflict over why its founders didn't support the current campaigns of a well-known national gay/lesbian organization. "I thought the [national organization] was a good organization promoting the gay movement; why are we opposed to them?" asked one member to general assent. Ideas flew about how attendees could figure out which stance was correct, perhaps by consulting gay magazines, talking to other activists, or reading the national group's literature. Ideas flourished until, suddenly, the conversation came to a stop when one member asserted that he had inside knowledge about national gay politics. He claimed that the national group was funding conservative organizations and political parties and therefore should be opposed, a statement that was accepted without objection. The group shelved the idea that it needed to learn more about national gay politics.

Grassroots groups value different kinds of knowledge, and possessing such information can position members as cognitively central. In an anti-police violence group, the knowledgeable one was "someone who grew up in the neighborhood" and thus knew intimately the level of police brutality toward young African Americans. For a Palestinian support group, it was someone with firsthand knowledge of suffering based on "situations there." In an environmental group that sought to form coalitions with similar groups, importance was accorded to those with broad knowledge of local, national, and international organizations, while in a civil rights group, it was someone who knew enough about a national organization to "translate" between them and the local group. For others, it was members who knew what sources of information to trust or dismiss.

The dynamics of establishing a "cognitively central" figure can be complicated, as seen in an anti-war group's discussion of the Iraqi election in early 2005. John opened with his analysis, insisting that "the elections didn't constitute a democracy" and reminding everyone—unnecessarily—that most Iraqis opposed the U.S. occupation. What happened then, drawn from author's field notes, shows how a cognitively central member like John can shape what activist groups try to learn.

> MEMBER 1 asks, of no one in particular, "Who was running [for office, in Iraqi election] and how were they elected?" but then turns to face JOHN awaiting an answer.
>
> JOHN provides a list of names.
>
> MEMBER 2 states that the United States hasn't revealed which Iraqis were running as candidates. JOHN, as if the statement had been a question, responds "Yes, that's right."
>
> MEMBER 3, agitated, concludes: "It's a farce! A council is being elected [in Iraq] to write a constitution under occupation." JOHN affirms that "Yes, elections are a cover that allows the U.S. to maintain a military presence in the Middle East." He then makes a lengthy statement predicting that the United States will let Iraq say that U.S. troops can leave and that President Bush may use that as an opportunity to invade Iran.

Cognitive centrality is self-reinforcing, as this example shows. Activist groups treat what such members say as important. And what cognitively central members say shapes the group's collective understandings, making these persons ever more central in the future. John became central when he demonstrated his knowledge of Iraqi politics. Not only was he recognized as the group's authority on Iraq, but his prediction that the United States would invade Iran also carried great weight, sparking the group's interest in knowing more about Iran, for which John was its main source.

Similarly, a member became cognitively central in another anti-war group because of her knowledge of military operations. Her centrality then made the group more attentive to military issues, such as the details of military campaigns and enlistment regulations that began to appear in its propaganda. And the need to produce these materials further strengthened her centrality in the group.

Cognitive centrality is not simply a product of matching the group's goals with individual aptitudes. It is not that an activist group wants to know more about the military, so the member who knows the most becomes cognitively central. Rather, goals and influence are intertwined. As a group changes its focus, who is cognitively central can shift or become further entrenched. Conversely, as someone becomes cognitively central, that person may alter the group's focus. An example is Street Medics Action Group (SMAG), a group that provided lay medical treatment during protest events, as related by a member.

> EMTs' (emergency medical technician) idea of a safe scene is a scene with lots of police officers on it—which is completely opposite of a protestor's idea [which is when] you see police, that's an unsafe scene. . . . We'll stay at the protest and we'll help people at the protest.

SMAG's founder envisioned it as "very activist oriented . . . just a bunch of activists who got medical training." In other words, its members would provide medical help, but its main concern was politics, not medicine: "People get very excited about the individual [protest] issues and they get excited when the issues succeed."

For a while, another member related, SMAG was "still sorting it out" and not clear "about the specifics of the way people were going to begin to relate to each other as we got to know each other better, how effective our decision-making process would be, how easy it was going to be to get funding, not sure, but pretty confident, that we're going to stick around, not going to just disappear." During this time, Judy, an experienced medic, moved to Pittsburgh and joined SMAG. Judy quickly became one of its most consistent members, as "other people get too busy or as other things come up, drift in and out." Moreover, Judy became a cognitively central member by asserting the importance of knowing medicine rather than knowing protest. As another member stated, "we know each other well enough to know where people are good at things. I'm not really good at questioning the wisdom of someone who has, like, a lot more training than I do." Judy's centrality further pushed SMAG toward valuing medical rather than political victories. In a post-mortem of a protest, for instance, there were many mentions of medical issues but little talk about the political issues that fueled the protest. In the words of one member, "the emotion [we feel after a protest] depends a lot on how much training we do. . . . We tried to have a training before people went down to Miami [for the protest]. It didn't go well. And people were pretty upset about that. But we're going to do it again. Do a mock training ourselves."

Activist groups develop ways to learn collectively, but often in very limited ways. Although individual members talk about activism as a way to learn more about political issues, grassroots groups quickly develop ways to reduce situations in which members engage in learning together.

CASE COMPARISON

How activist groups develop a political character is evident in the different paths taken by Stop Gun Violence (SGV) and Eliminating Police Violence Together (EPVT), groups that started with a similar sense of the problem, that of violence. Both began with a strong and directive founder and attracted about the same number of members to meetings. Attendance for SGV ranged from 6 to 15 people (mode = 10) and EPVT's varied from 4 to 14 people (mode = 5); both had equivalently larger attendance at their public events. But EPVT and SGV moved in different directions as they refined the problems they would address.

Despite their similar interest in stopping violence, SGV began with a wider scope than EPVT, seeing the problem as gun violence in general. As it quickly settled on the pending National Rifle Association (NRA) nationwide convention in Pittsburgh as a symbol around which to mobilize public interest, SGV recognized the advantage of keeping vague its sense of the causes of gun violence to rally a broad coalition of faith, peace and justice, and racial minority groups that might have different positions. In contrast, EPVT's focus began with a narrow interest in forcing the city to prosecute police involved in a series of killings of African American men. In EPVT, there was no sense that the cause of such violence needed discussion. It was presumed to be clear: over-zealous, fearful, and racist white police.

Over the course of a year, SGV and EPVT moved in opposite directions. SGV initially considered a variety of ideas about the problems behind gun violence but ultimately settled on what it regarded as a mainstream issue— the NRA—in order to reach a wide audience. It decided to save more contentious possibilities, such as ideas that militarism or homophobia fueled gun violence, for outreach to specific audiences, although such issues were never again raised. In contrast, EPVT's ideological field expanded over time, both internally and in its public presentations. It moved successively from defining the problem as white police assaulting African American strangers; to a sense that police of all races were hostile to African Americans; to a belief that male police officers engaged in widespread violence, including against their wives; to a sense of institutionalized societal racism for which the police were simply an instrument of violence (evidenced in a terminological shift from "killings" to "lynchings"); to a belief that there was a broad culture of violence (including violence within the African American community that heightened police fear and prompted displays of force); to a belief that violence was global (discussions of political prisoners like Mumia Abu-Jamal and the prison scandal in Iraq); and, ultimately, to a vague sense of an overall "lack of justice" that spawned all forms of violence.

How these two groups took such different paths can be seen in the stories they told about themselves and the social world.[23] From its beginning, Stop Gun Violence distanced itself from members' stories of personal tragedies; for instance, members were never asked if a personal event had brought them to the group. Instead, SGV's stories of gun tragedy were fashioned from items in the media and retold when they could be strategically appropriated for external audiences, as when news of a local child's accidental shooting of a postal worker was used to attract media to a press conference or when persons (unaffiliated with the group but known to have suffered from gun violence) were selected as speakers for events to give personal testimonies about gun violence.

Although it did not encourage members' personal stories, SGV initially discussed how it might widen its focus, and thereby its membership, to include groups disproportionately affected by gun violence, such as African Americans and battered women. Few efforts were made in this direction, but the discussion of outreach kept open the question of how to describe gun violence. The group talked of building a coalition of groups whose varied experiences would bring them to new understandings of gun violence and attract a more diverse membership. This possible broadening was interrupted, however, when SGV solicited assistance from a national gun violence group about protesting and was rebuffed. From that point, the character of its meetings changed: ideological discussions gave way to the details of event planning, such as the need to determine whether NRA delegates would be able to view the protest events from their meeting spaces. There was no more talk about identifying the problem or its causes. Also off the table was any discussion of recruiting new members since a broad base was no longer seen as a prerequisite for ideological clarity or even for a successful protest. The NRA protest ceased to be a mobilizing tactic for SGV and instead became its goal, with the group increasingly reactive to NRA plans, such as the announcement that Vice President Cheney would deliver the convention's keynote speech. In the end, technical and logistical issues swamped SGV, leaving little time or energy for a discussion of ways, other than through the NRA, that gun violence is promoted or manifested.

As occurred in SGV, the sequences of action and interpretation by Eliminating Police Violence Together (EPVT) were largely reactive to external events. Meetings and public events transpired in response to new killings or developments in existing legal cases. But while reactive sequences led away from broad-ranging ideological discussions in SGV, the reactive sequences in EPVT led the group to more extensive, spiraling, personal stories. Early storytelling in EPVT was highly personal and centered on the experiences of Marilyn, its founder and leader. Marilyn told the group, hesitantly at first and then repeatedly and boldly, how the police botched their investigation of her son's shooting, resulting in the shooter's release from jail, a story meant to demonstrate that the police are complicit in community violence. Later, when Marilyn became convinced that the district attorney (DA) would not pursue prosecution of the police officers accused in a particular case of police violence, and again when authorities initiated a probe of Marilyn and her family members for allegedly writing fraudulent checks (a charge later dismissed), the established place of Marilyn's stories in the group served to stretch its ideological horizons to consider other forms of officially sanctioned violence against African Americans. EPVT members then began to insert new stories of violence into meetings and public events, spiraling outward from the specific case of Marilyn and the Pittsburgh police to ever-broader ideas about the nature of violence and its causes.

Francesca Polletta argues that group narratives are more powerful when they are incomplete and thus require retelling.[24] Here, the constant twists and turns of ongoing legal cases and investigations fueled discussions within EPVT about the reasons behind these actions by the authorities. Such discussions evoked other, seemingly related stories. In an attempt to interpret the DA's refusal to prosecute the police in several cases, for example, one white female member described in vivid detail how the DA grew up to be a "brat" and a "mean kid" under the supervision of a father who "tried to shoot [her family's] chicken with a BB gun." The same member drew on her experiences in another city where she was an advocate for domestic violence survivors to explain a culture of acceptability that develops in racist police departments and leads to violence. Stories of personal abuse by the police led other members to tell stories of additional instances of abuse and mistreatment by authorities, spiraling the ideological scope of problems far beyond its initial focus on racist white police.

Their changing ideological paths had different consequences for the two groups. SGV embarked on a path of less and increasingly narrower ideological talk, less personal storytelling, a declining commitment of members, infrequent or no recruitment, and little talk about what the group might do after the NRA protest. Not surprisingly given its disintegrating membership, SGV's protest at the NRA convention was only lightly attended, by approximately 150 people in contrast to a turnout of 1,500 people (in heavy rain and cold) for an anti-war march the previous month. Although it did not officially disband, SGV did not meet after that event. EPVT's ideological expansion led it in a different direction. It retained a committed membership but became spread thinly over a widening range of issues, eventually including health care and the Iraq War, and faced difficulty mounting sustained or focused campaigns on police violence or other issues.

The path of what activist groups consider problematic both shapes their sense of possibilities and constrains their likely range of actions. What is problematic can metamorphose into the infinite, as in the case of EPVT, and leave the group floundering in a sea of competing directions and tactics. Alternately, the possibilities can disappear altogether, as they did in SGV, once the group abandoned its ideological talk and turned to tactics.

CONCLUSION

From the outset, activist groups create an ideological character. One way is by defining the problem they will work on. This process is complicated and often contentious as activist groups define their problem's scope, assess its moral status, talk about what they know, and consider how to learn more. As they do so, they set themselves on an ideological path that conditions what they will see as possible well into the future.

Activist groups start with a defined problem but rarely stay with this definition for long. Instead, they quickly mold the scope to allow them to act. Are they simply moving from broad goals (such as environmental quality) to nearer-term objectives (reducing automobile use) to practical tactics (add bike lanes)? Close observation of their internal dynamics shows they are not. Grassroots groups don't just pare down a problem to a manageable size; they redefine the problem to fit their possible actions. In the process, broader goals slip away and can be impossible to retrieve later. From a distance, these dynamics are difficult to see because in their public events activist groups generally project a broader sense of the problem. But internally, their political imaginations tend to narrow considerably over time.

As they develop a shared ideology, activist groups weigh the moral nature of the problem they want to address. This is true even if they never use moral frameworks in public. And since they are present from the beginning, moral frameworks can have long-lasting effects on how activist groups develop.

An ideological character requires activist groups to develop shared ways of knowing and assessing their knowledge, often by categorizing problems as representative or unique. Activist groups also learn together. Sometimes, their efforts are energetic and involve deep and broad political learning. Too often, though, grassroots groups push opportunities for collective learning to the side. Fearing internal friction, they avoid open discussions of new information and designate the task of information gathering and assessment to a few members.

This chapter highlights how the political imagination and theorizing of grassroots groups tend to narrow over time. What begins as broad discussions of politics erodes as the range of admissible topics shrinks and responsibility for charting the group's ideological direction comes to be the province of a small number of members. As the case studies of EPVT and SGV show, shifts in direction are possible in ideological trajectories, but such opportunities are not always seized.

Although activist groups tend to narrow their ideological focus over time, the way they engage in political talk also shows their democratizing potential. When members are talking about problems and how they might be resolved, they display a collective political imagination that, like collective intelligence, is a group-level phenomenon. Collective political imagination is often more expansive than that of any single member's, invigorating participants with new ideas and possibilities for action.

Although scholars more often look at how activists frame issues for an external public, this chapter shows that grassroots groups are actively involved in shaping political issues for themselves. They do not just adopt the definitions set by their founders. Nor do they rely on definitions used by other groups or larger social movements. Rather, they develop ways to collectively theorize about politics and political action.

CHAPTER 5

How Should We Treat Each Other?

Sam's passion for politics was evident in his cluttered living room, stacked high with papers from his years of grassroots activism. When I asked him to reflect on the many groups in which he had been involved, I was surprised that Sam didn't start by describing what they had achieved. Instead, pushing aside piles of activist literature, he launched into a vivid story of a group that "imploded" and "self-destructed":

> There was a lot of disagreements and in-fighting between some of the main members in the group. They just didn't want to come to any consensus—everybody wanted to do their own thing and they kept pushing really hard on that issue and essentially alienating a lot of people. . . . I don't think that the group ever really came together all that well as a group. It was still a group of individuals rather than a group.

Sam is not unique. When asked why their group worked or didn't work, activists not only mentioned strategies, ideologies, and opportunities; they also talked about how people treated each other. After meetings, activists conversed about which people were testy, why tempers flared, who cooperated or did not.

In *Talking about Politics*, Katherine Walsh contrasts voluntary groups in which people seek fellowship with those in which they have purposive goals, like promoting a cause or ideology.[1] In grassroots activism, these motives are entangled. Political commitment is important, of course, but people also are in grassroots groups because they like being around other activists. Relationships among members are not incidental to activism; they sustain or destroy it.

Before they join an activist group, people assess how they will get along with those already there. How a group *feels* is a sorting principle. It can usher people into activism or keep them on the sidelines, even people who agree with a group's politics and strategy and have personal ties to current members. How a group feels is also a self-reinforcing path, guiding people into one activist group rather than another and bolstering the expectation that this is what the group *is*.[2] An elderly white man recalled his hesitancy to join a civil rights group:

[I was] surprised that there wasn't more camaraderie; everyone would come to the meeting and we would talk about, well, this is on the agenda. And then it was, okay, the meeting's over. Bang. A few people would mingle around with each other and then they would go away. It reminds me a lot of professional actors when they're in a professional production and they're together and then once the show is over, it's time to strike the set, tear the goddamn thing down.

Expressions of friendship, respect, and fairness can unify emerging activist groups and make them work.[3] Indeed, emerging grassroots groups are buoyed through hard times by the positive feelings among activists. After a vicious confrontation with pro-military hecklers and feeling demoralized about it, members of one anti-war group decided to be friendlier with each other to counteract the nasty treatment they received from opponents at their public events. They congratulated themselves that they weren't like conservative groups in which, they presumed, people were as heavy-handed and hostile toward other members as they were to anti-war activists. The anti-war group could make a political point, one activist mentioned, simply by being an emotional oasis for its members. The group grabbed onto that idea, embarking on a trajectory of paying more attention to how its members got along. After staging an event, for instance, members now questioned each other about how "everyone felt" about the group as well as the political impact of the event.

A sense that members are highly engaged with each other is a self-reinforcing emotion that spills over into increased commitment to collective activism. A longtime activist in neighborhood organizing spoke enthusiastically about the dynamics in his group:

We found a lot of things in common, the concerns that we have for our communities and our families, and we admired each other for our brilliance. We have fun. We laugh. We talk about things. You get an opportunity to actually not be as serious as you are all the time. It was a no-brainer that we had to do this more, man.

In contrast to the lift people get from positive interactions, troubled exchanges drain energy from political action. Antagonism, betrayal, jealousy, and pressures to conform can drive people away and destroy even the most promising grassroots group.[4] As Sam's story shows, friction among members can cause groups to collapse, or leave activists feeling bruised and angry. Even if activists stay, negative interactions can reduce the time and energy they are willing to invest in a group. When activists talked to me about being "burned out" in grassroots politics, they weren't referring only to the enormous effort it takes to make social change. They also were upset about how people worked with each other and they struggled over whether to continue in groups whose difficult dynamics they saw no way to change. As a member of a reproductive rights group said,

> Aisha [another activist] also has become frustrated and maybe somewhat disenchanted. I know what that's like because it's happened to me from time to time too. I keep coming back. Not everybody does when that happens to them. I understand why. I almost didn't come back from my sabbatical, was not happy. I was depressed. I was anxious. I was worn out. Burned out. Frustrated.

Some found such tensions too much to bear, like a longtime activist who was on the brink of leaving a mass transit advocacy group because "sometimes when I walk into meetings in the evening, I almost feel like I'm going to the dentist office."

Activist groups develop characteristic ways in which people treat each other, what I term an *interpersonal* character. These are partly procedural, the implicit or explicit rules of how members should deliberate, make decisions, and take action. But there are more subtle dimensions as well, unspoken conventions about how members should interact on a personal, emotional level. As Craig Calhoun argues, social groups have "characteristic ways of relating emotions to each other, and of relating emotions to cognition and perception. . . . [They have] a sense of how to act, how to play the game, that is never altogether conscious or purely reducible to rules." Rules and conventions can knit a group together, creating "moral imperatives" and forging a sense of working as one unit to accomplish their goals. Or they can be sites of tension and conflict.[5]

A group's interpersonal character can be hard for outsiders to pinpoint. Any gathering is a swirl of micro-interactions that go off in different directions, with exchanges of support and anger, and interactions that are authoritarian as well as egalitarian. Even the smallest groups have subgroups with varying ways of interacting.[6] Despite such complexity, however, activists are readily able to summarize how a group "feels" and how its members "get along." They talk about some groups as warm, welcoming, and invigorating; others as depressing or unfriendly. It is this feel of the group's interaction that I term its interpersonal character.

This chapter not only looks at how activist groups build an interpersonal character. It also explores the *limitations* of how they do so, especially how activists can lose sight of how to change dynamics that become destructive. The focus is on two common trajectories for which observational data of group actions and interpretations are particularly well suited. The first trajectory is that of permissible talk, in which activist groups increasingly avoid collective discussion of how their members get along. The other is a path of increasing distinctions among members about who can speak and who should be listened to.

NOT TALKING ABOUT US

Activists place great importance on how people treat each other, but such talk becomes quickly submerged in their groups. In 295 activist group meetings, there were fewer than a dozen explicit discussions of how people got along, although the subject appeared often in side comments, furtive huddled chats at social events, and e-mail exchanges among activists and was expressed indirectly in voice tone and body language during meetings.[7] It was not uncommon for grassroots groups to frame themselves to audiences and potential recruits as friendly and welcoming, but such claims were rare in internal discussions. Occasionally, members made references to a group's dynamics in a quick aside. Positive ones might attract a few words of agreement but almost never spiraled into a sustained discussion. Critical comments generally were not followed up at all; they just ended with discomfort and unhappy silence.

It may be surprising to think of activist groups as avoiding talk on any topic, perhaps especially talk about their conflicts. As Gary Alan Fine notes, activism is "awash in talk"[8] and activists avidly relate tales of battles fought with opponents and skirmishes among comrades. But members generally raise such topics only outside the group; in their meetings, activists rarely talk about a group's internal dynamics. When one member proposed that a civil liberties group discuss the frictions that were so clearly evident, for instance, another simply declared that "we're not going to start that [kind of talk] now." The topic of discussion changed; a possible thread of talk about interpersonal conflict was halted.

At times, the absence of talk is quite striking. When its leader and principal financial backer, Salu, suddenly disappeared without explanation from the anti-violence group SGV, his departure was never mentioned. A few members whispered to each other in side talk, speculating on what might have happened, but no one brought it up at the meeting. When asked about it later, one member expressed concern, but said she wouldn't feel comfortable talking about this during the meeting. Over time, the silence in SGV became increasingly awkward, as the consequences of Salu's departure became more evident. A possible turning point arrived when no one was able to withdraw money from the group's bank account to pay for a rally permit because Salu was the sole signatory on their account. Faced with this crisis, members discussed whose name to add, but they did so gingerly, never mentioning Salu and sliding around the delicate issue of why he had left. They quickly returned to safer footing, shifting to a debate over whether it was constitutional for the city to require march permits.

Activist meetings commonly have undercurrents of worry, with no one voicing what everyone knows. As one activist stated bluntly, people are not willing to "own up to how they're feeling, and if they hear something they think is off-the-wall, say, 'hey, I think it's a bad idea.'" Indeed, even when more explicit talk would be useful, activists often take care to dodge it. A group protesting U.S. foreign policy, for instance, deftly moved to avoid what several members said would be an "uncomfortable climate" if they reflected on the tension that was so evident in their meetings.

In the face of awkward silence, activists tend to respond with uncharacteristic despair. If optimistic about their ability to change the world, they rarely feel empowered to alter how people get along in their own groups. Activists regard their group's interpersonal character from a perspective fixed in the present. They experience it as unchangeable, unable to imagine a time it was different in the past, or how it could be otherwise in the future. For that reason, some members openly bemoan collective talk about group dynamics as a waste of time. A middle-aged man got angry when he recalled a meeting of the Coalition for Progressive Action devoted to "endless amounts of time talking about what they should be like and [they] never really did anything." Initially, he held his annoyance in check by "writing notes back and forth" with his girlfriend. But eventually he "finally said, 'I had enough; this group sounds like it's more like the 'Coalition for Progressive Conversation.' And I got up, handed [his note] to the guy who was the chair of that group, and just walked away." A similar story was related by a neighborhood activist as she dismissed meetings that are "just talk about us," insisting that "if you're going to a meeting, you want to have something concrete to meet about." A leader of an animal rights group bristled at a member's suggestion that they talk through problems in their dynamics. To him, that would just undercut more essential work:[9]

> [Talking about] potlucks or parties or things like that to keep everybody connected. . . . There are so many more important things we could be doing rather than devoting our time and resources to that. . . . That doesn't really help animals.

When groups don't feel right on an interpersonal level, activists generally tend to see their choices as either leaving the group or accepting the situation. That is, they regard their options as loyalty or exit, but not voice,[10] a stance that is particularly ironic because activists work so hard to convince others to be vocal about problems in the society.

Members will voice their concerns about certain types of disagreements. Those who are disgruntled about the *ideological* direction of their group generally air their objections. The same is true when they don't like how a group defines itself *organizationally*. But members who deplore how people interact in a group tend to slip away or remain quiet, which simply reinforces problematic dynamics. Their sense of futility is evident in interviews in which they describe such problems in the most passive ways: "There isn't the solidarity that I expected. But, hey, I got along fine without it." Even hopeful sentiments lacked a sense of agency, like one man's "fantasy" that an anti-war group would have members with enough confidence in each other to "set a tone in the meeting in which debate was okay." When months went by and that time never arrived, he "started feeling impatient" and left the group.[11]

Avoiding talk is a self-reinforcing sequence. The longer groups shy away from such talk, the more they avoid any related comment lest it seem highly significant and be explosive. Joan and Eileen, the two founders of the national security policy group SECURE, were concerned about how its members would get along, given the scarring battles these founders had encountered in earlier activism. At the first meeting, they announced that SECURE would be different from other groups, with plenty of time to "talk through" any tensions. After a few meetings, though, no one said anything when they got to this item on the agenda. Joan and Eileen redoubled their efforts, reminding everyone that talking through concerns would keep things smooth. But members simply found new ways to resist, muttering among themselves, slipping out of the room, fidgeting, and grumbling audibly. Eileen offered a compromise: they would be able to drop the "talking through" time as soon as SECURE "came together" as a group. When the silence continued in subsequent weeks, however, this item simply disappeared from the agenda. It was never mentioned again.

If they cannot discuss conflicts, how do activist groups deal with tensions that bubble up in the group? Among emerging groups, the most common way is to plan new actions. In an environmental group, friction among members became so severe that people talked worriedly (although not openly in meetings) about whether the group might soon collapse. Facing crisis, the members decided to stop their "tired, repetitive actions" that "result in nothing" and try something different. Something more direct and striking, members agreed, would make them feel more unified and, the implication was clear, help reduce tension. Unable to change dynamics directly, activists sought to introduce new actions to create a turning point in the trajectory of conflict.

Fledgling activist groups turn to action because they assume that working together will stimulate positive interactions among members. As its founder whispered to me while a major conflict was brewing in a neighborhood rights group, members "will be able to bond" once they start organizing a protest. Conversely, unhappy members of a school reform group identified lack of action as the reason they couldn't seem to jell: "We just sat around and talked [but] people want to be active." Discussion of conflicts wasn't necessary; the group simply needed to get busy. The author's field notes written after a meeting of a civil liberties group show how activists interpret their changing interpersonal dynamics:

> Meetings had become sluggish and unfocused. Even agendas with little more than a few routine tasks took hours to accomplish as members fretted over what they were willing to do and sniped at each other. Almost overnight, however, these dynamics changed. Members now eagerly seized on tasks for which they could volunteer. The mood was light, friendly, and positive and they talked openly, for the first time in their history, about how they got along. Members expressed great excitement at their newfound ability to work in a spirit of cooperation, and speculated that they could now accomplish a great deal more. What did they see as the reason for their improved dynamics? That after a long period in which they made no headway with public officials, they had finally managed to engage in a dialogue with city representatives.

Activists say that action creates good dynamics because it gives people a common experience. The author's field notes of an anti-gun group described how it "becomes more excited . . . as the plans become more solidified and detailed." A young woman described the difficult dynamics as her group got started:

We only started in, maybe late October or early November. At first, there was that, we don't really know each other, what's really an okay question to bring up or not bring up? When is it okay to disagree with someone or not? Do I really know what I think about this? And all those kinds of things meant that the discussions were sometimes a little flat. It was just a matter of us all getting to know each other and having some common experiences that we could talk about and care about.

Action provided a way for them to get "to know each other" and have something in common they "care about." With practice, they had a template for working together so that members knew "what's really an okay question to bring up" and when it was "okay to disagree."

Activists also talked about the link between dynamics and activity in the opposite way: when groups get along, they can act. When I asked them why some meetings accomplished a lot while others did not, activists labeled as productive those times when people would "joke around," "feel comfortable with each other," "linger afterward" to talk, and "feel free to let off steam." When people didn't interact well, when members "were just sitting there," little got done. Grassroots groups reinforce this interpretation through stories. Unlike tales of "dramatic, politically relevant . . . disruptive, violent, [and] large-scale events" through which early gay liberation groups built a sense of themselves,[12] the often-repeated stories in Pittsburgh groups tended to center on their *efforts* more than their *events*. They featured *acting* more than *action*. An example is the anti-war group, No War Committee (NWC), whose disruptive protests, acts of civil disobedience, and attacks on military research facilities and recruitment stations were the subject of much media attention. In its meetings, however, NWC rarely recounted stories of high drama, except in the immediate aftermath of such an event. NWC's more frequent stories were about more mundane incidents. A frequently repeated tale is described in the author's field notes written after an NWC meeting:

They talked about when Homeville Library initially refused to show the film because it was too partisan. They [remembered being] shocked that the request was denied. Everyone said, "Way to go, Sadie," when she challenged the denial by stating that the library's rejection was based on partisan concerns. Ultimately, the library relented and let them have the space, but they still refused to endorse the film.

Several aspects of this story are significant. Certainly, it wasn't exciting; NWC was simply trying to show a film in a public library. Why would a film showing be so memorable, in comparison to the group's many episodes of civil protest, conflict, and arrests? Indeed, this wasn't even a story that others in the progressive community told about NWC; their stories about NWC featured its large crowds and confrontational tactics. The film story was odd too because it didn't end in a clear victory, since the library withheld its endorsement and publicity. But it illuminated how NWC could work together cooperatively and with persistence.

Are actions and good dynamics as entangled as activist groups think they are? To see, I compared the dynamics of meetings held during or close to a major event with the dynamics of meetings more distant from such events. I found that groups have somewhat more positive dynamics—a smoother flow of interactions, fewer visible power plays or destructive exchanges, and less strife—when they are busy with actions. But the differences were small, suggesting that action is not likely to fix a group's troubled dynamics.

Trajectories and Turning Points

As in all trajectories, there are turning points and exceptions in the path of permissible talk. Although most groups followed a trajectory of gradually diminishing talk about their interactions, one group disallowed any such talk from the start. FUTURE, a group focused on tax policy, operated on the assumption that it would need a stock of mutual trust and commitment in order to work out disagreements. Until it did, as one member framed it, it couldn't be sure that talking about internal issues would improve things rather than be a means for some members to criticize others. Thus FUTURE operated with a strict agenda that excluded any mention of the workings of the group or its members. When such ideas occasionally leaked into meetings, they were met with stony silence. Over time, and especially after several successful events, FUTURE's horizon of possibilities shifted. When one member suggested that the group assign a timekeeper to make sure that no one dominated the discussion, her comment drew widespread assent. This opened the door to further talk, including a discussion at the next meeting of how to evaluate the way members worked together that ended with the statement that such "feedback [will] improve our performance." At least for a while, FUTURE was on a trajectory toward greater discussion about its dynamics.

Given activists' expressions of futility about changing the dynamics of their groups, turning points in the trajectory of diminishing talk generally occurred only when groups saw themselves in crisis. In some, it was when they thought that conversing about their dynamics was necessary for them to act. A civil rights group's meeting had become little more than exchanges of information and committee reports after any prolonged discussion tended to erupt into conflict. But a suggestion by one member that it conduct business through e-mail was met with instant and near-unanimous disapproval. Doing so, others worried, would allow members to fade away and the group would do nothing. Face-to-face interactions, members told each other, were key to achieving the group's goals, a decision that briefly allowed talk about interpersonal difficulties. An environmental group opened a discussion when its long-standing fractiousness leaked into public view and threatened its reputation as a leader in progressive politics. When one member stated, bluntly, "there is a problem with our image," others quickly concurred, bemoaning that the group had become the subject of "groaning and snickering" throughout the movement. It couldn't be a "leader" among activist groups unless the progressive community saw it acting with solidarity and mutual respect. Similarly, the African American peace group, BAP, decided to talk things through when it faced dissolution. As one of its longtime members instructed the group, this change might work "because sometimes people just need to get things out."

Fledging activist groups quickly set up a trajectory of silence about their interpersonal dynamics. Not only does this not erase tensions in the group, but silence also makes tensions difficult to rectify. Activists come to see few options for changing the group. And, as they act on this assumption, they reinforce the normality of not talking about the group's dynamics. Over time, activists increasingly regard action as the only route for correcting interpersonal problems; earlier possibilities fade away.

WHO CAN SPEAK? WHOM DO WE LISTEN TO?

Activist group dynamics quickly reflect distinctions among members. Some members are listened to carefully, others are ignored. When one member presents an idea, it is discussed carefully and often followed. The suggestions of another merit little consideration. This happens through two processes. First, grassroots groups develop trajectories of credibility that accord some members greater standing to speak and act than others. Second, they silence any talk of inequities in how members are treated, which makes these distinctions difficult to identify or challenge.

Bestowing Credibility

Grassroots groups create inequities in their interpersonal dynamics that are based on an assessment, often tacit, of members' credibility. Activist credibility is similar to Karen Beckwith's notion of "political standing," what she describes as "explicitly articulated rationales of actors' position and presence in a movement that assert a status of legitimacy in making claims and demands."[13] In contrast to political standing, credibility is rarely explicit, although it is widely understood. It is a shared assumption by which a group operates without discussion or debate. Members who are regarded as credible are authorized to speak and to have others listen. Credibility is similar to power or legitimacy, but can be conferred for limited issues, enabling members to speak or act with authority on some topics but not others.[14] At any one time, a member regarded as highly credible also can be cognitively central or an official leader of a group, but such overlap is by no means universal.

One early basis for assigning credibility is recognition of what activists do or have done, what I term *credibility-by-action*. Some activist groups regard prior activism as conveying knowledge or skill or as proving an activist's mettle, and they treat experienced activists as particularly credible. Indeed, credibility from past action can be surprisingly broad. A woman who revealed that she was fired from a school district job was given substantial credibility by an education reform group for challenging the school system, even though the district was in another state and she was fired for a personal matter quite remote from the group's focus on student achievement.

Credibility-by-action also is bestowed by what activists are doing in the group now, although often more narrowly than for past work. Being willing to undertake "thankless" jobs can increase a member's credibility for issues closely connected to those tasks. Those who do the nuts and bolts work of arranging a rally, for example, gain standing in discussions of the rally, but not in discussions of other activities. The contrary is true as well: people who do not work on a task can lose standing to speak about that matter although not necessarily on other issues. As two young activists whispered to each other in an environmental group, unless people "got out and passed out flyers" they "shouldn't tell us what to do."

There are subtleties as to how credibility is assigned. Members with heavy job or family commitments can be credible by doing less work than others if their efforts exceed what the group expects of a person in that situation. As one activist told me, it's important to keep from becoming a group in which "the people who end up making the decisions are the people who stay around the meetings the longest . . . (so) it becomes the question of who has to get up for work the next day, who has kids that they have to go home and take care of, who doesn't have time to sit through what it takes. . . . It's like last one standing." Occasionally, members have reservations about their own credibility, as did a longtime, important member of an anti-gun group who announced that since he hadn't been active lately, others should do "whatever you want to do" and he would go along. However, such reluctance is uncommon.

Credibility also can be bestowed on members for who they are rather than what they do, what I term *credibility-by-connection*. Those with a connection (personal or by virtue of their social category) to the problem an activist group is working on generally are given some measure of credibility, although often only narrowly on those issues. Activist groups talk a great deal about this kind of credibility, asserting that ideas and plans are based on having members who experience these issues firsthand. Anti-war groups tout members who are veterans. Environmental groups claim to listen hard to those most likely to be damaged by industrial pollution or nuclear power. For civil liberties groups, the credible can be prisoners, or prisoner's family members or neighbors. Those with personal accounts of police brutality had added credibility in an activist group focused on police violence, as did those likely to experience police violence, such as African American men. Such credibility can enhance some and silence others, at least for a time. An African American reproductive rights group crackled with tension when male members angrily complained that they felt "castrated" during a film about wife battering. Annoyed by the men's response, women grumbled unhappily but did not object aloud. As one woman explained later, women aren't in a position to understand how men would feel in that situation.

Both types of credibility are shaped by social inequalities beyond the group. Credibility-by-action is more often attached to those from higher-status social groups, like whites and men. Just as Sherryl Kleinman found in her study of an alternative health organization, men with the same credentials as women are regarded more positively than the women.[15] Higher-status persons also assert their claims to credibility more boldly and insistently than do others. They cast their past experience in activism, or their current activity in the group, as more unique, onerous, or valuable than the prior work of other activists. Credibility-by-connection is more likely to be given to members with lower status and positions in society, at least in progressive groups that work on behalf of less powerful social groups.

Credibility-by-connection tends to be more circumscribed and flimsy than credibility from tasks. Those with credibility-by-action are given broader openings to speak and they are listened to, creating a cascading sequence that increases their credibility over time. Those with credibility-by-connection may also have substantial space to speak in activist group settings, but their words are less likely to direct the actions that the group undertakes, so there is less opportunity for this kind of credibility to expand over time.

Differences in credibility, especially credibility-by-action, enhance the social inequities of gender, race, age, and other factors that members bring into activist groups. Credibility is a channel through which distinctions of status and hierarchy flow into the dynamics of activist groups from the external environment.[16] Indeed, in almost every meeting of virtually every group—even those adamantly dedicated to social equality—white individuals routinely talked more often and more authoritatively, were listened to more attentively, and had their ideas alter the direction of the discussion more often than was true of members of other racial groups. The situation was similar for men compared to women; middle-class persons compared to working- or lower-class persons; and middle-aged or older members compared to younger ones. Of course, there were exceptions. Nonetheless, what Lynn Sanders terms "sneaky, invisible, and pernicious" hierarchies of gender, race, class, and age begin early in fledgling activist groups and expand quickly.[17]

Grassroots groups often publicly assert that getting people involved in political life will bolster democracy. But internally, many activist groups exhibit decidedly non-democratic interactions. In Sanders's terms, distinctions of credibility create a setting in which, "even if everyone can deliberate and learn how to give reasons—some people's ideas may still count more than others" and some people are "less likely than others to be listened to; even when their arguments are stated according to conventions of reason."[18] In the prickly atmosphere of an animal rights group, for example, members openly grumbled at any comment that was not precisely focused on action. As a result, its meetings became little more than a weekly distribution of tasks from the leader's checklist. The only exception was when Amy, a member who had been involved in numerous episodes of conflict with animal owners, wanted the floor. She was allowed to speak on any subject, and at length. The implicit rules of procedure did not apply to her.

Credible members also can make new rules, which further reinforces their credibility. Sarah, whose long history of GLBT activism gave her credibility in a new queer rights group, authoritatively dismissed another member's suggestion as "not worth discussing" because it was "not concrete enough." Without comment or complaint, this requirement became a new rule. Thereafter, talk was ruled out of order if it did not mention concrete action.

How social distinctions cascade and affect action and interpretation can be seen in a sequence of exchanges in a meeting of a progressive group. Alice and John, both white and middle class, deliberated about what they should do next to stop the U.S. invasion of Iraq. On one level, this seemed to be a debate between equals, with each member stating a view and defending it. But a closer look reveals that his words carried weight while hers were easily disregarded. The difference between Alice and John was not a matter of style or logic of argument. It was a matter of credibility.

The exchange began as Alice added another item to an ongoing discussion of the issues that the group should attend to:

We should also focus on the environmental devastation that wars cause.

John immediately countered:

No, we should only focus on the causes of war, such as militaristic culture and corporate greed, instead of on the effects of war.

In these two sentences, Alice and John presented contrasting ideas. She wanted the group to focus on the *effects* of war; he wanted it to focus on the *causes*. Their statements were equivalent and parallel, simply pushing the group in different directions. Both views were stated with conviction. They were even phrased in similar ways: what "we . . . should . . . focus on." But, as a closer look shows, Alice and John operated from different platforms of credibility. Alice framed her proposal as an *addition* to the group's current focus, asking members to focus *also* on environmental destruction. It was not necessary to understand or disagree with the group's current focus to adopt her suggestion. In contrast, John introduced a principle that would redirect the group, setting aside its current focus on the consequences of war.

Looking at the context of this exchange reveals additional layers. Although the group had met for some time, it never discussed whether to focus on the causes or consequences of war. It had simply operated on a shared, unarticulated sense that U.S. intervention in Iraq was wrong and politically disastrous. So when John proposed that members focus only on the causes of war, he was suggesting a major change in how the group should think about and act toward the war without stating it explicitly. His statement involved a claim larger than his surface request for a narrower focus. Without stating so outrightly, John was introducing a new principle of decision making for the group.

In the very next sentence, Alice both challenged and seemed to adopt the new principle. She rejected the idea that there were identifiable causes for war but hinted that the focus she initially proposed (environmental devastation) might be a cause as well as an effect of war and thus consistent with John's new principle:

But some societies have chronic warring, like Mayan culture. Sometimes the causes and effects of war are so blurred that it's difficult to disentangle them.

No one in the group weighed in, but John's principle triumphed. It would be an understanding from which the group operated in the future, although incorporated without any discussion or explicit acknowledgment. In his next statement, John refined his principle further: the group should not focus on all causes of war, only *economic* ones.

No, we should focus on U.S. economic interests (like thirst for oil) that are driving the war in Iraq.

The shift in the group's operating principles was evident as Alice continued. She no longer questioned the idea of focusing on causes—that wouldn't be brought up again by her or anyone. She now argued that the group shouldn't narrow their attention only to economic causes:

Previous U.S. military conflicts like [those in] Korea, Vietnam, Grenada had very little to do with economic interests, also Central America.

Their debate continued, but the terrain had changed. John added a corrective, reasserting the economic basis of war:

That is only partially right since the U.S. perceived the spread of Communism as a political and economic threat in those areas.

At that point, their dialogue ended. Without comment on the shift, the group moved on to discuss how to implement their new focus. After members briefly brainstormed how to educate the public about the economic causes of the Iraq war, especially war profiteering, Alice tried for the last word. Almost under her breath she reminded the group that economic causes were not the only relevant ones:

Environmental disasters in Rwanda and Haiti exacerbated military conflicts.

But the new principle—still unacknowledged—prevailed. The debate was over.

Since arguments in activist groups often trail off imperceptibly, as this one did, it is no wonder that activists expressed befuddlement when asked how one position or another took hold. Activists struggle to identify the origins of the social hierarchies that build up in their groups, leaving them with little sense of how to remedy these inequities.

Disavowing Leadership

At the same time that activist groups create distinctions among members, they make any mention of them off limits, so that members have difficulty questioning or confronting these status differences. In a conversational process described by Sophie Duchesne and Florence Haegel, any mention of inequities in the group is "dissolved in the free flow of a conversation where sentences follow on one another and ideas are juxtaposed, without anyone making any connection between them."[19] A group's ways of interacting becomes unquestionable. When a woman from Philadelphia came to observe a meeting of the protest support group SMAG, I asked for her impression of how they worked together. She hastened to say that she supported the group and its work but was distressed to see how often some members talked down to or interrupted others, especially given SMAG's commitment to collective decision making. Although its problems were dramatic enough to be visible to a casual visitor, SMAG's members acted puzzled when asked about them. They were concerned but couldn't explain what caused, or how to correct, these troubled dynamics.

Leadership is one of the earliest topics to become unmentionable in activist groups.[20] In private, activists acknowledge that their groups have leaders and they are consistent in who they identify as leaders. Activists also generally agree that leaders are necessary as long as regular members have input into how the group works. As a young woman in an environmental group told me, "meetings [are] where decisions and debates should happen. . . . I hate being part of a group that, when you show up, it seems like everything's been talked about and decided on, and you just like are there, kind of, like, what's going on?"

However, if activists value leadership, almost nobody says anything positive about it in activist groups. Actually, few people say much about leadership at all. The topic generally comes up only when the group elects officers, and even then conversation tends to diminish the value of leaders, evident in the undercurrents in discussions of whether to replace titles of president or chair with those of coordinator or facilitator. Open talk of leadership, even by those with official positions in a group, often is not sanctioned. When Janice acted openly as its leader by chastising members of Ecology Now who "really dropped the ball" at a failed protest, members shook their heads and made eye contact with each other, registering their discontent. Several got up and abruptly left the meeting.

Activist groups often claim to have leaders in name only. Bill had exercised strong, consistent, and uncontested leadership in CONCERN since the group began. The author's field notes identified him as the one who scheduled, organized, and ran every meeting and he served as the group's public spokesperson. However, when a new member looked to him after someone suggested a radical change in tactics, Bill berated her indignantly: "Why are you looking at me? I'm not the leader!" Similar incidents appeared in other groups. Even in groups with strong leadership, based on my coding of leadership dynamics in 251 meetings, it was virtually never acknowledged.

Sometimes, activist groups take steps to maintain the sense that they are leaderless. In the anti-drug group Death by Heroin, one member made critical decisions between meetings without consulting anyone else. In one such incident, he radically shifted the group's neighborhood focus by committing it to host a community-wide event downtown and setting up a press conference to announce the plan. Members not only went along with these commitments but redefined them as having been group decisions. The community event was brought up as a "possibility" at a meeting, with no mention that it was already under way; the group dutifully discussed whether this would be a good direction for them. No one objected or raised a question. Such reactions were decidedly off the table. Within months, the move toward a community focus had been adopted in group lore as a direction that "we" decided to take.

Leadership is not only unmentionable in politically progressive emerging groups, where equality among members might be expected to be a concern but also in conservative ones. Across the political spectrum, most new activist groups operate as if minimizing leadership will help hold the group together. A member of another conservative anti-drug group put it this way:

> Even with some of the conflicts of personalities, we stayed a grounded group, meaning that we have been successful in knowing that no one else is [more] important than the other and no one else is higher than the other and no one's opinion is more than another. And because of that we have been able to really keep it together—we've been really able to keep our relationships together.

Openly expressing apprehension about leadership is possible in emerging groups since formal positions and hierarchies among members are not yet normalized. It particularly flares up when members are sought for official roles, like chair or president. In addition to worrying about the workload, members shy away from leadership to avoid being criticized by other members. The popular connotation of a leader is positive, someone with a vision whom others will follow. But in fledgling grassroots groups, the idea of a leader is more problematic, implying control and undeserved power.

That grassroots groups do not want to see themselves as having central leaders does not mean that leadership is not exercised. It certainly is. But it tends to be unacknowledged, even denied. Even when there are obvious struggles for leadership, such as in one school reform group in which two women battled for control, many new activist groups studiously avoid the topic. Leadership, like other aspects of their interpersonal dynamics, can be carefully sidestepped even when its importance is clear. It is another trajectory of avoidance that shapes the interpersonal character of activist groups.

Trajectories and Turning Points

Activist groups have a difficult time addressing problematic dynamics for a more practical reason: activists worry about the fallout from doing so. In their interviews, most activists portray their groups as fragile and vulnerable to collapse. As one put it, "Every organization I'm working with is an inch away from disappearing off the face of the earth." Criticizing the group, they fret, might destroy it. Moreover, they see voicing conflict as likely to undermine a group's ability to act (as one activist put it, to "stop the group from being able to move forward") and thereby create more conflict.

An AIDS activist group fell into trouble when its founder and leader, Anna, seemed to lose interest. She stopped sending reminders of meetings, then announced that she had brought no new ideas from a conference she had attended in Washington, D.C., on the group's behalf. At first, members grumbled privately. Eventually, several erupted in anger at a meeting, complaining that Anna was "dumping" her jobs on everyone else with little notice. As others brought up additional incidents, an explosive spiral of anger seemed inevitable. Yet, suddenly the discussion stopped after a member declared that "this kind" of talk could be harmful. People continued to grumble among themselves but not openly at meetings. Ironically, however, members' efforts to stem conflict led the group to a fatal impasse. Since they had decided not to talk about what was wrong for fear of creating "negative emotion," activists couldn't take steps to redistribute the work previously done by Anna. Over the next couple of meetings, the discussion increasingly spun off in tangents. The fragile organization fell apart. Within a month, it stopped meeting at all.

A few groups were able to change their ways of interacting, at least to a small extent. The most common method was to adopt new rules of behavior without talking about why these were needed. An example is REBORN, whose members were visibly exasperated when a newcomer dominated the meeting in spite of subtle efforts to keep him in check. When the problem snowballed in the next meeting, one member wrote out and displayed what he claimed to be the group's rules:

> No one should repeat him/herself
> No philosophical treatises
> Don't go on and on about the same issue
> Let others speak

Although these, or any other rules, had never been discussed, his action provided an opening to handle the newcomer's behavior and other members eagerly jumped in with other rules:[21]

> No side conversations
> People should respect each other
> People should realize that everyone was "donating time" at the meeting

A few groups made more strenuous efforts to change their dynamics. Sometimes, they were able to resolve problems; more often, the discussion broke down. In an anti-imperialist group, a longtime member interrupted the flow of a meeting to declare that the group had "serious internal problems": over the last six months, members had shown a decided "lack of respect" for the "unspoken differences" among them. Although she was deliberately vague about the nature of the problem, other women jumped in to clarify. "In spite of the group's best efforts," one declared, "sexism is still an issue." A few members seemed surprised, others just dismayed or weary. After a few more heated exchanges, the discussion fizzled out.

Grassroots groups do have openings when another trajectory is possible. When a member openly stated that things in the group were "tense," RISE did not revert to its usual pattern of dismissing tension as nothing more than the press of pending deadlines. This time, a couple of people spoke up and agreed. For once, there was an opening to discuss the dramatic conflict that had plagued RISE for months and was widely noted by activists in other progressive groups. But RISE couldn't decide what was wrong. How could it "turn things around," as one member insisted they do, if members didn't know why things had turned sour? Without a clear problem, the group couldn't identify a specific solution. Instead, activists latched onto generalities. "If we're kind," one member insisted as others nodded, "things will work out." By using "courtesy rules" like not interrupting, another suggested, they could make things better. But that didn't work.

An anti-police violence group broke its trajectory by organizing a pasta dinner at a large Baptist church to discuss its internal problems. An atmosphere that might have encouraged open discussion, however, had the opposite effect. Comments that fit the night's "celebratory" mood were built upon by others; those that were "emotionally heavy" were ignored. Instead of the direct talk that members expected, the night became filled with praise for themselves as "people who want justice." They acknowledged their problems only obliquely, picking out members who treated each other with kindness and proposing an award for one who was "always there" for other members.

Distinctions among members cascade in activist groups. As some are accorded greater credibility, they gain opportunities to speak and their words are listened to carefully. Those deemed less credible have fewer opportunities to display or increase their credibility. Such self-reinforcing sequences build disparities into group dynamics, while paths of silence and avoidance make these inequities literally unmentionable.

CASE COMPARISON

It is possible to see how activist groups develop an interpersonal character over a longer time by comparing the different emotional trajectories of two groups whose members were similar in many respects. Planet Protection Society (PPS) attracted young, gender-diverse, and mostly university students interested in environmental issues. The members of Animal Liberation League (ALL), whose campaign against foie gras was detailed in Chapter 2, were similar. The two groups might be expected to exhibit comparable emotional characteristics. But they did not. PPS became inclusive, tightly knit, and mutually supportive—what its members described as a "fun" group, attracting 22 to 50 people to its meetings (mode = 30)—while ALL developed a rigid, sober, and tense emotional style, with an attendance that varied from 1 to 20 people (mode = 8).

The idea of launching PPS began with a small group of friends and fellow students who wanted to create a broad citizen's environmental movement. The emotional tenor of its initial meetings varied widely, as founding members alternated between efforts to excite new recruits and expressions of frustration that the group had not gotten "moving" on specific campaigns. After three meetings, it was not clear that PPS would get off the ground. Fearful of defeat, the founding members decided—but did not announce to the general membership—that they would constitute themselves as an executive board to handle bureaucratic and logistical matters, leaving general membership meetings free for creative brainstorming and decision making. This proved to be an emotional, as well as tactical, turning point for the group. From that time on, PPS flourished with its emotional tenor divided: executive meetings had a serious, businesslike cast, while general meetings had substantial camaraderie and informal talk among members.

The upbeat emotional style of PPS's general meetings was encouraged through a variety of means, some planned by the executive board and others carried forward by members. Meetings began with introductions—a practice that continued throughout the year, even when no one new was present, and sometimes evoked laughter as when members were asked to state their name and best Halloween costume. This was followed by small-group brainstorming sessions and report-backs, giving leaders an opportunity to praise the contributions of members and reinforce the idea that PPS was not like other student-dominated groups that did not "do much." With a leadership group, rather than a single leader, a variety of emotional tactics were employed to encourage enthusiasm among members, from invitations to a "group hug" to cheerleading that "this is just the starting point!"

Over time, the light emotional style promoted by PPS's founders was adopted by members. One who became the group's unofficial jester interrupted a discussion with the suggestion that the group "wear uniforms with badges," eliciting the jovial response by a leader that "we'll kick you out, [but] we encourage you to express yourself." PPS-sponsored parties and social events were popular and frequent. One indication of the group's affective cohesion was its ability to adjust its leadership. After eight months, several members of the then-unacknowledged executive board announced their pending resignations, forcing the founders to solicit board members from the regular membership. The revelation that the group had an inner core of leadership was greeted by the membership with surprise, but also humor. Jokes were bandied around about members versus leaders, including a founder's acknowledgment that he was the group's "self-appointed president." The pattern of resolving conflict with humor was sufficiently established that this transition was completed without incident.

Planet Protection Society's emphasis on creating solidarity among members through positive emotional appeals shaped a shared sense of the group and its members as "fun" but also constrained its external use of hot-button emotions like anger, outrage, or resentment. Such negative emotional appeals declined over time in PPS's campaigns and within six months were virtually absent, even for issues like environmental deregulation, in which acrimonious emotions might garner public attention and support. Those perceived as anti-environment, such as President Bush or recalcitrant university officials, continued to be subjects of derision and salacious humor in meetings, creating laughter and goodwill. But in exchanges with outsiders, even those seen as enemies, PPS insisted on a cautious, respectful tone and what they referred to as "appropriate behavior." Minor concessions by officials were followed by expressions of gratitude, including thank-you notes passed around at meetings for the signatures of members. For example, one university administrator was the subject of frequent hostility and ridicule in PPS meetings for her refusal to respond to their demands. Calls for a sit-in at her office or an effort to rally influential community members against her were met with boisterous approval. When it was time to craft a response, however, the tone of the discussion shifted. A few leaders and members expressed the desire to have the group "be taken seriously," which was clarified to mean having "thorough research [and] the proper format." Members who had proposed angrier or more confrontational means of achieving success quickly backed down, amid a series of joking comments that restored the lighthearted solidarity of the group.

As negative emotions and confrontational tactics in PPS became increasingly off limits in meetings, the group's sense of what was possible and what it should do took on a narrower and more mainstream political cast. PPS's goals changed from curbing corporate control over environmental policies to promoting local use of wind energy and hybrid cars in the university motor pool. But as this emerging sense of itself as an emotionally attractive group cascaded, it ultimately limited the range of tactics and goals that PPS saw as possible.

Like PPS, ALL began as a student group based on circles of friends. Yet unlike the positive style that attracted and retained members in PPS, the rigid and unfriendly style in ALL meant that new recruits often felt unwelcome and rarely returned. From its inception, ALL's strong leader, Heather, perceived her role as planning the group's strategies and goals and providing the knowledge and motivation that would encourage others to adopt these goals and commit energy to the group. Due to the dense web of interpersonal ties among ALL's founding members, Heather's vision went unchallenged and meetings were largely instructional and devoid of emotional exchanges among members. Even meetings after major events— media coverage of ALL, arrests of ALL activists, and concessions by the targets of ALL's protests—evidenced little impassioned discussion.

Concerned that the group could not sustain its current projects, Heather lectured members about her frustration that they were reluctant to commit sufficient time and that the group was unable to attract new members. But emotional exchanges between Heather and members were one-way. No one responded to Heather's lecture or, at a subsequent meeting, to her complaints about being treated rudely by restaurant owners when she approached them about altering their menus. Moreover, the scope of Heather's emotional talk was limited, focused entirely on her feelings about the group's ability to achieve its goals, as, for example, in her annoyance when the group wanted to take on too many projects or when the targets of the group's protests did not acquiesce to its demands.

Despite its minimal emotional content in meetings, ALL was quite willing to use emotional appeals in other venues.[22] Through e-mail, Heather circulated vivid descriptions of animal abuse meant to arouse passionate responses, one so graphic that a recipient asked to be removed from the list. ALL also used emotional language in its propaganda, attacking its targets as either uninformed or immoral—such as university lab administrators (who experimented on animals "without regard to their care"). People need to be confronted, ALL insisted, with the realities of animal abuse. As ALL's propaganda became more emotionally charged, its actions became increasingly provocative. Attempts to negotiate with university officials or others were halted in favor of picketing with signs that graphically depicted animal cruelty. ALL's emotional paths within the group and toward its audiences were very different, and both were self-reinforcing.

Planet Protection Society and Animal Liberation League show that similar groups can adopt very different ways of interacting. In PPS, emotional banter was strong within the group, but emotions were rare and dwindled over time in its political campaigns. In contrast, ALL had little emotional interaction internally but deployed increasingly intense emotional appeals to its audiences.

CONCLUSION

Activist groups develop ways of interacting that rest on a myriad of subtle conventions as well as official and informal rules; these shape a group's interpersonal character. They set out expectations for how members should get along personally and how they should work together. Such assumed ways of interacting cascade over time by setting some kinds of interactions as off limits and making others seem normal. Friendly groups become even friendlier; in the same way, those in which interactions are tense find these relations becoming more fractious over time. Friendly groups attract members, energy, and commitment; the converse is true for those that are antagonistic or unwelcoming. And, as the contrasting trajectories of PPS and ALL show, a group's interpersonal character makes actions seem more or less possible.

This chapter focused on two trajectories by which activist groups create shared understandings about how their members should treat each other.

One is a path of permissible talk. From their earliest days, activist groups limit discussions of their internal dynamics in open meetings. This contrasts sharply with activists' intense attention to these issues when talking to each other in private and outside the group setting. Within a group, however, members learn to avoid talking about its dynamics. Their avoidance shapes a path of expected talk, making the topic more and more difficult to raise over time. Even when group dynamics are problematic, activists see little way to talk about or rectify them. The only option they perceive is to initiate new actions that will give members a sense of common purpose and mend conflicts. But, as the observational data show, this strategy is not likely to work since there is little connection between actions and the dynamics of group meetings. Generally, turning points in the trajectory of diminishing talk come only at times of crisis. When groups face immediate collapse, their members can reopen long-submerged topics of conversation, including how they interact with each other.

The second trajectory is toward distinctions among members. Activist groups develop ways of interacting that give greater weight to what some members say than to the ideas of others. They do so by according some members greater credibility, based on their actions or connections to the issue the group is working on, as well as their social status in the larger society. Credibility snowballs as more credible members have greater influence in shaping how the group will interact, positioning them to become even more credible. At the same time, activist groups develop ways of ignoring the existence of internal distinctions by, for example, making the issue of leadership difficult for members to openly acknowledge.

How patterns of interaction develop in grassroots activism gives insight into broader issues as well. It shows that what is missing in group dynamics, what isn't talked about or what doesn't happen, is the product of prior actions and interpretations as much as what is discussed and what does happen. Activist groups create silence and inaction by identifying what is permissible for discussion and what is not. And such silence and inactivity have trajectories over time, just as talk and action do. They build upon themselves, reducing incrementally the sense of what is possible.

Paths of interpersonal character also show that over time, activists have a declining sense of how much they can affect their groups. Even activists who feel able to change their group's political direction, or reshape how it is constituted, often see little hope for changing troubled interpersonal dynamics. The time orientations in which they talk about how people treat each other reveal a sense of futility: the members remain fixedly in the present, seemingly incapable of drawing lessons from a better time in the past or envisioning a better functioning group in the future.

These findings have implications for the democratic potential of grass-roots activism. Dynamics that privilege the ideas and actions of some activists over others and limit the possibility of confronting such inequities are problematic. But might these dynamics be confined to fragile, emerging grassroots groups and unlikely to continue into groups that become established? It's not clear.

On the one hand, groups with particularly troubled dynamics might tend to dissolve, so established groups might be likely to have emerged from fledgling groups with some measure of positive feeling and equity among members. On the other hand, deeply problematic dynamics also exist in many established activist organizations. If activists have little hope of changing difficult dynamics in groups that are just forming and in flux, they may face an even tougher challenge in changing organizations whose patterns are more firmly settled.

CHAPTER 6

Lessons

Grassroots activism should be a democratizing force. It creates space in civic life for ideas and actions that exist nowhere else, encouraging people to envision how the world can be transformed into something better. It reinvigorates the sense that what ordinary citizens do matters. It gives activists a sense of common purpose. And it provides an alternative to the apathy and disengagement that characterize much of modern political life.[1]

To a certain extent, this study confirms the democratizing qualities of grassroots activism. Pittsburgh's fledgling activist groups generated a collective euphoria that emboldened their members to acts of conscience and political will that they would otherwise never have dreamed of. Activists acted on what they saw as *ideal* and *right,* even as it put them at odds with powerful institutions and persons.[2] At times, they displayed leaps of imagination that forged a new understanding of social life and themselves as political actors.

Unfortunately, that is not the whole story. Pittsburgh's fledging activist groups were also unfocused and their progress was halting at best. Often they failed to live up to their potential. They missed precious openings for action and stumbled over how to define themselves. Their political imaginations narrowed quickly, often leaving them unable to envision more than minor tinkering with social ills. Members interacted in ways that left them depleted and anxious rather than energized about shaping a new direction for society.[3] Some of these problems arose because the groups were new; emerging groups are more tentative and fragile than they will be later, if they survive. But others foreshadowed troubles that would likely deepen over time since emerging groups are more open, imaginative, and democratic than they are likely to be later.

How does the democratic potential of grassroots activism erode so quickly? At least some of the answer lies in the dynamics of fledgling activist groups. Like the sequences of action that constitute large-scale historical processes, what happens inside new activist groups is path dependent. Just as a city that allows oil wells precludes recreational tourism, activist groups cut off options with which they began. The analogy is not perfect; the micro-level, cultural paths of fledgling group activity are less entrenched than the macro-level, structural paths of geographic development. But thinking about activist group dynamics as path-dependent sequences helps explain why they fall into routines and how a sense of possibility can stagnate. Similar to the way a declining city can become vibrant again, activist groups have opportunities to alter their trajectories, but these turning points are frequently missed.

That fledgling activist groups operate in path-dependent sequences has implications for both scholars and activists. This final chapter builds from Ruth Wilson Gilmore's challenge that "in scholarly research, answers are only as good as the further questions they provoke, while for activists, answers are as good as the tactics they make possible."[4] It opens by suggesting lessons for scholars that raise new questions, then offers implications for tactics by which grassroots activists can more effectively make democracy.

IMPLICATIONS FOR SCHOLARSHIP

This study suggests four lessons for scholars of activism.

One lesson is the importance of what doesn't happen and what isn't said. Activism isn't made only by what groups decide and what actions they take. Equally as significant is what they fail to do or say—and what they fail even to consider. It is a mistake for scholars to focus only on visible events and pronouncements. As the trajectory of Pittsburgh's activist groups illustrates, what happens is deeply shaped by what cannot happen and what is left unsaid. Groups do not make decisions from an unlimited range of options but from a set of choices that they have played a part in restricting.

Scholars of activism rarely study what is missing in social life. Yet it is possible to do so by using techniques of comparison. Comparing sequences of action and interpretation over time can show what was possible earlier and then was lost. Comparing these sequences across groups can indicate what is possible in one group but not in a similar one. In Pittsburgh's activist groups, these comparisons revealed that the sequences of inactivity and silences operate with the same dynamics of path dependency as do sequences of activity and talk. For instance, inactivity and silences tend to cascade: what activist groups disallow tends to expand over time as, after a period of not talking about a leader's absence, a group will find it increasingly difficult to raise the subject later. Too, inactivity and silences constrain the future: activist groups sidelined topics, categorized issues as not relevant, and ignored what they wanted to avoid. And in activity and silence, timing matters: activist groups were shaped, in subtle and nearly invisible ways, by what they decided to avoid in their earliest days.

A second lesson is about agency. Pittsburgh's activists and groups displayed intentional creative action in extensive and subtle ways that are rarely explored in scholarship. Their agency was exhibited not only in efforts that throw a group's trajectory off course;[5] it existed also in purposive, meaningful action that moved in more familiar directions. Agency is found in stasis as well as change.[6]

However, the study of fledgling activism shows that agency is more complex than it is often depicted. Activists don't just exert agency, or fail to do so. They act with purpose and intention in greater and lesser degrees, and with more or less of a sense that their actions will matter. Agency has temporality. It is more likely at earlier points along a sequence, less likely later. And agency can be collective as well as individual. Collective agency is deliberate and creative, like individual agency, but it also is coordinated, resting on a foundation of shared purpose among activists.

The collapse of alternatives in many of Pittsburgh's grassroots groups shows that the agency of activism should not be exaggerated. The dynamics of grassroots groups can limit agency as much as provide an arena for its exercise. Yet the diminishment of agency is neither inevitable nor unstoppable. Activists can change the trajectories of their groups by introducing new interpretations and proposals for action, as the many examples in this book show. Returning to Christian Smith's observation that humans are self-conscious about their intentionality,[7] activists can collectively reflect on the decline of alternative possibilities in their groups and act to reverse it. ALLIES 2007, the anti-violence group, deliberatively revisited topics and decisions from earlier meetings and welcomed the input of new members. In so doing, their discussions continued to draw on a wide range of possibilities over time. Path-dependent trajectories in the dynamics of activist groups can stifle the range of possibilities they consider, but activists can alter these trajectories.

A third lesson is that small events, even those that occur by happenstance, can profoundly affect trajectories. An example is Norman Cantor's story of Princess Joan, daughter of England's King Edward III whose rise seemed unstoppable in nineteenth-century Europe. On her way to marry a Spanish prince and cement an immense dynasty, however, Princess Joan succumbed to the plague. Cantor writes that the "bacillus from a flea-ridden rat or consumption of beef from a sick cow that killed her altered the course of European political development for the next hundred years."[8] If a single flea bite could alter the historically robust trajectory of an entire European monarchy, it is no wonder that tiny serendipitous events can radically change the course of fragile emerging activist groups.

Seen through a tight lens, the impact of small incidents is quite striking.[9] For example, when a single member skips a meeting to see his girlfriend, a group can suddenly shift direction, taking on a character that it wouldn't have done otherwise but will come to regard as obvious and indubitable. In like fashion, a marital split or clash among friends can change alliances in an activist group in unexpected ways, setting it on a path that no one would have predicted but that everyone feels unable to stop. The same is true of a sound system that fails, an unexpected rain shower, a chance conversation that changes the time a group will meet.

Happenstance includes intentional action as well as twists of fate that emerge from inside groups or intrude from the outside. It involves incidental events, decisions, and interactions that have major and long-term consequence, setting groups in new directions that then take on a momentum of their own.[10] Yet activist groups and the scholars that study them easily lose sight of the power of early, small acts. Duncan Watts observes that "it is always possible, after the fact, to come up with a story about why things worked out the way they did."[11] In the case of grassroots activism, such retrospective stories generally stress the influence of larger events and those closer in time to the story's end. As the trajectories of Pittsburgh's groups show, however, what Javier Auyero and Débora Alejandra Swistun call a "continuing pileup of things" can accumulate and have large consequences without anyone noticing.[12]

A final lesson is the broad scope of activism. In recent years, scholars have *widened* the study of activism by paying attention to the actors, institutions, and cultural milieu around activist groups. Just as valuable is *lengthening* the study of activism by following groups from their beginnings to understand the assumptions, trajectories, and ways of being that are established in early days.

Following groups from the beginning makes it possible to see the unfolding of group-level properties like collective intelligence and imagination.[13] It captures activism as a process, the dynamics by which groups make choices, develop routines, advance alternatives, and lose them. It avoids attributing a solidity to activist groups that happens when we assume that they have a constant purpose, membership, agenda, and dynamics over time. It also moves away from relying on taxonomies of activism (as identity based or ideological, for instance) to explain how groups work. And it preserves what Rhys Isaac argues is an obligation of scholars of activism, "to proclaim the deep truth that the world is what it is because of the particular sequence of what has been done . . . [to affirm that] the shape of the world to come remains to be made by human action in circumstances that can never be foretold."[14]

IMPLICATIONS FOR MAKING DEMOCRACY

Grassroots groups are an important source for democratic renewal. At their best, they provide a forum for the invigorating political talk and action that become scarce in political parties beholden to donors and organized special interests. Activist groups don't just support democratic institutions; when they are open to a full array of new possibilities, grassroots groups make democracy anew.

The dazzling potential of grassroots activism is rarely achieved, at least in the modern United States. Some scholars attribute this to external factors, such as the staggering hurdles that activist groups face when they seek to alter entrenched structures of power and social inequality. Others identify internal problems, like a tendency for organizations to become oligarchical over time.[15] This book adds a new element, showing how early cultural dynamics can undermine the democratizing potential of activism as grassroots groups fall into routines that erode their imagination and engagement. This happens as early dynamics quickly become self-reinforcing, reducing their horizons of possible talk and action and moving them toward homogenization. Recruits tend to be similar to current members, information is sought from familiar sources, members interact as they are accustomed to doing. Such settled ways of being create a character, a foundation, a predictability that allows a group to continue and to act collectively. But these ways of being also quash the possibility of other ideas and ways of acting. Moreover, such paths are difficult to correct because they are assumed, constituting the invisible fabric of group life.

Yet there is hope. The paths of action and interpretation in activist groups, even those that steer in non-democratic directions, are created by members. They are not inevitable outcomes of structural conditions. Nor are they simply the product of larger external forces. Divisions of social status and privilege in the Pittsburgh groups, for instance, didn't just flow in from the outside. They were built into the dynamics of these groups by identifiable paths of action and interpretation. They were neither automatic nor unchangeable.

Two findings about Pittsburgh's activists suggest how diminishing horizons of possibility can be challenged or reversed. One is that ordinary activists extensively theorize about the social world and themselves as political actors. Members of activist groups don't simply adopt the understandings of founders as their own. Nor do they just import ideas from other groups or rely on leaders or spokespersons to do so. Rather, the intellectual work of activism—interpreting the world, developing a shared ideology, and shaping frames that will translate the particular problems of an aggrieved group into universal conditions appealing to a broader public[16]—engages members of emerging groups at all levels.

Theorizing in emerging activist groups is complex and often not linear. Members cobble together analyses, ideologies, and frames in fragmented discussions that meander across terrains of morality, epistemology, and ontology as well as politics. Activists draw on implicit ideas of ethics and morality as well as prior beliefs and experiences. They ponder epistemological issues as well as political ones, assessing what is known, what is knowable, and how it can be known.

Such explicit theorizing doesn't always last long. As activist groups form the assumptions on which they will operate, discussing the nature of the social world or the potential of political action seems less urgent. Grassroots groups come to rely on what Raymond Geuss terms "concepts that are in common use and present themselves as self-evidently univocal, internally coherent, well grounded, and rational to use."[17] Over time, the intellectual work of activism parses out—or is claimed—as the province of certain members, those earlier described as cognitively central, credible, or leaders.[18] Memory of an earlier and more participatory process starts to fade. But at least at the beginning, the intellectual energy of activist groups is broad.

The other hopeful finding is that some Pittsburgh groups were able to escape paths of diminishing possibility through self-conscious efforts. Their members worked hard to bring ideas back onto the table that had slipped away by reminding each other about earlier discussions and ideas that they hadn't pursued. They designed strategies to keep themselves open to the input of new members by being explicit about what had happened in the past and why they made the decisions they had. They encouraged others to voice their concerns openly and without recrimination. They talked about what they could do differently and how. They struggled to make their actions and ideas explicit.

Forgetting is part of how groups cohere.[19] Losing track of previous options helps forge shared understandings. It takes once-contentious possibilities off the table and makes the group—as it is now—seem inevitable.

But there are perils to erasing what once was. Activist groups remain vital and democratic when they work against the process of forgetting, excavating the roots of what has become habitual and normative and reopening possibilities that have eroded or been closed.[20] Activists need to expose the forgotten and challenge the dynamics that make forgetting possible. Grassroots activism can be a democratizing force. But it isn't a matter only of creating activist groups and getting people to participate. Activists also need to take steps to ensure that their groups fulfill their democratic potential. Grassroots activism can only strengthen democracy when it nurtures a broad sense of possibility.

I end with a reflection on the ethics of writing about activism. Gilmore's challenge to find questions for scholars and tactics for activists implies that scholars and activists have different interests. For the racist movements I studied earlier, that is certainly the case; scholars generally seek to disable racist movements while racist activists seek to strengthen them. In this study of Pittsburgh's grassroots activists, however, my interests and those of activists overlap considerably. All these activists are working toward politically palatable goals; many of which I support. For studies like this, scholars should work toward both better questions and better tactics.[21]

Unfortunately, the quest for better questions can undermine, at least in the short run, the search for better tactics. Exposing the problems of emerging activist groups generates new questions for scholars but also casts fragile grassroots groups in a critical light that may undermine them. Activist groups today, especially those with progressive agendas, face immense obstacles in the form of new repressive laws, heightened intensity of surveillance and policing, the growing power of corporate media, and the increasing strength of conservative political parties, movements, strategists, and funders. In such a climate, scholars have an ethical responsibility to highlight the value, richness, and contributions of grassroots activism, and I hope this book does so. But scholars of activism also have an ethical responsibility to point out how activist groups can inspire audiences while crushing the spirits of their members, how they can move society in new directions while their own horizon of possibility collapses. Doing so may open conversations that, however difficult, are essential for the project of making democracy.

APPENDICES

These appendices are for scholars and students who want details of the design and methodology of this study. As an aid to readers, Appendix A lists the names, acronyms, and issue focus for all groups named in the book. Appendix B provides information on sampling strategies, data collection techniques, coding, and analysis. Appendices C–F are templates used in data collection through observation, interviewing, questionnaires, and inventories of Web sites and publications. These templates changed over time as new questions emerged from initial data collection, but the general structure and nature of the questions remained consistent. Appendix G lists the deductive analytic codes.

Appendix A

ACTIVIST GROUPS MENTIONED BY NAME IN THE BOOK		
Name at time of mention*	Acronym	Issue focus at time of mention*
AID/S		world AIDS crisis
Allies 2007		end violence among African American youth
Animal Liberation League	ALL	end animal abuse
Antiwar Campus Now		college students for peace
Black Antiwar Pittsburgh	BAP	mobilize African Americans against U.S. military in Iraq
Center for Progressive Values	CPV	resource and organizing center
Civil Liberties Defense Committee	CLDC	civil liberties
Coalition for Progressive Action		
CONCERN		conservative issues
CONSERVE		conservative issues
Death by Heroin		anti-drug
DebtFree		advocate forgiveness for debt of poor countries
East Side Progressive Coalition		progressive issues
Ecology Now	EN	environmental issues
Eliminating Police Violence Together	EPVT	stop police violence against civilians
End War and Occupation Committee	EWOC	anti-war
FUTURE		reform tax policy
GAYVOTE		oppose anti-gay policies
Greenview against Drugs	GAD	stop illegal drugs

continued

Name at time of mention*	Acronym	Issue focus at time of mention*
Liberty Now	LN	advocate conservative issues
Marriage Now	MN	advocate same-sex marriage in Pennsylvania
New Army of Revolution	NAR	build progressive movement in Pittsburgh
New Dawn		stop violence among black youth
No War Committee	NWC	anti-war
People Opposing Drugs		anti-drug
Pittsburgh Antiwar Network	PAN	anti-war
Planet Protection Society	PPS	environmental issues
Queer Organizing Network		queer rights
QUERE		queer advocacy
Race Equality	RE	racial civil rights
REBORN		queer rights
RISE		African American community empowerment
Street Medics Action Group	SMAG	protest support
SECURE		security policy
Stop Gun Violence	SGV	build movement against gun violence
Stop the Killing	StK	against black-on-black violence
Women against War	WAW	women for peace

*Activist groups do not maintain the same name and issue over time. This doesn't include the many other groups that are described, but not named, in the book.

Appendix B: Research Strategy

This project used a multi-method design to collect data on activist groups and their environments. The data are from documents and media coverage of Pittsburgh activist groups/organizations, social movement incubators, and foundations; ethnographic observations and documents from emerging activist groups and several established groups for comparison; and interviews/questionnaires with activists and possible recruits. Thus, data are nested as community-level, group-level, and individual-level information.

Sampling Methods

I used a two-stage sampling strategy to create a quasi-sampling frame (since there is no comprehensive list of activist groups, especially new and emerging groups) from which to select groups.

Stage One: In this stage, we (I and a team of students) enumerated all emerging activist groups in Pittsburgh over a one-year period. I began by defining emerging activism as collective public groups in the early stages of organizing protests or other challenges to existing state or non-state authorities, using means other than those of conventional politics.[1] Initially, I included only groups that were actively recruiting, but this excluded those that accepted new members but did not engage in public recruiting. I thus redefined emerging activism as new groups that are (1) public (advertising for members or publicizing themselves); or (2) open to new members, even if with restrictions; and (3) trying to change society. I included both progressive and conservative groups to allow comparison across political agendas.

I identified emerging groups in three ways: (1) by systematically monitoring all local newspapers, including general readership papers and specialized papers directed to the city's African Americans, Latino/as, LGBT persons, Catholics, Jews, artists, and homeless populations; (2) by contacting community officials, leaders, and activists who would likely know about incipient organizing efforts; and (3) by monitoring public and commercial spaces where activism is publicized, including coffeehouses and bars, music venues, parks, and spaces of public activism like demonstrations such as Rock against Racism and the LGBT Pride Days.[2]

Stage Two: I selected emerging activist groups for intensive study through an iterative sample strategy. First, I selected a set of groups that represented a "meaningful range"[3] of political agendas and member demographics. After preliminary analysis of data from these groups pointed to the importance of factors such as traditional versus faith-based orientations and incubator organizations, I selected another set of emerging groups that varied on these dimensions. Ultimately, 69 activist groups were included for intensive study at some point. I do not list these groups by name because this would identify activists who were promised confidentiality.

Data Collection

From the 69 sampled emerging groups, we collected three kinds of data: observational, interview, and documentary.

Observational Data

We collected very detailed data through regular observation of meetings and public events of the emerging activist groups. As a context for understanding the dynamics of groups, direct observation has a number of advantages over written minutes of meetings.

First, meeting minutes often simply record the final decisions, while observation captures the process of decision making, changes in the rules as they occur, the logic of deliberation, the nature of compromise or the exertion of power, and the discussions and actions through which decisions are made or left unmade. Observations show a group's deliberation, not just its decisions.

Second, observation reveals whose voices are most respected and taken most seriously, who verbalizes the sense of the group, and who represents particular factions within the group. In contrast, meeting minutes often screen out the names of speakers so the actual practice of leadership (as opposed to the formal position of leader) or entrepreneurship is difficult to discern.

Third, through observations it is possible to track who does *not* attend a meeting, while minutes show—incompletely—only those who attend. With observation, I can see who is dropping away or leaving the group, especially if they leave without directly voicing dissent or disillusion. Observations reveal behaviors that are contrary to expectations, thus allowing tests of emerging hunches, whereas minutes do not. Observations make it possible to link members' actions and talk over time whereas few individual names appear in minutes.

I have observations of 378 events of the 69 activist groups between 2003 and 2007. The majority (295) were group meetings. Of the remaining 83 events, 58 were protests or vigils and 25 were miscellaneous occurrences, including press conferences, workshops, and group-sponsored social or educational events. The attendance at meetings averaged 12.7 persons; for protests, it was 138. Women made up a slightly larger proportion (56%) of meeting attendance than did men.

Observational data were collected by me or by students I trained—a form of what Calvin Morrill and his colleagues term "team ethnography." Team ethnography is particularly suited to collecting data on a large number of groups simultaneously and for providing multiple perspectives on the complicated dynamics and actions of these groups.[4] To check reliability, two researchers periodically attended the same events and compared their notes; discrepancies were analyzed at weekly staff meetings and resulted in adjustments to the observational template.

Observations were semi-structured, using a template for field notes that was continually refined over time to include new issues and address emerging hypotheses (Appendix C).[5] The template guided collection of general data on the event and group as well as specific discursive and interactional data about interpersonal, ideological, and organizational characteristics of the group. For example, prompts in the template reminded the observer to be alert for information on alliances and frictions (interpersonal), what was recognized as expertise (ideological), and incidents in which rules were evoked or broken (organizational). Periodically, conversation at a meeting was recorded for in-depth analysis.

To collect data that were systematic as well as responsive to the qualitative research strategy of simultaneous data collection and interpretation, part of the observational template was fixed and part evolved over time as some lines of inquiry were resolved and other lines of inquiry were opened by earlier observations and analyses. Put another way, observational data collection was shaped both deductively, by analytic concepts and questions derived from existing scholarship and theories, and inductively, by concepts and questions that emerged from prior observations.

To capture the immediacy of group dynamics as well as record what happened or failed to happen over time, the template was organized in three segments. Initial data about the group and event were recorded prior to the observation (name of group, how we found out about the event, etc.). A second set of observations, largely about the characteristics and immediately observable dynamics of the event such as power struggles, emotions expressed, rules invoked, decision making, and discussions of audiences, was recorded during the event or meeting. A third set of observations, mostly reflections on what the group accomplished, what did not happen that might be expected to happen, and the overall tenor and rhythm, was recorded afterward. For selected periods of time, we also assessed the formalization, leadership strength, membership consistency, and moves toward action of each meeting or event. Observational data also extended beyond the predetermined categories of the template, as we recorded unanticipated aspects of activist group dynamics and preserved information whose descriptive value was not immediately clear.[6]

Interview Data

We conducted semi-structured, face-to-face individual interviews with members, leaders, new recruits, marginal members, defectors from the group, and those approached to join who declined to do so. Interviews solicited demographic and organizational information as well as the informant's interpretations of group processes, operation, and other issues as they arose.[7]

Fifty-three activists were interviewed, some repeatedly. Of these, 33 (62%) were white, 12 (23%) were African American, and the remaining 8 (15%) were Asian or Asian American, Middle Eastern, or Latino/a. Their median age was 35, with 21 (60%) in their 20s; the others ranged in age up to 70 years. Most (47, or 88%) had a history of activism prior to joining the group in which they were currently involved and 35 (66%) were currently involved with more than one group. The semi-structured format allowed me to collect comparable data across all interviews and garner unanticipated information. The interviews were conducted in a conversational manner, with respondents encouraged to expand on their comments and provide detailed narratives; all interviewees were asked to respond to a common set of questions listed on the interviewing template (Appendix D). All interviews were recorded and transcribed in full.

In addition, short questionnaires were distributed after meetings of selected groups, some repeatedly (Appendix E), and focus groups were conducted with one predominantly African American and one predominantly white activist group to assess the impact of the 2004 presidential election campaign on their groups.

Contextual Data

Activist groups operate within local activist environments that constrain and enable the actions of activists and dynamics of groups. To understand this environment, we collected several kinds of data on the wider context of Pittsburgh activism:

Indymedia: Data (including police attendance, violence, size, target, etc.) on all protest events, and surrounding dialogues among activists that were displayed as photographs or text on the Web site of Pittsburgh Indymedia, an independent progressive media source. Its extensive footage of protests constitutes what Chris Atton refers to as the data of "native observations."[8] These data covered 290 events between September 2003 and May 2005.

Newspapers/media: Data (including location, size, composition, message, etc.) on all events sponsored by local progressive groups (not only those covered in the observational data) that were reported in any newspaper or other media between September 2003 and April 2005, totaling 1,258 events by 133 groups.

Three Rivers Community Foundation: Characteristics (history, mission, goals, media usage, Web site characteristics and links, funding) and proposed actions (intent, plan, budget, etc.), and if funded, the results of the proposed action for all groups that sought funding from this local progressive philanthropic foundation in 2003, 2004, and 2005, totaling 178 proposals by 153 different activist groups.

Activism bi-annual inventory: An inventory of all activist groups and organizations in Pittsburgh, with basic data on their stated purpose, leadership, relationship to activist group incubators or other groups, location, and major public events (Appendix F). This was done every six months, from October 2003 through April 2006, resulting in data at six points in time. These data document activist group appearance and disappearance as well as changes in activities, mission, leadership, location, and relationship to incubators and other groups.

Documents

We collected published materials and Web sites of all activist groups in the study, plus a selection of e-mail and Web-based discussions from a subset of the groups used for a "virtual ethnography"[9] of mediated talk. Additionally, we analyzed all issues of *The New People*, a monthly progressive newspaper of the Center for Progressive Values (CPV), between 2003 and 2007—a total of 60 issues or approximately 600 pages.

CODING AND ANALYSIS

Coding and analysis of data from observations, interviews, documents, and other sources took place simultaneously, following established procedures for qualitative methodology.[10] To increase reliability, a sample of material was coded by different coders and discrepancies were used to adjust the instructions to coders.

All written data were entered into the qualitative data management program N6 (and, later N7) and coded for themes, relationships, and patterns in small (1–2 sentences or less) textual segments linked to contextual information about the group, event, and speakers. All data were coded in full twice. First, a list of theoretical and empirical categories were generated deductively from prior research to elicit information on how groups develop interpersonal, organizational, and ideological characteristics (Appendix G). Then, a list of themes and categories was generated inductively from several systematic readings of all data to capture nuances and develop new lines of inquiry. All data were coded with the resulting inductive codes.

Deductive and inductive coding schemes included both overt content and silences/omissions. Codes for overt content were used when a group commented about a topic or engaged in action connected to that topic. Thus, an overt code for conflict was applied when groups talked about conflict or when they were engaged in conflictual talk or actions. Codes for silences/omissions were used when a group might have talked or acted in some way, but did not. A silence/omitted code for conflict designated when groups might have engaged in conflict (based both on their earlier actions and talk and those of other groups in comparable situations), but did not.

Analysis was longitudinal and comparative. I examined activist group characteristics over time within groups to assess how these change, and how earlier actions enable or constrain subsequent ones. I examined characteristics across groups to assess difference by type, composition of members, issues, and other factors and to test emerging hypotheses.

Appendix C: Observational Template

Record at Beginning of Event:

> Date of Observation
> Group Name
> Where did we hear about this meeting/event (flyer, event, verbal comment)
> Did we have a person who referred us? Who?
> Where Observed
> Information on Membership/Attendance (size, composition)
> How Group Is Recruiting
> Group Goals (and source of evidence)
> Public Events (held or planned)

Take Notes During Event On:

1) Conflicts:
2) Power Struggles:
3) Identifiers/Qualifiers:
4) "Us" Talk or "Enemy" Talk:
5) Emotions Invoked or Displayed:
6) Talk of Problems in the Group:
7) "Rules" Are Evoked or Broken:

Write About Later:

1) General impressions about group
2) Pre-existing ties
3) Alliances, frictions, in/out group
4) Dynamics within meeting
5) What is "accomplished" in group identity, goals, strategies? How?
6) Who is seen as recruitable?
7) Leadership—overt or backstage
   * differentiate between leader; organizer; coordinator
   * specify actions that lead you to list a person in one of these roles
8) What are spoken and unspoken norms?
9) Friction—what happens?
10) Talk about other groups
11) Who sets agenda? Monitors it? Does it shift?
12) Anything expected that does not happen?
13) What didn't you [or someone else] understand?
14) How are people authorized to speak/act?
15) What is assumed (e.g., young people are good to recruit) and is there ever clarification/challenge to these assumptions?

Appendix D: Interviewing Schedule

Record on Template, Do Not Tape:

> Demographic Information (age, race, sex):
> Current activism (including role in the group):
> History of activism in Pittsburgh and elsewhere (record chronologically; probe for descriptions of groups):

In a minute, I'll turn on the tape for a series of questions. I'll ask you a series of questions about

(1) your former groups
(2) your memory of when you first joined [current group]
(3) your impressions of how [group] is working, internally
(4) your role in [group] and as an activist

Begin Taping

(1) Your Former Groups
    What led the group to end (or you to leave)?
    How well did that group function?
    * What were its strengths and weaknesses?
    * Give an example that shows group's strength and weakness
    Which group(s) do you think worked best?
    * worst?
    What kinds of groups are you most comfortable in?

What groups in Pittsburgh do you rely on now? WHY?

What groups in Pittsburgh do you most respect, or see as a model? WHY?

(2) When You First Joined [Current Group]

What attracted you to the group? [Or how did you organize it?]

If Brought In:

* How were you recruited?

    (Did you know someone in the group?)

    (How would you characterize your relationship with that person at the time?)

    (What did they say/do that convinced you?)

* Did anyone discourage you from joining [starting the group]?

* (Were other people being recruited at the same time? Who and how?)

If Started It:

* Who did you bring in at the beginning?

* What groups were they from?

* Who did you try to convince, but didn't join at the beginning?

What do/did you think about how the group worked when you first came?

* What impressed you, or worried you?

    What expectations did you have about how the group would work before you joined?

* Did you think you might become a leader of the group, eventually?

* Did you think this would be a supportive group of people?

    When did you start thinking of yourself as a member of this group?

    When did you start thinking of yourself as a [identity marker; e.g., antiwar activist]?

    How similar or different were your ideas (politics?) from others in the group when you first joined?

* How similar are they now?

* What are some points of disagreement?

(3) Your Impressions of [Group]

One thing we're interested in is how groups change over time:

How has group changed over time?

What do you see as its turning points? (DETAILS)
Were the expectations you originally had for the group met?
Could someone change the goals of the group at this point?
* What could be changed?
* What could not be changed?

We are interested in knowing how groups decide how to recruit, and when:

At what points did the group work to recruit new people?
What kinds of people have you/the group tried to recruit?
* How successful?
Are there kinds of people you didn't try to recruit, but should have?
* Why didn't you?
How does the group try to identify new members?
How successful has the group been in retaining new members?
    (Example)
What attracts people to the group, do you think?
* Give me an example of someone who was successfully recruited
If you had a specific project or issue for which you needed more help,
    who could you enlist?
If the group needed more members, where would you look for them?
What leads people to stay or leave, do you think?
* Give me an example of someone who stayed (Details)
* Give me an example of someone who left (Details)

We are interested in how groups work internally, their dynamics:

What do you like best about how the group works?
Could you walk me through what a good meeting would be like,
    when people get along?
What do you like least about how the group works?
Could you walk me through what a not-so-good meeting would be
    like, when people are not getting along?
What are the "unspoken rules" of the group? [prompt]
* What issues/ideas are "off-limits"?
How would you describe the nature of personal relationships in the
    group?
* Do people socialize with each other outside the group?
* Do you regard other members of the group as friends?
* Do you think these personal ties help the group or not?

Do you think you could be honest about personal issues in the group?
* Or to individual members?

How often do you think emotions get expressed in the group?
* When do happy emotions show up?
* When do angry or upset emotions show up?
* Give an example of a time that felt uncomfortable in the group and how it was resolved

Do you think there are tensions around gender? race? age? sexuality?
* Give an example of when these came up and what happened
* Give an example of conflict in the group, and how it got resolved

What has been the most fulfilling aspect of being in this group for you?
* Give an example of a time you felt fulfilled

What has been the most frustrating aspect of being in this group for you?
* Give an example of a time you felt frustrated

Have you ever thought about quitting the group? (Details)

Also, we are interested in understanding how people might see a groups differently: Can you describe your understanding of what the group is about?

* What purpose does the group serve in "the larger scheme of things"?
* What needs in the community/world does the group fulfill?
* Who, specifically, are you trying to reach with your message?
* Are you successful?

Walk me through an event that you thought was particularly good
Walk me through an event that you thought was not so good
What do you think the groups' future will be?

We are also interested in understanding how groups develop leadership:

Who do you think of as leaders in the group?
* What makes them leaders?
* Who generally delegates tasks?

Could you be a leader? Would you want to?
Who do ideas come from, usually? (Leader, members, others)
What gives someone the credibility to be listened to?
When (over what) do people disagree with the leaders?

We are interested in understanding how the group works outside of meetings:

What kinds of decisions or plans do you think are made outside of meetings (or committee meetings)?

Which people do you think are most involved in planning or making decisions between meetings?

Would you be interested in being more involved in this kind of work for the group? (If so) How would you go about doing so?

(4) Your Role in [Group] and as an Activist

What is your role in the group?

* What exactly, do you do in the group? (Example)

* Changed over time?

How is your role likely to change in the future?

What have certain people in the group taught you? Who?

What have you taught others in the group?

Do you think your activism has hurt you in other areas of your life? (Example)

Does your family (partner) encourage or discourage your activism?

Are there ways that your activism has paid off for you in other areas? (Example)

(For interviewee with multiple memberships)

Do you ever feel a conflict between your involvement in X and Y groups?

Do they make conflicting demands?

(If so) How do you handle this? (Probe for example)

With what group or issue would you like to be involved in the future?

Can we re-interview you in the future, perhaps in about 6 months?

Appendix E: Short Questionnaire

1. How did you find out about this group?
2. What attracted you to the group?
3. What impresses you about how the group is working?
4. What worries you about how the group is working?
5. What other political or social change groups do you currently belong to?
6. What groups in Pittsburgh do you most respect, or see as a model? WHY?

Age
Gender
Race

Appendix F: Group Inventory Template

1. What does the group want to change (goals, etc.)?
2. Does the group meet on a regular basis?
3. How is the group organized? How are tasks delegated? Are there officers or leaders? Who takes responsibility in the group?
4. Where does the group get members?
5. Does the group have events? Does the group work with others on events?
6. Does the group advertise meetings?
7. How does the group stay together? How does the group stay in contact?
8. Does the group try to get media coverage? How does the group interact with the media?
9. Does the group have a website? What does it look like?
10. When did the group start meeting? Whose idea was it originally to form the group? What triggered the group's formation? How long did it take for the group to coalesce?
11. Are there paid staff?
12. Where does the group meet?

Appendix G: Deductive Codes

Accomplishments
Accountability (to other groups; to members)
Agendas
Allies
Arenas of action
Assumptions
Audiences (external; internal)
Authorities
Becoming an activist
Blame
Central activists
Centralization
Compromises
Conflict (interpersonal; ideological)
Culture (shared beliefs; sense of justice; meaning frames)
Decentralization
Decision-making (backdoor)
Defining what is problematic
Delegation of tasks
Democratic practices (basis of authority; deliberation)
Diversity
Division of labor
Emotions (subcultures; expression; socialization into)
Ethics (dilemmas)
Evaluation of group
Exit

Expectations (of success)
Experts (expertise)
External pressures
Form vs. content
Future (vision; expectations)
Goals (group; shifts; individual)
Group dynamics
Identities (individual; collective; identity qualifiers)
Imagined options
Inchoate circumstances
Initial mobilization (expectations; how; when; who)
Issues suppressed
Joining group (how; why; when)
Knowledge
Loyalty claims
Manners
Media
Members (desired recruits; new; founding; composition; size)
Money
Motivated by opportunities
Multiple memberships
Movement sustainability
Movement interaction (alliances; bridging organizations; coalitions;
    overlapping members; friction)
New ideas
Perceived benefits (costs; opportunities)
Power struggles
Protests (contestation; intentionality; collective identity)
Public events
Reactive sequences
Reflexivity
Relations among members (deferential; hostile; tutelage; friendship)
Repertoires (modular; innovative; rejected)
Resources
Rewards for participation
Rhythm to resolve issues
Rules
Self-reinforcing sequences
Silencing
Sliding categories
Staff

Storytelling about group
Stratification (race; status; age; gender; sexuality)
Structural constraints
Submerged networks
Support in group
Tactic types (identity-oriented; strategy-oriented)
Tactic interaction (coercion; facilitation; insider; outsider; bargaining; violence)
Tactics (shift in; taste in)
Temporal markers
Time, sense of
Top down leadership
Turning points
Worries about group

END NOTES

CHAPTER 1

1. There is an impressive scholarship on avoidance in political life, including Katherine Cramer Walsh, *Talking about Politics: Informal Groups and Social Identity in American Life* (Chicago: University of Chicago Press, 2004); Katherine Cramer Walsh, *Talking about Race: Community Dialogues and the Politics of Difference* (Chicago: University of Chicago Press, 2007); Robert D. Putnam, *Bowling Alone: The Collapse and Revival of American Community* (New York: Simon & Schuster, 2000); Sophie Duchesne and Florence Haegel, "Avoiding or Accepting Conflict in Public Talk," *British Journal of Political Science* 37:1 (2007):1–22; Diana C. Mutz, *Hearing the Other Side: Deliberative versus Participatory Democracy* (New York: Cambridge University Press, 2006); and, especially, Nina Eliasoph, *Avoiding Politics: How Americans Produce Apathy in Everyday Life* (New York: Cambridge University Press, 1998).

2. Marc W. Steinberg, "Toward a More Dialogic Analysis of Social Movement Culture," in *Social Movements: Identity, Culture, and the State*, edited by David S. Meyer, Nancy Whittier, and Belinda Robnett (New York: Oxford University Press, 2002), 224; Robin D. G. Kelley, *Freedom Dreams: The Black Radical Imagination* (Boston: Beacon Press, 2002b), 9; Marcel Stoetzler and Nira Yuval-Davis discuss this as engaging "the 'deeper' realms of the 'social imaginary'" in their "Standpoint Theory, Situated Knowledge and the Situated Imagination," *Feminist Theory* 3:3 (2002):326.

3. Étienne Balibar, "Historical Dilemmas of Democracy and Their Contemporary Relevance," lecture at Citizenship in the 21st Century: An International Colloquium, Pittsburgh, March 18, 2008; H. Van Gunsteren, *A Theory of Citizenship: Organizing Plurality in Contemporary Democracies* (Boulder, CO: Westview, 1998), 526–527. Also see Kenneth Andrews et al., "Civic Associations That Work: The Contributions of Leadership to Organizational Effectiveness," paper presented at the annual meeting of the American Sociological Association, Montreal, August 2006.

4. As Andrea L. Smith warns, we should not rush to "celebrate 'activism' in an undifferentiated sense without looking at how different activisms often reinscribe racism, sexism, and colonialism more than they resist it" (*Native Americans and the Christian Right: The Gendered Politics of Unlikely Alliances* [Durham, NC: Duke University Press, 2008], xxx). Also Stefan-Ludwig Hoffman, "Democracy and Associations in the Long Nineteenth Century: Toward a Transnational Perspective," *Journal of Modern History* 75 (2003):269–299;

Benedict Anderson, *Imagined Communities* (New York: Verso, 1991); and James Jasper, *The Art of Moral Protest: Culture, Biography, and Creativity in Social Movements* (Chicago: University of Chicago Press, 1997). For examples of anti-democratic collective action, see Kathleen Blee, *Women of the Klan: Racism and Gender in the 1920s* (Berkeley: University of California Press, 1991); Kathleen Blee, *Inside Organized Racism: Women in the Hate Movement* (Berkeley: University of California Press, 2002); and Kathleen Blee, "Racial Violence in the United States," *Ethnic and Racial Studies* 28:4 (2005):599–619.

5. Whether internal democracy declines over time in activist groups as they bureaucratize and/or focus on survival has been the subject of considerable debate. See Frances Fox Piven and Richard A. Cloward, *Poor People's Movements: Why They Succeed, How They Fail* (New York: Vintage, 1979) and William Gamson, *The Strategy of Social Protest* (Belmont, CA: Wadsworth, 1975/1990). In an important later study, *Freedom Is an Endless Meeting: Democracy in American Social Movements* (Chicago: University of Chicago Press, 2002a), Francesca Polletta finds that participatory democracy can be the outcome of social movements.

6. A good discussion of how members "count" in activism is Michael W. Foley and Bob Edwards, "How Do Members Count? Membership, Governance, and Advocacy in the Nonprofit World," in *Exploring Organizations and Advocacy: Governance and Accountability,* edited by Maria D. Montilla and Elizabeth J. Reid. Retrieved November 17, 2005 (http://www.uipress.org).

7. Howard S. Becker, *Tricks of the Trade: How to Think about Your Research while You're Doing It* (Chicago: University of Chicago Press, 1998), 120. Grassroots activism is defined in contrast to electoral and institutional politics, but its groups, goals, tactics, and ideas about politics can overlap those of more conventional civic groups. See Lee Ann Banaszak, Karen Beckwith, and Dieter Rucht, "When Power Relocates: Interactive Changes in Women's Movements and States," in *Women's Movements Facing the Reconfigured State,* edited by Lee Ann Banaszak, Karen Beckwith, and Dieter Rucht (New York: Cambridge University Press, 2003), 1–29; Robert J. Sampson, Doug McAdam, Heather MacIndoe, and Simón Weffer-Elizondo, "Civil Society Reconsidered: The Durable Nature and Community Structure of Collective Civic Action," *American Journal of Sociology* 111:3 (2005):673–714; and Doug McAdam, Robert J. Sampson, Simon Weffer, and Heather MacIndoe, "'There Will Be Fighting in the Streets': The Distorting Lens of Social Movement Theory," *Mobilization: An International Journal* 1:1 (2005):1–18.

8. The median household income in Pittsburgh in 2000 was $28,588, compared to $41,994 nationally.

9. To focus on how groups decide what they want to be, I excluded groups that lacked the freedom to do so, such as those considerably influenced or controlled by another group and what Silke Roth (*Building Movement Bridges: The Coalition of Labor Union Women* [Westport, CT: Praeger, 2003]) calls "insider organiza-tions." For example, I don't include Justice for Janitors because of its close ties to the Service Employees International Union, anti-abortion groups connected to Catholic churches, or pro-gun groups that are accountable to the Republican Party. This criterion may have excluded a proportionately larger number of conservative than progressive activist groups because of the large number of politically active conservative churches in Pittsburgh. I also exclude self-help groups, like yoga societies or infertility support networks, since these are not

activist in the sense of challenging existing authorities. I don't include groups focused solely on self-expression or individual behavior, like vegetarian societies or tattooing groups. A useful discussion of how to distinguish activism for social change from other forms of activism is David S. Meyer, "Social Movements: Creating Communities of Change," in *Feminist Approaches to Social Movements, Community, and Power: Conscious Acts and the Politics of Social Change*, Vol. 1, edited by Robin L. Teske and Mary Ann Tétreault (Columbia: University of South Carolina Press, 2000), 35–55.

10. Randall Collins, "Social Movements and the Focus of Emotional Attention," in *Passionate Politics: Emotions and Social Movements*, edited by Jeff Goodwin, James M. Jasper, and Francesca Polletta (Chicago: University of Chicago Press, 2001), 34.

11. Bert Klandermans, *The Social Psychology of Protest* (Cambridge, MA: Blackwell, 1997), 213.

12. Ruud Koopmans, "The Missing Link between Structure and Agency: Outline of an Evolutionary Approach to Social Movements," *Mobilization: An International Journal* 10:1 (2005):22; Charles C. Ragin and Howard S. Becker, *What Is a Case? Exploring the Foundations of Social Inquiry* (New York: Cambridge University Press, 1992), 6; and Stephen Valocchi, *Social Movements and Activism in the USA* (New York: Routledge, 2009).

13. Alberto Melucci, *Challenging Codes: Collective Action in the Information Age* (New York: Cambridge University Press,1996), 40; Steinberg, "Toward a More Dialogic Analysis," 209; and Connie J. G. Gersick, "Time and Transition in Work Teams: Toward a New Model of Group Development," *Academy of Management Journal* 31:1 (1988):9–41.

14. Doug McAdam, "Beyond Structural Analysis: Toward a More Dynamic Under-standing of Social Movements," in *Social Movements and Networks: Relational Approaches to Collective Action,* edited by Mario Diani and Doug McAdam (New York: Oxford University Press, 2003), 281–298; Jasper, *The Art of Moral Protest*, 77; Charles Kurzman, *The Unthinkable Revolution in Iran* (Cambridge, MA: Harvard University Press, 2004); and Koopmans, "The Missing Link." Important studies of culture building in activist groups include Paul Lichterman, *Elusive Togetherness: Church Groups Trying to Bridge America's Divisions* (Princeton, NJ: Princeton University Press, 2005), Nina Eliasoph, *Making Volunteers: Civic Life after Welfare's End* (Princeton, NJ: Princeton University Press, 2011), Ann Mische, *Partisan Publics: Communication and Contention across Brazilian Youth Activist Networks* (Princeton, NJ: Princeton University Press, 2009), Richard L. Wood, *Faith in Action: Religion, Race, and Democratic Organizing in America* (Chicago: University of Chicago Press, 2002), Sherryl Kleinman, *Opposing Ambitions: Gender and Identity in an Alternative Organization* (Chicago: University of Chicago Press, 1996), and Stephen Hart, *Cultural Dilemmas of Progressive Politics: Styles of Engagement among Grassroots Activists* (Chicago: University of Chicago Press, 2001).

15. Becker, *Tricks*, 85; Scott A. Hunt and Robert D. Benford, "Collective Identity, Solidarity, and Commitment," in *The Blackwell Companion to Social Movements*, edited by David A. Snow, Sarah A. Soule, and Hanspeter Kriesi (Malden, MA: Blackwell, 2004), 438; McAdam, "Beyond Structural Analysis." As Francesca Polletta (*It Was Like a Fever: Storytelling in Protest and Politics* [Chicago: University of Chicago Press, 2006], 183) argues, "we should scrutinize the points at which we choose to begin and end our accounts, and consider whether our

analysis might be different if the story started or ended at a different point." In her retrospective analysis of the early civil rights movement ("The Long Civil Rights Movement and the Political Uses of the Past," *Journal of American History* 91:4 [2005]:1233–1263), Jacquelyn Dowd Hall argues for considering the early days of a movement as the beginning of its history, not as a prehistory. There are good studies that trace social movements from their origin, but these generally focus on the factors that predict persistence, not their dynamics. In particular, the studies by John D. McCarthy, Bob Edwards, and their collaborators that trace the evolution of peace movements and Mothers against Drunk Driving chapters and Mario Diani's study of the Italian environmental movement show that strategy, organizational ties, and agency, as well as resources, matter to group survival—but not exactly *why* these matter. See Bob Edwards and John D. McCarthy, "Strategy Matters: The Contingent Value of Social Capital in the Survival of Local Social Movement Organizations," *Social Forces* 83:2 (2004):621–651; Bob Edwards, "Semi-Formal Organizational Structure among Social Movement Organizations: An Analysis of the U.S. Peace Movement," *Nonprofit and Voluntary Sector Quarterly* 23:4 (1994):309–333; John D. McCarthy and Mark Wolfson, "Resource Mobilization by Local Social Movement Organizations: Agency, Strategy, and Organization in the Movement against Drinking and Driving," *American Sociological Review* 61 (1997):1070–1088; and Mario Diani, *Green Networks: A Structural Analysis of the Italian Environmental Movement* (Edinburgh, Scotland: Edinburgh University Press, 1995). An important theoretical argument about the origins of collective action is Doug McAdam, "Revisiting the U.S. Civil Rights Movement: Toward a More Synthetic Understanding of the Origins of Contention," in *Rethinking Social Movements: Structure, Meaning, and Emotion,* edited by Jeff Goodwin and James M. Jasper (Lanham, MD: Rowman & Littlefield, 2004), 201–232.

16. Gene Burns, *The Moral Veto: Framing Contraception, Abortion, and Cultural Pluralism in the United States* (New York: Cambridge University Press, 2005), especially 180; Becker, *Tricks*, 85.

17. Paul Routledge, "Critical Geopolitics and Terrains of Resistance," *Political Geography* 15:6–7 (1996):523. The moments when all seems possible in activism are described in Melucci, *Challenging Codes*, 350–351; Kelley, *Freedom Dreams*; Francesca Polletta, "'It Was Like a Fever . . . ': Narrative and Identity in Social Protest," *Social Problems* 45:2 (1998):137–159; Javier Auyero, *Contentious Lives: Two Argentinian Women, Two Protests, and the Quest for Recognition* (Durham, NC: Duke University Press, 2003); Temma Kaplan, *Taking Back the Streets: Women, Youth, and Direct Democracy* (Berkeley: University of California Press, 2004); and Denis O'Hearn, *Nothing But an Unfinished Song: Bobby Sands, the Irish Hunger Striker Who Ignited a Generation* (New York: Nation Books, 2006). One consideration for activists in new groups is how similar or different from existing groups they want these to be. For a parallel argument, focused on social movements, see Doug McAdam, "'Initiator' and 'Spin-Off' Movements: Diffusion Processes in Protest Cycles," in *Repertoires and Cycles of Collective Action,* edited by Mark Traugott (Durham, NC: Duke University Press, 1995), 217–239; and Debra C. Minkoff and John D. McCarthy, "Reinvigorating the Study of Organizational Processes in Social Movements," *Mobilization: An International Journal* 10:2 (2005):289–308.

18. See Eliasoph, *Making Volunteers*. The impact of established social practices on the form of activism is seen in the early civil rights movement, detailed in Aldon D. Morris,

The Origins of the Civil Rights Movement: Black Communities Organizing for Change (New York: Free Press, 1984). A group's "tastes in tactics" is one example of how legacies of action linger after their original proponents are gone, explored in Jasper, *The Art of Moral Protest*, 229; also see Megan Meyer, "Organizational Identity, Political Contexts, and SMO Action: Explaining the Tactical Choices Made by Peace Organizations in Israel, Northern Ireland, and South Africa," *Social Movement Studies* 3:2 (2004):167–197. Organizational research, too, finds that early actions can be influential long afterward, a process these scholars term "imprinting." A striking example of organizational imprinting is the finding by James Baron and his colleagues that the number of women currently hired into scientific and engineering jobs in California's Silicon Valley technology companies depends in part on "organizational blueprints" put into place by the company's founders, even if these have been long forgotten, in James N. Baron, Michael T. Hannan, Greta Hsu, and Ozgecan Kocak, "Gender and the Organization-Building Process in Young, High-Tech Firms," in *The New Economic Sociology: Developments in an Emerging Field,* edited by Mauro F. Guillén, Randall Collins, Paula England, and Marshall Meyer (New York: Russell Sage Foundation Press, 2002), 245–273. Another important work on the legacies of early moments in a historical trajectory by Michael T. Hannan and his colleagues is Michael T. Hannan, M. Diane Burton, and James N. Baron, "Inertia and Change in the Early Years: Employment Relations in Young, High Technology Firms," *Industrial and Corporate Change* 5:2 (1996):503–536. Sociological theories of historical legacy are developed in Howard S. Becker, "The Power of Inertia," *Qualitative Sociology* 18:3 (1995):301–309; Harvey Molotch, William Freudenburg, and Krista E. Paulsen, "History Repeats Itself, but How? City Character, Urban Tradition, and the Accomplishment of Place," *American Sociological Review* 65:6 (2000): 791–823; and Charles Tilly, *Durable Inequality* (Berkeley: University of California Press, 1999).

19. See David Diehl and Daniel McFarland, "Toward a Historical Sociology of Social Situations," *American Journal of Sociology* 115:6 (May 2010):1717. Michael T. Heaney and Fabio Rojas ("The Place of Framing: Multiple Audiences and Antiwar Protests Near Fort Bragg," *Qualitative Sociology* 29 [2006]: 503) call for more research on the "filtering process" in frame development. On framing processes, see David A. Snow and Robert D. Benford, "Ideology, Frame Resonance, and Participant Mobilization," in *International Social Movement Research, from Structure to Action: Comparing Social Movement Research across Cultures,* Vol. 1, edited by Bert Klandermans, Hanspeter Kriesi, and Sidney Tarrow (Greenwich, CT: JAI Press, 1988), 197–217; David A. Snow, "Master Frames and Cycles of Protest," in *Frontiers of Social Movement Theory,* edited by Aldon Morris and Carol McClurg Mueller (New Haven, CT: Yale University Press, 1992), 133–155; and Robert D. Benford, "An Insider's Critique of the Social Movement Framing Perspective," *Sociological Inquiry* 67:4 (2007):409–430.

20. Bert Klandermans and Dirk Oegema, "Potentials, Networks, Motivations, and Barriers: Steps towards Participation in Social Movements," *American Sociological Review* 52 (August 1987):519–531; David S. Meyer, "Claiming Credit: Stories of Movement Influence as Outcomes," *Mobilization: An International Journal* 11:3 (2006): 202.

21. Martha Ann Carey and Mickey W. Smith, "Capturing the Group Effect in Focus Groups: A Special Concern in Analysis," *Qualitative Health Research* 4:1 (1994):123–127.

22. Minkoff and McCarthy, "Reinvigorating the Study," 303.
23. Jean-Pierre Reed and John Foran, "Political Cultures of Opposition: Exploring Idioms, Ideologies, and Revolutionary Agency in the Case of Nicaragua," *Critical Sociology* 28:3 (2002):358.
24. Paul Lichterman, "What Do Movements Mean? The Value of Participant-Observation," *Qualitative Sociology* 21:4 (1998):403.
25. Ira Katznelson describes such information as "experience-near," in *Working-Class Formation: Nineteenth-Century Patterns in Western Europe and the United States* (Princeton, NJ: Princeton University Press, 1986), 16.
26. Lichterman, "What Do Movements Mean?" 403. Here, I take Patricia Ewick and Susan Silbey's advice to "focus less on the precipitating events and, instead, excavate the gradual transformations" in "Narrating Social Structure: Stories of Resistance to Legal Authority," *American Journal of Sociology* 108:6 (2003):1365–1366. The need to study processes and mechanism in social life directly is explored in Elizabeth A. Armstrong and Mary Bernstein, "Culture, Power, and Institutions: A Multi-Institutional Politics Approach to Social Movements," *Sociological Theory* 26:1 (2008):74–99; Doug McAdam, Sidney Tarrow, and Charles Tilly, *Dynamics of Contention* (New York: Cambridge University Press, 2001); Laurie R. Weingart, "How Did They Do That? The Ways and Means of Studying Group Process," *Research in Organizational Behavior* 19 (1997):189–240; Renée R. Anspach, *Deciding Who Lives: Fateful Choices in the Intensive-Care Nursery* (Berkeley: University of California Press, 1993); and Marshall Ganz, *Why David Sometimes Wins: Leadership, Organization, and Strategy in the California Farm Worker Movement* (New York: Oxford University Press, 2009). A provocative discussion of the issue of weighing knowledge and assessing its credibility is Barry Barnes and David Bloor, "Relativism, Rationalism and the Sociology of Knowledge," in *Rationality and Relativism*, edited by Martin Hollis and Steven Lukes (Cambridge, MA: MIT Press 1982), 21–47.
27. Ewick and Silbey ("Narrating Social Structure," 1365–1366) describe the importance of unrealized actions, what they term "plots that appear to lead nowhere but that may accumulate to produce new social relations and yet newer narratives." Michel Foucault, *The History of Sexuality* (New York: Vintage, 1976), 27; Eliasoph, *Avoiding Politics*. Other important work on silences in social life are Eviatar Zerubavel, *The Elephant in the Room: Silence and Denial in Everyday Life* (New York: Oxford University Press, 2006); Alford A. Young Jr., *The Minds of Marginalized Black Men: Making Sense of Mobility, Opportunity, and Future Life Chances* (Princeton, NJ: Princeton University Press, 2004); Kleinman, *Opposing Ambitions*; and Hart, *Cultural Dilemmas*.
28. David Diehl and Daniel McFarland usefully theorize interaction as "composed of an iterative, interrelated process of actors orienting and reorienting themselves, both interpersonally and temporally, to each other and to the shared activity of the situation" in "Toward a Historical Sociology," 1744; Lichterman, "What Do Movements Mean?" 412; Colin Barker, "Fear, Laughter, and Collective Power: The Making of Solidarity at the Lenin Shipyard in Gdansk, Poland, August 1980," in *Passionate Politics,* edited by Goodwin et al.; Melucci, *Challenging Codes,* 391; Joann Carmin and Deborah B. Balser, "Selecting Repertoires of Action in Environmental Movement Organizations: An Interpretive Approach," *Organization and Environment* 15:4 (2002):365–388; and Walsh, *Talking about Politics,* 35.
29. On the cultural dynamics of collective narration and sense-making, see Polletta, *It Was Like a Fever*; Ewick and Silbey, "Narrating Social Structure"; Andrew J. Perrin,

Citizen Speak: The Democratic Imagination in American Life (Chicago: University of Chicago Press, 2006); and Steinberg, "Toward a More Dialogic Analysis." Also see Andrew Abbott, Time Matters: On Theory and Method (Chicago: University of Chicago Press, 2001), 121; Carey and Smith, "Capturing the Group Effect"; and Jenny Kitzinger and Clare Farquhar, "The Analytical Potential of 'Sensitive Moments' in Focus Group Discussions," in Developing Focus Group Research: Politics, Theory and Practice, edited by Rosaline S. Barbour and Jenny Kitzinger (London: Sage, 1999), 156–172.

30. Christian Smith, Moral, Believing Animals: Human Personhood and Culture (New York: Oxford University Press, 2003), 41, 43. See also Lichterman's discussion of group reflexivity in Elusive Togetherness.

31. Barbara J. Risman, "Gender as a Social Structure: Theory Wrestling with Activism," Gender & Society 18:4 (2004):432.

32. Magali Sarfatti Larson and Silvia Sigal, "Does 'The Public' Think Politically? A Search for 'Deep Structures' in Everyday Political Thought," Qualitative Sociology 24:3 (2001):286. Pierre Bourdieu calls this doxa, the "commonplace 'sense of limits'" that make the social world appear self-evident to social actors, in Distinction: A Social Critique of the Judgement of Taste (Cambridge, MA: Harvard University Press, 1984), 471, cited in Tim Cresswell, In Place/Out of Place: Geography, Ideology, and Transgression (Minneapolis: University of Minnesota Press, 1996),19. Lichterman, "What Do Movements Mean?" 402. Also see Zerubavel, Elephant in the Room.

33. See Judith Butler, "Imitation and Gender Insubordination," In Inside/Out: Lesbian Theories, Gay Theories, edited by Diana Fuss (New York: Routledge, 1991), 13–31, and Steven Seidman, "Identity and Politics in a 'Postmodern' Gay Culture: Some Historical and Conceptual Notes," in Fear of a Queer Planet: Queer Politics and Social Theory, edited by Michael Warner (Minneapolis: University of Minnesota Press, 1993), 105–142.

34. Alfred North Whitehead, cited in James M. Jasper, Art of Moral Protest, 363.

35. Andrew Abbott terms this "microtransformation" in "What Do Cases Do? Some Notes on Activity in Sociological Analysis," in Ragin and Becker, eds., What Is a Case? 53–82. Also Abbott, Time Matters, 42.

36. Angela N. H. Creager, Elizabeth Lunbeck, and M. Norton Wise, eds., Science without Laws: Model Systems, Cases, Exemplary Narratives (Durham, NC: Duke University Press, 2007), 13.

37. Abbott, Time Matters, 41. As Alberto Melucci (Challenging Codes, 21) argues, social movements aren't things in themselves but rather analytic concepts. Moreover, as Joann Carmin and Deborah B. Balser ("Selecting Repertoires of Action") note, interpretations change as group members and external environments change. See also Erika Effler Summers, Laughing Saints and Righteous Heroes: Emotional Rhythms in Social Movement Groups (Chicago: University of Chicago Press, 2010).

38. Steven Hitlin and Glen H. Elder Jr., "Time, Self, and the Curiously Abstract Concept of Agency," Sociological Theory 25:2 (2007):183.

39. Jacques Revel cautions as well about treating context and objects of inquiry as "distinct levels of observation," in "Microanalysis and the Construction of the Social," in Histories: French Constructions of the Past, edited by Jacques Revel and Lynn Hunt (New York: New Press, 1995), 500; Linda M. G. Zerilli talks about being politically enabled through "outsidedness" in her "Toward a Feminist Theory of Judgment," Signs: Journal of Women in Culture and Society 34:2

(2008):312. As Nicholas Pedriana ("Rational Choice, Structural Context, and Increasing Returns: A Strategy for Analytic Narrative in Historical Sociology," *Sociological Methods & Research* 33:3 [2005]:349–382) argues, context may be particularly important in highly detailed, "zoomed in," studies. An example is the study of hate crimes. If a young white man stabs a black man, should we consider this a racial hate crime? Not necessarily. What if the men had argued earlier? Or the white man was showing off to his buddies? Or he planned to rob someone and the black man was next to a subway stop that provided the white man a quick avenue of escape? Context is necessary to define hate crimes because it provides the meanings of action, as explored in Kathleen Blee, "The Microdynamics of Hate Violence: Interpretive Analyses and Implications for Responses," *American Behavioral Scientist* 51:2 (2007):258–270.

40. Doreen Massey, "The Political Place of Locality Studies," *Environment and Planning* 23 (1991):267–281. Important empirical and theoretical works that connect issues of space and collective politics include Byron A. Miller, "Collective Action and Rational Choice: Place, Community, and the Limits to Individual Self-Interest," *Economic Geography* 68:1 (1992):22–42; Byron A. Miller, *Geography and Social Movements: Comparing Antinuclear Activism in the Boston Area* (Minneapolis: University of Minnesota Press, 2000); John A. Agnew, *Place and Politics: The Geographical Mediation of State and Society* (Boston: Allen and Unwin,1987); Krista E. Paulsen, "Making Character Concrete: Empirical Strategies for Studying Place Distinction," *City and Community* 3:3 (2004):243–262; Steve Pile, "Introduction: Opposition, Political Identities, and Spaces of Resistance," in *Geographies of Resistance*, edited by Steve Pile and Michael Keith (New York: Routledge, 1997), 1–32; Anton Rosenthal, "Spectacle, Fear, and Protest: A Guide to the History of Urban Public Space in Latin America," *Social Science History* 24:1(2000):33–73; and William H. Sewell Jr., "Space in Contentious Politics," in *Silence and Voice in the Study of Contentious Politics*, edited by Ronald R. Aminzade, Jack A. Goldstone, Doug McAdam, Elizabeth J. Perry, William H. Sewell Jr., Sidney Tarrow, and Charles Tilly (New York: Cambridge University Press, 2001), 51–88.

41. Kathleen Blee and Ashley Currier, "How Local Social Movement Groups Handle a Presidential Election," *Qualitative Sociology* 29:3 (2006):261–280.

42. Donatella della Porta and Dieter Rucht, "Left-Libertarian Movements in Context: A Comparison of Italy and West Germany, 1965–1990," in *The Politics of Social Protest: Comparative Perspectives on States and Social Movements,* edited by J. Craig Jenkins and Bert Klandermans (Minneapolis: University of Minnesota Press, 1995), 233. A review of different ways of defining the field of action that surrounds activist groups is found in Minkoff and McCarthy, "Reinvigorating the Study," 290. The importance of the external organizational field for social movements is demonstrated empirically in Rory McVeigh, Carl Neblett, and Sarah Shafiq, "Explaining Social Movement Outcomes: Multiorganizational Fields and Hate Crime Reporting," *Mobilization: An International* Journal 11:1 (2006):23–49; Debra C. Minkoff, "Bending with the Wind: Strategic Change and Adaptation by Women's and Racial Minority Organizations," *American Journal of Sociology* 104:6 (1999):1666–1703; Verta Taylor, "Social Movement Continuity: The Women's Movement in Abeyance," *American Sociological Review* 54:5 (1989):761–775; and Bob Edwards and Michael Foley, "Social Movement Organizations beyond the Beltway: Understanding the Diversity of One Social Movement Industry," *Mobilization: An International* Journal 8:1 (2002):87–107.

43. A sense of a progressive social movement family is evidenced in the considerable overlap in the two directories of activist groups in Pittsburgh, one produced by an anarchist activist, the other by a liberal environmental group. There is a vast literature on how activist groups form links with each other and define themselves as a common movement. Among the richest works are Donatella della Porta and Massimiliano Andretta, "Changing Forms of Environmentalism in Italy: The Protest Campaign on the High Speed Railway System," *Mobilization: An International Journal* 7:1. (2002):59–77; Kenneth T. Andrews, "The Impacts of Social Movements on the Political Process: The Civil Rights Movement and Black Electoral Politics in Mississippi," *American Sociological Review* 62:5 (1997):800–819; and Elizabeth A. Armstrong, "From Struggle to Settlement: The Crystallization of a Field of Lesbian/Gay Organizations in San Francisco, 1969–1973," in *Social Movements and Organization Theory*, edited by Gerald F. Davis, Doug McAdam, W. Richard Scott, and Mayer N. Zald (New York: Cambridge University Press, 2005), 161–188.

44. This foundation's mission is to fund small, emerging, and controversial groups working for progressive social change. My analysis of 178 proposals submitted to the foundation by 153 groups shows more funding for mainstream and established activist organizations than for small and emerging groups in absolute numbers, but fewer as a proportion of proposals submitted. See Kathleen Blee and Lisa C. Huebner, with the assistance of John Nigro, "Three Rivers Community Foundation Funding Patterns, 2003–2005," unpublished document, 2008.

45. David S. Dobbie, "More than the Sum of Their Parts? Labor-Community Coalitions in the Rust Belt," Ph.D. dissertation, University of Michigan Department of Sociology (2008), 208; also see Judith Donaldson, Gloria Rudolf, and Cynthia Vanda, "Environmental Scan of Progressive Work in Southwestern Pennsylvania," unpublished report to the Three Rivers Community Foundation, Pittsburgh, 2008.

46. All group names are pseudonyms to protect the privacy of those I interviewed.

47. Taylor, "Social Movement Continuity."

48. Paul Bagguley, "Contemporary British Feminism: A Social Movement in Abeyance?" *Social Movement Studies* 1:2 (2002):169–185; and Minkoff and McCarthy, "Reinvigorating the Study."

49. Provocative arguments about agency and structure in activism are made by Marc Steinberg, "Toward a More Dialogic Analysis"; Jeffrey C. Alexander, *The Civil Sphere* (New York: Oxford University Press, 2006), especially 216, 224; and Melucci, *Challenging Codes*.

CHAPTER 2

1. The idea of collective intelligence is a foundation of modern statistics, since the average of individual estimates is more correct than any individual estimate. Its application to task teams is detailed in Anita William Wooley, "Collective Intelligence," presented at the Center for Interdisciplinary Research on Teams, Carnegie-Mellon University, Pittsburgh, PA, February 27, 2009. Grassroots groups are not perfectly analogous to task teams since members of task teams are not self-selected or motivated by political zeal and generally have a pre-determined task and timetable. As noted by Richard Klimoski and Susan Mohammed ("Team Mental Mode: Construct or Metaphor?" *Journal of Management* 20 [1994]:404), "All teams are groups, the converse is not necessarily so." Nonetheless, task teams and activist groups similarly emphasize group identity, interdependent action, and

organizational context and work to develop shared understandings. Studies of task teams that are particularly useful for scholars of activist group research are John R. Katzenbach and Douglas K. Smith, "The Discipline of Teams," *Harvard Business Review* 71 (1993):111–120; Richard A. Guzzo and Marcus W. Dickson, "Teams in Organizations: Recent Research on Performance and Effectiveness," *Annual Review of Psychology* 47 (1996):307–338; Karl E. Weick and Karlene H. Roberts, "Collective Mind in Organizations: Heedful Interrelating on Flight Decks," *Administrative Science Quarterly* 38 (1993):357–381; and Gersick, "Time and Transition." Critics of task team research, however, point to the limitations of studies outside of a natural setting. These issues, along with other problems of experimental and quasi-experimental methods in the study of natural groups are discussed in Roy Baumeister, Kathleen D. Vohns, and David C. Funder, "Psychology as the Science of Self-Reports and Finger Movements," *Perspectives on Psychological Science* 2:4 (2007):396–403, and Richard Moreland, "How Often Is Behavior Actually Measured by Social Psychologists Who Study Small Groups," presented at the Center for Interdisciplinary Research on Teams, Carnegie-Mellon University, Pittsburgh, PA, February 27, 2009.

2. James Mahoney ("Revisiting General Theory in Historical Sociology," *Social Forces* 83:2 [2004]:459–489) notes that since culture is a property of social groups rather than individuals, groups have emergent features that cannot be reduced to the attributes of individuals. Important statements on groups and organizations in activism are Klandermans, *The Social Psychology of Protest*, 121; Beth Schafer Caniglia and JoAnn Carmin, "Scholarship on Social Movement Organizations: Classic Views and Emerging Trends," *Mobilization: An International Journal* 10:2 (2005):201; Elizabeth S. Clemens and Debra C. Minkoff, "Beyond the Iron Law: Rethinking the Place of Organizations in Social Movement Research," in *Blackwell Companion*, edited by Snow et al., 158; Charles Tilly, *Why? What Happens When People Give Reasons . . . and Why* (Princeton, NJ: Princeton University Press, 2006); Walsh, *Talking about Politics*; and Robin Stryker, "Beyond History versus Theory: Strategic Narrative and Sociological Explanation," *Sociological Methods & Research* 24:3 (1996):304–352.

3. Melucci, *Challenging Codes*, 388; James M. Jasper, "A Strategic Approach to Collective Action: Looking for Agency in Social Movement Choices," *Mobilization: An International Journal* 9:1 (2004):1–16; James M. Jasper, *Getting Your Way: Strategic Dilemmas in the Real World* (Chicago: University of Chicago Press, 2006); and Meyer, "Claiming Credit." In their *Voices of the Valley, Voices of the Straits: How Protest Creates Communities* (New York: Berghahn Books, 2008), Donatella della Porta and Gianni Piazza talk of social movement organizations as "not only mobilisation agents, but also as spaces of deliberation and value construction."

4. Steinberg, "Toward a More Dialogic Analysis," 208; McAdam, "Beyond Structural Analysis," 290. The discussion of "brute fact" is in George Steinmetz, "Odious Comparisons: Incommensurability, the Case Study, and 'Small N's' in Sociology," *Sociological Theory* 22:3 (2004):378, in a discussion of Charles Taylor's article "Interpretation and the Sciences of Man." An excellent empirical study of the intertwining of action and interpretation is Javier Auyero, *Contentious Lives: Two Argentine Women, Two Protests, and the Quest for Recognition* (Durham, NC: Duke University Press, 2003).

5. Gary Alan Fine, "Public Narration and Group Culture: Discerning Discourse in Social Movements," in *Social Movements and Culture*, edited by Hank Johnston and Bert Klandermans (Minneapolis: University of Minnesota Press, 1995):128–129.

6. Melucci, *Challenging Codes*, 393; also Bourdieu, *Distinction*, 471, and Michèle Lamont and Virág Molnár, "The Study of Boundaries in the Social Sciences," *Annual Review of Sociology* 28 (2002):167–195.

7. Barrington Moore's classic study of nation-state development, *Social Origins of Dictatorship and Democracy: Lord and Peasant in the Making of the Modern World* (Boston: Beacon Press, 1966), is a similar analysis. Theories of path-dependent sequences in the discipline of geography are known as *time geography* but for clarity I use *path dependency,* the term more common in sociology.

8. Allan Pred, "Of Paths and Projects: Individual Behavior and Its Societal Context," in *Behavioral Problems in Geography Revisited*, edited by Kevin R. Cox and Reginald G. Golledge (New York: Methuen, 1981), 231.

9. Allan Pred, "Presidential Address: Interpenetrating Processes: Human Agency and the Becoming of Regional Spatial and Social Processes," *Papers of the Regional Science Association* 57 (1985):8.

10. Joseph M. Bryant and John A. Hall, "Theories and Methods Applied: Research Exemplars in Historical Social Science," in *Historical Methods in the Social Sciences,* Vol. 4, edited by John A. Hall and Joseph M. Bryant (London: Sage, 2005): vii; Pred, "Presidential Address," 15.

11. Pred, "Presidential Address," 8; Paul C. Adams, "Protest and the Scale Politics of Communications," *Political Geography* 15:5 (1996):419–441.

12. William Sewell, "Three Temporalities towards an Eventful Sociology," in *The Historic Turn in Human Sciences*, edited by Terrence J. McDonald (Ann Arbor: University of Michigan Press, 1996), 262–263.

13. Molotch, Freudenburg, and Paulsen, "History Repeats Itself, but How?"; James Mahoney, "Path Dependence in Historical Sociology," *Theory and Society* 29:4 (2000):507–548; Paulsen, "Making Character Concrete."

14. See Nicholas Pedriana, "From Protective to Equal Treatment: Legal Framing Processes and Transformation of the Women's Movement of the 1960s," *American Journal of Sociology* 111:6 (2006):1718–1761; Stryker, "Beyond History versus Theory"; Christopher Rhomberg, *No There There: Race, Class, and Political Community in Oakland* (Berkeley: University of California Press, 2004); Jeffrey Haydu, "Making Use of the Past: Time Periods as Cases to Compare and as Sequences of Problem Solving," *American Journal of Sociology* 104:2 (1998):339–371; and Rhys Isaac, "History Made from Stories Found: Seeking a Microhistory That Matters," *Common-Place* 6:1. Retrieved November 8, 2005 (www.common-place.org).

15. Douglass C. North, *Institutions, Institutional Change and Economic Performance* (Cambridge, MA: Cambridge University Press, 1990), 98–99.

16. Becker, "Power of Inertia"; Tilly, *Durable Inequality*.

17. Molotch, Freudenburg, and Paulsen, "History Repeats," 819 (authors' italics); see also Steve Pile, "Introduction: Opposition, Political Identities, and Spaces of Resistance," in *Geographies of Resistance*, edited by Steve Pile and Michael Keith (New York: Routledge, 1997),1–32; and Rhomberg, *No There There*. This provides one solution to the inattention of social movement theory to processes that create stability, as noted by Neil Fligstein and Doug McAdam in "Toward a General Theory of Strategic Action Fields," *Sociological Theory* 29 (2011):1–26.

18. Charles Tilly, *Big Structures, Large Processes, Huge Comparisons* (New York: Russell Sage, 1984), 14 (italics in original).

19. Wanda J. Orlikowski, "Material Knowing: The Scaffolding of Human Knowledge-ability," unpublished paper, retrieved October 19, 2010 (http://seeit.mit.edu/Publications/Orlikowski_OKLC_write-up_2006.pdf).

20. Charles Tilly, "Future History," *Theory and Society* 17:5 (1988):703–712. Paul Krugman, "History and Industry Location: The Case of the Manufacturing Belt," *American Economic Review* 81:2 (1991):80–83; Dwight B. Billings and Kathleen M. Blee, *The Road to Poverty: The Making of Wealth and Hardship in Appalachia* (New York: Cambridge University Press, 2000); Becker, *Tricks*, 50; and Dana Colleen Reinke, "Assessing Place Character in Response to Wal-Mart," Ph.D. dissertation, University of Pittsburgh Department of Sociology (2006).

21. Andrew Abbott, *Time Matters: On Theory and Method* (Chicago: University of Chicago Press, 2001); and Paul Pierson, "Increasing Returns, Path Dependence, and the Study of Politics," *American Political Science Review* 94:2 (2000):251–267.

22. Moloch, Freudenburg, and Paulsen, "History Repeats," 795; Clifford Geertz, *The Interpretation of Cultures* (New York: Basic Books, 1973). This is similar to what Jack Katz terms "retrodiction," an analytic method of looking at sequences of action from one time to a later time; see "From How to Why: On Luminous Description and Causal Inference in Ethnography (Part 1)," *Ethnography* 2:4 (2001): 443–473. Also see David J. Harding, Cybelle Fox, and Jal D. Mehta, "Studying Rare Events through Qualitative Case Studies: Lessons from a Study of Rampage School Shootings," *Sociological Methods and Research* 31:2 (2002):174–217; James Mahoney, "Revisiting General Theory in Historical Sociology," *Social Forces* 83:2 (2004):459–489; and the discussion of both/and methodology in Patricia Hill Collins, *Black Feminist Thought: Knowledge, Consciousness, and the Politics of Empowerment* (Boston: Unwin Hyman, 1990).

23. In *Getting Your Way*, James Jasper argues that groups involve multiple lines of strategic actions among various sets of competing and cooperating players who pull in different directions. This is true as well in grassroots activism. To show the patterns of path dependency in these groups, I focus on lines of action that shape the overall direction of the group, like decisions to recruit new members, change the group's issue focus, or create structures of leadership. However, there are considerable levels of complexity in the overlapping and conflicting strategic actions, interactions, and goals of individual activists and subsets of activists. These are not brought into focus by this analysis but are worthy of attention.

24. Mutz, *Hearing the Other Side*, 127; also see Mahoney, "Path Dependence." This dynamic is similar to the narrowing paths of action that Effler (*Laughing Saints*) identifies in activist groups, but she traces the origins of paths to obstacles that groups confront. I envision the origin of paths more broadly, since sequences of action can cumulate in paths without an identifiable obstacle.

25. Renée Anspach notes how the "social situations of participants influence not only their sense of the 'right' course of action but the 'facts' they select as relevant, and hence what they choose to designate as 'data'" (*Deciding Who Lives*, 49).

26. My focus is *how* grassroots groups operate in path-dependent ways and the consequences that follow. Although it is beyond the scope of this book to explain *why* they do so, individual psychology no doubt is a factor. As social psychologists document, people have a bias for the status quo in their decision making. Group-level factors matter too. In *Freedom Is an Endless Meeting* (21), Francesca Polletta notes that for social movements, "a tactical option or an organizational form may be appealing because it is similar to what we are used to." See also Rhomberg, *No There There*; Daniel A. McFarland, "Resistance as a Social Drama: A Study of Change-Oriented Encounters," *American Journal of Sociology* 109:6 (2004):1249–1318; Weick and Roberts, "Collective Mind in Organizations"; and

James N. Baron, Michael T. Hannan, and M. Diane Burton, "Labor Pains: Change in Organizational Models and Employee Turnover in Young, High-Tech Firms," *American Journal of Sociology* 106:4 (2001):960–1012; Becker, "The Power of Inertia," 304.

27. Paul Pierson. "Not Just What, but When: Timing and Sequence in Political Processes," *Studies in American Political Development* 14 (2000):76.

28. John Walton (*Storied Land*, 281) terms these "situational contingencies of action"; also see Neil Ferguson, "Crossing the Rubicon: Deciding to Become a Paramilitary in Northern Ireland," *International Journal of Conflict and Violence* 2:1 (2008):130–137.

29. William H Sewell Jr., "A Theory of Structure: Duality, Agency, and Transformation," *American Journal of Sociology* 98:1 (1992):1–29.

30. Path-dependency ideas have been used in social movement studies in a limited way, mostly to describe structural features that affect the outcomes of social movements like how policies of taxation channel social movement organizations toward a narrow range of structures, reported in John D. McCarthy, David W. Britt, and Mark Wolfson, "The Institutional Channeling of Social Movements by the State in the United States," in *Research in Social Movements, Conflicts and Change: A Research Annual*, Vol. 13, edited by Louis Kriesberg and Metta Spencer (Greenwich, CT: JAI Press, 1991), 45–76. Also see Paul Almeida, "The Sequencing of Success: Organizing Templates and Neoliberal Policy Outcomes," *Mobilization: An International Journal* 13:2 (2008):165–187.

31. Charles Tilly, "Contentious Repertoires in Great Britain, 1758–1834," in *Repertoires and Cycles of Collective Action*, edited by Mark Traugott (Durham, NC: Duke University Press, 1995), 15–42; also Minkoff, "Bending with the Wind," 1691; and Meyer, "Organizational Identity," 184.

32. Joseph. T. Mahoney, *Economic Foundations of Strategy* (Thousand Oaks, CA: Sage, 2005), and Sara Shostak, Peter Conrad, and Allan V. Horowitz, "Sequencing and Its Consequences: Path Dependence and the Relations between Genetics and Medicalization," *American Journal of Sociology* 114:1 (2008):287–316.

33. Abbott, *Time Matters*; Pierson, "Increasing Returns"; Ronald R. Aminzade, "Historical Sociology and Time," *Sociological Methods & Research* 20:4 (1992):456–480; and Katz, "From How to Why."

34. Activist groups are much quicker to change from a path on which they embark than are the deeply embedded macro structures like nation-states or modes of production that are the usual focus of path-dependency theories. As well, internal factors may be more likely to dislodge activist groups from their paths while external factors may be more influential in altering paths of macro social structures.

35. See Andrew Abbott, "On the Concept of Turning Point," *Comparative Social Research* 16 (1997):89–109, and his discussion in *Times Matters*, as well as Mueller and McCarthy, "Cultural Continuity and Structural Change," 258. On an individual level, turning points are narrated in life stories to denote transition, conversion, awakening, and salvation and are generally defined in hindsight, as in Tamara K. Hareven and Kanji Masaoka, "Turning Points and Transitions: Perceptions of the Life Course," *Journal of Family History* 13:1 (1988):271–289, or Thomas DeGloma, "The Social Logic of 'False Memories': Symbolic Awakenings and Symbolic Worlds in Survivor and Retractor Narratives," *Symbolic Interaction* 30:4 (2007):543–565. Studies of people engaged in extremist politics commonly use crises and turning points as explanatory concepts, as in Neil

Ferguson's account ("Crossing the Rubicon," 135–136) of the experiences of paramilitary insurgents in Northern Ireland as "they made the transition from civilian to insurgent." Drawing on work of the philosopher Karl Jaspers, Ferguson makes a compelling case for examining "the decision making processes an individual experiences when faced with a critical incident or boundary situation which causes them to self-reflect and imagine an altered future in which they purposely challenge the status quo and strive to act in a manner which will alter the socio-political situations." My work on U.S. racist groups (*Inside Organized Racism*), however, suggests that narrated accounts of such transitions may be highly influenced by subsequent experiences. See also Minkoff, "Bending with the Wind"; Deborah B. Balser, "The Impact of Environmental Factors on Factionalism and Schism in Social Movement Organizations," *Social Forces* 76:1 (1997):199–228; Minkoff and McCarthy, "Reinvigorating the Study"; and Morris, *Origins of the Civil Rights Movement*.

36. Abbott, "On the Concept of a Turning Point," 99. For macro-level studies, as Chris Rhomberg points out (*No There There*, 205), Jeffrey Haydu's reiterated problem-solving model ("Making Use of the Past") is a way out of the determinism of traditional path-dependency models; it shows that solutions used at one time become part of the context when the next problem is faced, so reiterated problem-solving structures generate problems that are solved differently at different times. Moreover, in contrast to path dependency, which positions problems as accidental and exogenous, Haydu's reiterated problem-solving approach shows how decisions at one time create a fault line for future problems and options for new solutions. See also Carol McClurg Mueller and John D. McCarthy, "Cultural Continuity and Structural Change: The Logic of Adaptation by Radical, Liberal, and Socialist Feminists to State Reconfiguration," in *Women's Movements Facing the Reconfigured State*, edited by Lee Ann Banaszak, Karen Beckwith, and Dieter Rucht (New York: Cambridge University Press, 2003), 219–241; Effler, *Laughing Saints*; and Pred, "Presidential Address." Beyond this study, but worth investigating, is whether turning points are more likely when internal and external rhythms of change operate in synch, what organizational scholars call "entrainment." See Ganz, "Why David Sometimes Wins," and Gersick, "Time and Transition," 16.

37. Sewell, "Three Temporalities."

38. Abbott, "On the Concept of Turning Point," 89.

39. On logics of action, see Donatella della Porta, *Social Movements, Political Violence, and the State: A Comparative Analysis of Italy and Germany* (New York: Cambridge University Press, 1995) and Larson and Sigal, "Does 'The Public' Think Politically?"

40. Mustafa Emirbayer and Ann Mische, "What Is Agency?" *American Journal of Sociology* 103:4 (1998):962–1023 (italics in original). Steven Hitlin and Glen Elder's life course perspective on agency and the self ("Time, Self, and the Curiously Abstract Concept of Agency," *Sociological Theory* 25:2 [2007]:173) also suggests that time is key to locating turning points in micro-level interactions: as actors are oriented in time, they implicate different aspects of an "active, socialized, meaning-making" self:

As actors become more or less concerned with the immediate moment versus long-term life goals, they employ different social psychological processes and exhibit different forms of agency. The intra-personal perception of what might be termed a "time horizon," a concentrated focus on a particular zone of temporal space, is a response to social situations and conditions of agentic action. Agency is exerted differentially depending on the actor's salient time horizon.

Agency, in this theory, is bound to how actors are oriented in time, and this shifts according to problems encountered in interaction. Two types are particularly applicable to activism. One is "pragmatic agency," which is situated in the present. It is expressed in actions that are chosen when habitual patterns are not possible. Such choices shape and express a coherent sense of "what we are 'really' like." I choose to do one action and not another because I am, biographically and now, the kind of person who will do that. I act a certain way because I am that kind of person, a sense of self-identity that is made firmer with each action taken on this basis. That I am *this* kind of person is an assessment of the past. Events or actions are selectively cobbled together to show that I am—in my essence—honest, talented, maternal, or spiritual.

Hitlin and Elder develop the concept of "pragmatic agency" to describe the time orientation of individual action, but a similar idea applies to collective action. Activist groups forge actions that build a sense of their collective character. They see themselves—therefore they *are* and will act—confrontational or accommodating, laid-back or eager, broad or focused. This sense of a collective self has direct implications for what activists see themselves as able to do. They consider confrontational tactics always, or almost never. They press for rapid action, or entertain endless discussion. They draw information from many sources, or from the same sources repeatedly.

Hitlin and Elder's concept of "life course agency" is also useful for understanding activist groups. Life course agency describes the time horizon of actors who reach beyond pragmatic choices of the present, engage a longer view of time, and take action to move toward a distant future. This kind of agency incorporates aspects of the self beyond those activated in pragmatic action, such as a sense of capability to reach goals. The converse is true as well: those who see little possibility of directing their future are unlikely to have long-term plans or to engage in actions of life course agency.

41. Emirbayer and Mische, "What Is Agency?" 966, 968.
42. Emirbayer and Mische ("What Is Agency?") allow the possibility that their theory could apply to collective actors. However, it is important to be cautious when using theories of individual agency to understand groups because the conflicting agendas of individuals can lurk beneath what appears to be a unitary collective. Moreover, there is a long debate about whether social groups, or only individuals, can be said to act. Although I use individual-level concepts to examine group-level phenomena, I do not claim that these are parallel. In my view, activist groups do not act—or have a self—as a unified entity. They are constituted by individual actors who act and interact in a group context but are not reducible to the group. At the same time, activist groups are more than the sum of their individual actors. Even more so than task teams—whose dynamics are clearly shown to be more than an aggregate of team members—grassroots activist groups work to develop collective interpretations and action. They might not "act" as a group in an ontological sense, but activist groups are oriented temporally in their collective actions. If they lack a singular self, they have (at least partially) shared time horizons.

43. Robin D. G. Kelley. "Finding the Strength to Love and Dream," *Chronicle of Higher Education* 7 (2002a).

44. Jasper, *Art of Moral Protest*, 65.

45. Piven and Cloward, *Poor People's Movements*; Frances Fox Piven and Richard A. Cloward, *Regulating the Poor: The Functions of Public Welfare* (Ann Arbor: University of Michigan, 1993); and J. B. Shank, "Crisis: A Useful Category of Post-Social Scientific Historical Analysis?" *American Historical Review* 113 (2008):1090–1099. Dave Elder-Vass ("Reconciling Archer and Bourdieu in an Emergenist Theory of Action," *Sociological Theory* 25:4 [2007]:325–346) notes that it is not only in crisis that habitus doesn't provide a usable response. However, activist groups define a situation in which their usual responses don't work as, in fact, a crisis.

46. Larson and Sigal, "Does 'The Public' Think Politically?"; Kurzman, *The Unthinkable Revolution in Iran*, 171; and Rhomberg, *No There There*, 205.

47. Kurzman, *The Unthinkable Revolution in Iran*, 9; Sidney Tarrow, "Cycles of Collective Action: Between Moments of Madness and the Repertoire of Contention," in *Repertoires and Cycles of Collective Action*, edited by Mark Traugott (Durham, NC: Duke University Press, 1995), 89; Stephen Downing, "The Social Construction of Entrepreneurship: Narrative and Dramatic Processes in the Coproduction of Organizations and Identities," *Entrepreneurship: Theory and Practice* 29:2 (2005):185–204; and Smith, *Moral, Believing Animals*, 31.

48. This is similar to the hermeneutical analysis of action as text, a model for which is developed in Kathleen Blee and Dwight Billings, "Reconstructing Daily Life in the Past: An Hermeneutical Approach to Ethnographic Data," The Sociological Quarterly 27:4 (1996):443–462. See Paul Ricoeur, "The Model of the Text: Meaningful Action Considered as Text," *New Literary History* 5:1 (1973):91–117; Diane Vaughan, *The Challenger Launch Decision: Risky Technology, Culture, and Deviance at NASA* (Chicago: University of Chicago Press, 2006); and Mayer N. Zald, "Ideologically Structured Action: An Enlarged Agenda for Social Movement Research," *Mobilization. An International Journal* 5:1 (2000):1–16.

49. Becker, *Tricks*, 61–62; Diane Vaughan, *Uncoupling: Turning Points in Intimate Relationships* (New York: Oxford University Press, 1986). Also see Howard Becker, "Notes on the Concept of Commitment," *American Journal of Sociology* 66:1(1960):32–40. This is similar to Andrew Abbott's "pattern-based approach," which begins with clusters of cases with similarities in "On the Concept of Turning Point."

50. Allan Pred ("Presidential Address," 8) argues that "by limiting and enabling what people can do, power relations also limit and enable what people know (and are able to say) and how they perceive and think" although his analysis mostly focuses on structure, not interpretation.

51. Emirbayer and Mische, "What Is Agency?" 1011. Also see Marshall Ganz, "Resources and Resourcefulness: Strategic Capacity in the Unionization of California Agriculture, 1959–1966," *American Journal of Sociology* 105:4 (2000):1003–1062, and Ganz, "Why David Sometimes Wins."

52. Tilly, *Big Structures*; Pierson, "Increasing Returns"; and Pierson, "Not Just What, but When." This is what Bryant and Hall ("Theories and Methods Applied," ix) consider an example of 'deep lines' of causality, like how early choices have strong effects. In "Reversals of Fortune: Path Dependency, Problem Solving, and Temporal Cases" (*Theory & Society* 39:1 [2010]:28), Jeffrey Haydu notes that "variable-based accounts underestimate the role of serendipity in historical outcomes."

53. Kwame Anthony Appiah, *Experiments in Ethics* (Cambridge, MA: Harvard University Press, 2008), 6.

54. For a similar argument, see Francesca Polletta, *It Was Like a Fever: Storytelling in Protest and Politics* (Chicago: University of Chicago Press, 2006).

55. Jeff Goodwin, "'The Struggle Made Me a Nonracialist': Why There Was So Little Terrorism in the Antiapartheid Struggle," *Mobilization: An International Journal* 12:2 (2007):193–203.

56. Quotations from different people in a single meeting, from author's field notes.

57. Nina Eliasoph and Paul Lichterman, "Culture in Interaction," *American Journal of Sociology* 108:4 (2003):735–794.

CHAPTER 3

1. Randall Collins, *Interaction Ritual Chains* (Princeton, NJ: Princeton University Press, 2004), 36. The term originally appears in Emile Durkheim, *The Elementary Forms of Religious Life* (New York: Free Press, 1912/1995), xli.

2. Smith, *Moral, Believing Animals*, 52–53.

3. Lichterman (*Elusive Togetherness*, 15) writes about "group-building customs" by which activist groups define membership without explicit statements.

4. All activist groups wrestle with who they are, especially in their early days, but the intensity with which they do so varies. For some, it becomes a major focus, even a point of conflict. In others, self-definition generates little discussion and no friction.

5. Tilly, "Contentious Repertoires"; Melucci, *Challenging Codes*; and Kimberly Dugan and Jo Reger, "Voice and Agency in Social Movement Outcomes," *Qualitative Sociology* 29:4 (2006):467–484.

6. For example, one group developed a strong collective identity as guardians of civil liberties, but this identity dissolved over time as its members began to discard the group's plans of action in favor of individual contacts with local officials who, they thought, would pass a referendum.

7. Not all grassroots groups exclude current members who don't fit their emerging self-definition as REBORN did. Many search for labels that broadly encompass all members and shy away from those that would exclude any.

8. Smith, *Moral, Believing Animals*, 43.

9. Ibid., 41; also see Kathleen Blee and Amy McDowell, "Social Movement Audiences," *Sociological Forum* 27:1 (2012), forthcoming.

10. Nira Yuval-Davis, "Belonging and the Politics of Belonging," *Patterns of Prejudice* 40:3 (2006),197. Rhomberg (*No There There*) makes a similar point about the perils of assuming that groups persist with the same actors.

11. Expediency logics of a different sort are evident in the effort to import repertoires of tactics and ideas from other activist groups, as well as the use of trial and error in action sequences; see Tilly, "Contentious Repertoires" and Francesca Polletta, "How Participatory Democracy Became White: Culture and Organizational Choice," *Mobilization: An International Journal* 10:2 (2005):271–288.

12. Yuval-Davis, "Belonging," 204. Also see McVeigh, Neblett and Shafiq, "Explaining Social Movement Outcomes"; Noel Ignatiev, *How the Irish Became White* (New Brunswick, NJ: Rutgers University Press, 1996); and Karen Bodkin, *How Jews Became White Folks: And What That Says about Race in America* (New Brunswick, NJ: Rutgers University Press, 1998). An important theory of social boundaries is Lamont and Molnár, "The Study of Boundaries"; also see Lamont, *Dignity of Working Men*.

13. Jasper, *Art of Moral Protest*, 244.
14. Verta Taylor's substantial body of work on emotion in activist cultures develops these ideas more fully. See "Watching for Vibes: Bringing Emotion into the Study of Feminist Organizations," in *Feminist Organizations: Harvest of the New Women's Movement*, edited by Myra Marx Ferree and Patricia Yancey Martin (Philadelphia: Temple University Press, 1995), 223–233; *Rock-a-by Baby: Feminism, Self-Help, and Postpartum Depression* (New York: Routledge, 1996); and "Emotions and Identity in Women's Self-Help Movements," in *Self, Identity, and Social Movements*, edited by Sheldon Stryker, Timothy J. Owens, and Robert W. White (Minneapolis: University of Minnesota Press, 2000), 271–299.
15. Kathleen Blee and Ashley Currier, "Character Building: The Dynamics of Emerging Social Movement Groups," *Mobilization: An International Journal* 10 (2005):129–144, and Blee and Currier, "How Local Social Movement Groups."
16. Ethnomethodologists like Harold Garfinkel have been successful in bringing such categories to the surface. See his *Seeing Sociologically: The Routine Grounds of Social Action* (Boulder, CO: Paradigm, 2005).
17. Lichterman (*Elusive Togetherness*) points out that the meaning of membership comes from the larger culture; it is not something that activist groups create. This chapter examines how they do so.
18. Ronald R. Aminzade and Doug McAdam, "Emotion and Contentious Politics," in *Silence and Voice in the Study of Contentious Politics*, edited by Ronald R. Aminzade, Jack A. Goldstone, Doug McAdam, Elizabeth Perry, William H. Sewell Jr., Sidney Tarrow, and Charles Tilly (New York: Cambridge University Press, 2001), 27.
19. Jasper's "extension dilemma," which counterposes expanding a group with the loss of unity (*Getting Your* Way, 127–129), captures some of this debate although StK wrestled with a broader sense of how to define itself. Its questions about personal commitment and the group's likely longevity, in particular, were raised as hopeful expectations rather than dilemmas.
20. Albert O. Hirschman, *Exit, Voice, and Loyalty: Responses to Decline in Firms, Organizations, and States* (Cambridge, MA: Harvard University Press, 1970).
21. Even in formalized social movement organizations, membership can have a variety of definitions, including tacit supporters on e-mail or mailing lists, those who attend occasional events, and financial donors, as well as those engaged in decision making and agenda setting. As Michael W. Foley and Bob Edwards note about nonprofit organizations, "membership is an extremely slippery and value-laden concept," in Foley and Edwards, "How Do Members Count?" 12.
22. Yuval-Davis, "Belonging," 197. Also see James Downton Jr. and Paul Wehr, "Persistent Pacifism: How Activist Commitment Is Developed and Sustained," *Journal of Peace Research* 35:5 (1998):531–550.
23. To assess the emotional mood of activist groups, the research team coded the emotional content of exchanges in meetings for a subset of 12 activist groups that had widely varying rates of attendance over time. We found a slightly higher number of negative dynamics (expressions of frustration, helplessness, anger) in meetings in which the attendance was lower than the previous meeting, but the effect was quite modest.
24. David Knoke and Nancy Wisely, "Social Movements," in *Political Networks*, edited by David Knoke (New York: Cambridge University Press, 1990), 57–84.

CHAPTER 4

1. Alexander, *Civil Sphere*, 277. Snow and Benford's "Ideology, Frame Resonance, and Participant Mobilization" is an excellent example of this literature on framing.

2. Alexander, *Civil Sphere*, 219; Steinberg, "Toward a Dialogic Analysis," 224; Polletta, "Plotting Protest," 33; Gayatri Chakravorty Spivak, "Can the Subaltern Speak?" in *Marxism and the Interpretation of Culture*, edited by Cary Nelson and Lawrence Grossberg (Urbana: University of Illinois Press, 1988), 271–313.

3. Cristina B. Gibson, "From Knowledge Accumulation to Accommodation: Cycles of Collective Cognition in Work Groups" *Journal of Organizational Behavior* 22:2 (2001):121–134; Steinberg, "Toward a Dialogic Analysis," 209. As many studies show, a shared sense that a problem can be remedied through collective action is the foundation for solidarity and collective identity in activist groups. Among these, see Adams, "Protest and the Scale Politics"; Charles Tilly, "Contentious Repertoires"; William A. Gamson, "Commitment and Agency in Social Movements," *Sociological Forum* 6:1(1991):27–50; Alberto Melucci, "The Process of Collective Identity," in *Social Movements and Culture*, edited by Hank Johnston and Bert Klandermans (Minneapolis: University of Minnesota Press, 1995), 41–63; and David A. Snow and Doug McAdam, "Identity Work Processes in the Context of Social Movements: Clarifying the Identity/Movement Nexus," in *Self, Identity and Social Movements*, edited by Sheldon Stryker, Timothy J. Owens, and Robert W. White (Minneapolis: University of Minnesota Press, 2000), 41–67.

4. Walsh, *Talking about Politics*; Nina Eliasoph and Paul Lichterman, "We Begin with our Favorite Theory . . . : Reconstructing the Extended Case Method," *Sociological Theory* 17:2 (1999):230, italics in original; Pamela E. Oliver and Hank Johnston, "What a Good Idea! Ideologies and Frames in Social Movement Research," *Mobilization: An International Journal* 5:1 (2000):44–45.

5. Eliasoph and Lichterman, "Culture in Interaction," 736.

6. There is considerable research on the ideologies of social movement groups, especially on how these connect group beliefs to the concerns of members, potential recruits, and audiences and how the ideologies of groups affect strategies, recruitment, actions, and outcomes; less studied, however, is how these ideologies come to be. See Snow and Benford, "Master Frames and Cycles of Protest"; Snow and Benford, "Ideology, Frame Resonance"; Blee, *Inside Organized Racism*; Bert Klandermans, "The Formation and Mobilization of Consensus," in *International Social Movement Research, From Structure to Action: Comparing Social Movement Research across Cultures*, Vol. 1, edited by Bert Klandermans, Hanspeter Kriesi, and Sidney Tarrow (Greenwich, CT: JAI Press, 1988), 173–196.

7. Marcel Stoetzler and Nira Yuval-Davis, "Standpoint Theory, Situated Knowledge and the Situated Imagination," *Feminist Theory* 3:3 (2002):321, 325, 326 (italics in the original).

8. Such expansive political imaginations are found among activist groups in Donatella della Porta's study of the global justice movement, "Making the Polis: Social Forums and Democracy in the Global Justice Movement," *Mobilization: An International Journal* 10:1 (2005):73–94.

9. A similar problem arises as activist groups want a scope sufficiently narrow to make it possible to take action but broad enough that their actions will result in social change, although this is often a strategic and instrumental question rather

than an interpretive one. A variety of such dilemmas are theorized in Jasper, *Getting Your Way.*

10. Duchesne and Haegel, "Avoiding or Accepting Conflict."

11. Ricouer, "The Model of the Text."

12. Jasper, *Art of Moral Protest*, 135. On political opportunity, see works by David S. Meyer, especially his "Protest and Political Opportunities," *Annual Review of Sociology* 30 (2004):125–145; Meyer and Douglas R. Imig, "Political Opportunity and the Rise and Decline of Interest Group Sectors," *Social Science Journal* 30:3 (1993):253–270; and Meyer and Debra C. Minkoff, "Conceptualizing Political Opportunity," *Social Forces* 82:4 (2004):1457–1492.

13. Susan Neiman, *Moral Clarity* (Princeton, NJ: Princeton University Press, 2009), 5.

14. Kwame Anthony Appiah, *Experiments in Ethics* (Cambridge, MA: Harvard University Press, 2008),159. Moral concerns underlie many facets of activism, beyond the issues they address. As Daniel McFarland ("Resistance as a Social Drama") argues, for instance, the very nature of social interaction creates a "moral imperative" that shapes action. Also see Hart, *Cultural Dilemmas.*

15. Another type of indirect moral clam is exemplified by a member of a same-sex marriage group who insisted that members should want to change the law because they are "horrified that such an injustice has not been corrected yet," not because they have a personal investment in the cause.

16. Activist groups rely on a variety of information sources, of which they have differing levels of trust. Some, but not all, of the progressive groups believed the accounts on Indymedia, the alternative, left-oriented Web site, but greeted mainstream media reports with skepticism. Yet activists do not simply dismiss most media sources, even those they regard as biased. They also rely on them for some news and as venues to publicize events and reach a larger public. An anti-war group, for instance, talked about presenting its views as "simply as possible" to the press so they wouldn't confuse their various issues or have one issue "obscure the other." A peace group decided that since the "regular media" were "keeping alive" the prisoner abuse scandal at Guantanamo, they did not need to spend energy on the issue. An animal rights group that was openly ridiculed in local newspapers decided that even these negative depictions were a "minor victory" in providing publicity. Indeed, almost all activist groups judged the effectiveness of their actions in part by how they are covered in mainstream media. Nonetheless, relations with the mainstream media can be contentious. One group dissolved in acrimony when a media person came to a meeting. After he left, recriminations flew, one woman accusing unspecified others of inviting him although "I thought we had agreed: no media at our meetings," others yelling that "I don't feel comfortable [with him here]," that "we need to be open to the media," that "they [media] are unscrupulous," and that the media will "use our comments against us."

17. Carol Heimer, "Cases and Biographies: An Essay on Routinization and the Nature of Comparison," *Annual Review of Sociology* 27 (2001):47–76.

18. It wasn't simply that members feared retribution by the perpetrators of violence; in fact, they provided very explicit information when asked about an incident and openly disparaged those who went along with the "Stop Snitching" campaign then raging in Pittsburgh's poor neighborhoods.

19. Paul Lichterman, "Talking Identity in the Public Sphere: Broad Visions and Small Spaces in Sexual Identity Politics," *Theory and Society* 28:1 (1999):101–141. This

is similar to Alison Assiter's notion of "epistemological communities" in which people, unified by political values and mutual respect, "shape their access to knowledge collectively rather than individually," detailed in her *Enlightened Women: Modernist Feminism in a Postmodern Age* (New York: Routledge, 1996), 77; 200. Also see Marcel Stoetzler and Nira Yuval-Davis, "Standpoint Theory, Situated Knowledge and the Situated Imagination," 320.

20. Vaughan, *Challenger Launch Decision*.
21. Paul Lichterman. "Talking Identity," 104.
22. Norbert L. Kerr and R. Scott Tindale, "Group Performance and Decision Making," *Annual Review of Psychology* 55 (2004):638.
23. Polletta, *Freedom Is an Endless Meeting*; Francesca Polletta, "Plotting Protest: Mobilizing Stories in the 1960 Student Sit-Ins," in *Stories of Change: Narrative and Social Movements*, edited by Joseph E. Davis (Albany: SUNY Press, 2002), 31–52.
24. Ibid.

CHAPTER 5

1. Walsh, *Talking about Politics*.
2. The idea of sorting principles in activism is based on the work of Mario Luis Small in his *Unanticipated Gains: Origins of Network Inequality in Everyday Life* (New York: Oxford University Press, 2009). On the issue of how people decide to be activists or not, see Meyer, "Social Movements"; David Meyer, "Restating the Women Question," in *Women's Movements Facing the Reconfigured State*, edited by Lee Ann Banaszak, Karen Beckwith, and Dieter Rucht (New York: Cambridge University Press, 2003), 277; and Mahmut Bayazit and Elizabeth A. Mannix, "Should I Stay or Should I Go? Predicting Team Members' Intent to Remain in the Team," *Small Group Research* 34:3 (2003):290–321.
3. Polletta (*Freedom Is an Endless Meeting*) finds that friendship can also limit and create problems in activist groups. I focus on expressions of solidarity within the group—that is, the group's feeling—rather than the existence of social ties among members outside the group.
4. There is a substantial literature on how interpersonal ties among participants and between participants and outsiders impact social movement recruitment, retention, and outcomes. See Valocchi, *Social Movements and Activism*; della Porta, *Social Movements, Political Violence, and the State*; William A. Gamson, *Talking Politics* (New York: Cambridge University Press, 1992); Doug McAdam, "Recruitment to High-Risk Activism: The Case of Freedom Summer"; and David A. Snow, Louis A. Zurcher Jr., and Sheldon Ekland-Olson, "Social Networks and Social Movements: A Microstructural Approach to Differential Recruitment," *American Sociological Review* 45 (1980):787–801. Such ties can be domineering or supportive, enduring or fleeting, strong or weak—characteristics that affect the movement's collective identity, members' understandings of grievances and opportunities, retention of recruits, and culture. There are also a number of significant studies of the role of emotion in activism, especially Mary Bernstein, "The Contradictions of Gay Identity: Forging Identity in Vermont," in *Social Movements: Identity, Culture, and the State*, edited by David S. Meyer, Nancy Whittier, and Belinda Robnett (New York: Oxford University Press, 2002), 85–104; Kathleen M. Blee, "Managing Emotion in the Study of Right-Wing Extremism," *Qualitative Sociology* 21 (1988):381–399; Wini Breines, *Community and Organization in the New Left, 1962–1968: The Great Refusal* (New York:

Praeger, 1982); Lory Britt and David Heise, "From Shame to Pride in Identity Politics," in *Self, Identity and Social Movements*, edited by Sheldon Stryker, Timothy J. Owens, and Robert W. White (Minneapolis: University of Minnesota Press, 2000), 252–268; Craig Calhoun, "Putting Emotions in Their Place," in *Passionate Politics*, 45–57; Myra Marx Ferree, "The Political Context of Rationality: Rational Choice Theory and Resource Mobilization," in *Frontiers in Social Movement Theory*, edited by Aldon Morris and Carol Mueller (New Haven, CT: Yale University Press, 1992), 29–52; Myra Marx Ferree, "Soft Repression: Ridicule, Stigma, and Silencing in Gender-Based Movements," paper presented at the Collective Behavior and Social Movement Section of the American Sociological Association workshop, "Authority in Contention," Notre Dame, IN, August 2002; Jeff Goodwin, James M. Jasper, and Francesca Polletta, "Introduction: Why Emotions Matter," in *Passionate Politics*, 1–24; Rebecca Klatch, *A Generation Divided: The New Left, the New Right, and the 1960s* (Berkeley: University of California Press, 1999); Verta Taylor and Nancy Whittier, "Analytic Approaches to Social Movement Culture: The Culture of the Women's Movement," in *Social Movements and Culture*, edited by Hank Johnston and Bert Klandermans (Minneapolis: University of Minnesota Press, 1995), 163–187; Deborah Gould, *Moving Politics: Emotion and ACT UP's Fight against AIDS* (Chicago: University of Chicago Press, 2009); and Nancy Whittier, *Feminist Generations: The Persistence of the Radical Women's Movement* (Philadelphia, PA: Temple University Press, 1995).

5. Craig Calhoun, "Putting Emotions in Their Place," in Goodwin et al., *Passionate Politics*, 53, 55. Calhoun further notes that people's emotions can be shaped by the actions and interactions in social groups: "Movements produce emotions; they do not simply reflect emotional orientations brought to them by members." Also see Daniel A. McFarland, "Resistance as a Social Drama: A Study of Change Oriented Encounters," *American Journal of Sociology* 109:6 (2004):1249–1318. Anne Kane discusses the "emotional habitus" of activism in "Finding Emotion in Social Movement Processes: Irish Land Movement Metaphors and Narratives," in Goodwin et al., *Passionate Politics*, 251–266. Relatedly, Aminzade and McAdam ("Emotion and Contentious Politics") posit the notion of a collective "economy of affection." My focus on the construction of interpersonal dynamics is in contrast to studies that illuminate how these are strategically shaped by leaders of social movements. I draw on Randall Collins's theory of "emotional attachment" ("Social Movements") and Deborah Gould's study of AIDS activism (*Moving Politics*), as well as Francesca Polletta and Ed Amenta, "Conclusion: Second that Emotion? Lessons from Once-Novel Concepts in Social Movement Research," in Goodwin et al., *Passionate Politics*, 303–316. See also Sidney Tarrow, "Silence and Voice in the Study of Contentious Politics: Introduction," in Aminzade et al., *Silence and Voice*,1–13, and Verta Taylor, "Emotions and Identity."

6. See Diehl and McFarland, "Toward a Historical Sociology," and Aminzade and McAdam, "Emotion and Contentious Politics," especially p. 27.

7. Carey and Smith, "Capturing the Group Effect."

8. Fine, "Public Narration and Group Culture," 142.

9. This is an example of what Jasper (*Getting Your Way*, 125) describes as the "Janus dilemma," in which the effort to keep a group working together conflicts with the effort to work toward external goals.

10. Hirschman, *Exit, Voice, and Loyalty.*

11. This is in sharp contrast to the internal dynamics that scholars describe in other activist groups, perhaps especially those in the 1970s and 1980s, as, for example, Barbara Epstein's *Political Protest and Cultural Revolution: Nonviolent Direct Action in the 1970s and 1980s* (Berkeley: University of California Press, 1991).

12. Elizabeth A. Armstrong and Suzanna M. Crage, "Movements and Memory: The Making of the Stonewall Myth," *American Sociological Review* 71 (2006):726.

13. See Karen Beckwith, "Women's Movements at Century's End: Excavation and Advances in Political Science," *Annual Review of Political Science* 4 (2001):371–390, and Cathryn Johnson, Timothy J. Dowd, and Cecilia L. Ridgeway, "Legitimacy as a Social Process," *Annual Review of Sociology* 32 (2006):53–78. This is also similar to what Lynn M. Sanders talks about as "epistemological authority" in which speakers are able to have statements acknowledged by others in the process of collective deliberation in her "Against Deliberation," *Political Theory* 25(3): 349. Most scholarship on credibility in activism focuses instead on how activists assert their credibility to outside audiences, as does Steven Epstein, "The Construction of Lay Expertise: AIDS Activism and the Forging of Credibility in the Reform of Clinical Trials," *Science, Technology & Human Values* 20 (October 1995):408–437, and Wood, *Faith in Action*.

14. There are many facets of how credibility is assigned that are relevant but not considered here in order to allow a more pointed focus on the main issues raised in activist groups. But these broader aspects of credibility surely play some role. For instance, Mary Bernstein and James M. Jasper ("Interests and Credibility: Whistleblowers in Technological Conflicts," *Social Science Information* 35:3 [1996]:565–589) discuss how credibility is reduced to the extent that the speaker is considered to have a personal interest in the topic.

15. Sherryl Kleinman, *Opposing Ambitions: Gender and Identity in an Alternative Organization* (Chicago: University of Chicago Press, 1996).

16. Sanders, "Against Deliberation," 370.

17. Sanders, "Against Deliberation," 355. Bettina F. Aptheker's autobiography—*Intimate Politics: How I Grew Up Red, Fought for Free Speech, and Became a Feminist Rebel* (Emeryville, CA: Seal Press, 2006)—provides a powerful account of how credibility is tied to social status as she relates that people were more willing to believe her stories of abuse by the FBI than by her famous and well-regarded father.

18. Sanders, "Against Deliberation," 353, 349, 365. Sanders points to other factors that shape how equitable the dynamics of groups will be, such as how a group defines its task. She notes that studies of courtroom juries find that "verdict-driven" juries (which push for a quick resolution) are less likely to have broad input into their deliberations than "evidence-driven" juries (which weigh possible verdicts more extensively). Among activist groups, the pattern is less clear. To some extent, groups with looming deadlines and intense pressure to accomplish tasks are more likely than less driven groups to have status inequities in their dynamics, but the direction of causality is unclear since high-status members might push groups to be verdict-driven.

19. Duchesne and Haegel, "Avoiding or Accepting Conflict," 8.

20. There is a robust literature on leadership in activist groups, including Ronald R. Aminzade, Jack A. Goldstone, and Elizabeth J. Perry, "Leadership Dynamics and Dynamics of Contention," in *Silence and Voice*, 126–154; Polletta, *Freedom Is an Endless Meeting*; Belinda Robnett, *How Long? How Long? African-American Women and the Struggle for Civil Rights* (New York: Oxford University Press, 1999); Sharon Nepstad and Clifford Bob, "When Do Leaders Matter? Hypotheses on

Leadership Dynamics in Social Movements," *Mobilization: An International Journal* 11:1(2006):1–22; and Klandermans, "Formation and Mobilization."

21. Less explicit, but commonly enforced in emerging activist groups, are conventions that comments must follow the topic under discussion, that comments should not cause the meeting to continue longer than necessary, that discussions should remain civil, and that important matters should have more time than smaller, unimportant points.

22. Elizabeth J. Perry, "Moving the Masses: Emotion Work in the Chinese Revolution," *Mobilization: An International Journal* 7:2 (2002):111–128.

CHAPTER 6

1. Andrew J. Perrin (*Citizen Speak: The Democratic Imagination in American Life* [Chicago: University of Chicago Press, 2006], 2) says that it is "in conversation with others" that a "democratic imagination" is born. Also see Raymond Geuss, *Politics and the Imagination* (Princeton, NJ: Princeton University Press, 2010), and Cornel West, *Democracy Matters: Winning the Fight against Imperialism* (London: Penguin Press, 2004).

2. Appiah, *Experiments in Ethics*; Smith, *Moral, Believing Animals*.

3. Their understandings are captured in Kwame Anthony Appiah's argument (*Experiments in Ethics*, 22) that "if you say somebody *ought* to do something, you must be supposing that it is something they *can* do." When activist groups evaluate what they ought to do, they take into account their capacity to do so.

4. Ruth Wilson Gilmore, *Golden Gulag: Prisons, Surplus, Crisis, and Opposition in Globalizing California* (Berkeley: University of California Press, 2007), 27.

5. At times, activist groups can enable possibilities that were previously uncharted and unleash what Jeffrey Goldfarb calls "zones of political freedom and creativity" in his *The Politics of Small Things: The Power of the Powerless in Dark Times* (Chicago: University of Chicago Press, 1996), 68.

6. The intentional and innovative nature of such efforts can be difficult to see from a distance, the former seeming habitual and the latter appearing to be simple unsettledness. See Joan Wallach Scott, *Only Paradoxes to Offer: Feminism and the Rights of Man* (Cambridge, MA: Harvard University Press, 2008), 17.

7. Smith, *Moral, Believing Animals*.

8. Norman F. Cantor, *In the Wake of the Plague: Black Death and the World It Made* (New York: Perennial/Harpers Collins, 2002), 218.

9. Observing activism up close, through a zoom lens rather than a panoramic one, can uncover subtleties that are otherwise invisible. As Cantor (*In the Wake*, 122) writes of the natural sciences, "Galileo, Newton, and above all Einstein knew that truth was in the details, that knowledge of nature was gained by the closest possible scrutiny of very small segments of natural processes." See also Giovanni Levi, "On Microhistory," in *New Perspectives on Historical Writing*, edited by Peter Burke (University Park: Pennsylvania State University Press, 1991), 93–113; Carlo Ginzburg, "Latitudes, Slaves, and the Bible: An Experiment in Microhistory," in *Science without Laws*, 243–263; and Kevin M. Kruse, *White Flight: Atlanta and the Making of Modern Conservatism* (Princeton, NJ: Princeton University Press, 2005), 11.

10. Melucci (*Challenging Codes*, 185) calls this the "paradox of small interventions producing big effects."

11. Duncan J. Watts, "Is Justin Timberlake a Product of Cumulative Advantage? The New Theory of the Hit Record," *New York Times Magazine* (April 25, 2007):22–25.

12. Javier Auyero and Débora Alejandra Swistun, *Flammable: Environmental Suffering in an Argentine Shantytown* (New York: Oxford, 2009), 144.
13. Such a focus has limitations, of course. Looking at activist groups rather than subgroups or individuals might suggest more consensus and unity of purpose than is the case. It misses evidence that is beyond or within the level of group experience, such as the motives, emotions, and perspectives of each activist and broader cultural process that give meaning to what happens in the group.
14. Isaac, "History Made."
15. Robert Michel, *Political Parties* (New York: Free Press, 1966).
16. Alexander, *The Civil Sphere*; Snow, "Master Frames and Cycles of Protest"; Snow and Benford, "Ideology, Frame Resonance, and Participant Mobilization"; and Douglas Bevington and Chris Dixon, "Movement-Relevant Theory: Rethinking Social Movement Scholarship and Activism," *Social Movement Studies* 4:2 (2005):185–208.
17. Geuss, *Politics and the Imagination*, 87.
18. In a few groups, these positions overlapped; the same member or small set of members was considered cognitively central and highly credible and held official or semi-official leadership positions. More often, different persons held these roles. It is possible, although beyond the scope of these data, that these roles increasingly overlap as activist groups become settled and formally established.
19. Appiah quotes the nineteenth-century French philosopher Ernest Renan as saying, "forgetting, and I would even say historical error, is an essential element in the creation of a nation" in his *Experiments in Ethics*, 6.
20. Geuss, *Politics and the Imagination*, 87.
21. Kathleen Blee and Ashley Currier, 2011. "Ethics beyond the IRB: An Introductory Essay," *Qualitative Sociology* 34:3 (2011):401–413; Valocchi, *Social Movements and Activism*.

APPENDIX

1. Meyer, "Social Movements."
2. The spaces of mobilization are explored in Dingxin Zhao, "Ecologies of Social Movement: Social Mobilization during the 1989 Prodemocracy Movement in Beijing," *American Journal of Sociology* 103:6 (1998):1493–1529.
3. Jennifer Mason, *Qualitative Researching* (Thousand Oaks, CA: Sage, 2002), 123–125.
4. Calvin Morrill, David A. Snow, and Cindy H. White, *Together Alone: Personal Relationships in Public Places* (Berkeley: University of California Press, 2005), x.
5. Robert M. Emerson, Rachel I. Fretz, and Linda L. Shaw, *Writing Ethnographic Fieldnotes* (Chicago: University of Chicago Press, 1995).
6. Biologists have demonstrated repeatedly the value of such descriptive detail to science, as discussed in Creager et al., *Science without Laws*. Sociologists should similarly value basic data about social processes. See also Abbott, *Time*.
7. Kathleen M. Blee and Verta Taylor, "Semi-Structured Interviewing in Social Movement Research," in *Methods of Social Movement Research*, edited by Bert Klandermans and Suzanne Staggenborg (Minneapolis: University of Minnesota Press, 2002), 92–117.
8. Chris Atton, "Reshaping Social Movement Media for a New Millennium," *Social Movement Studies* 2:1 (2003):10.
9. Nicole Constable, *Romance on a Global Stage: Pen Pals, Virtual Ethnography, and "Mail Order" Marriages* (Berkeley: University of California Press, 2003).
10. Mason, *Qualitative Researching*.

BIBLIOGRAPHY

Abbott, Andrew. 1992. "What Do Cases Do? Some Notes on Activity in Sociological Analysis." Pp. 53–82 in *What Is a Case? Exploring the Foundations of Social Inquiry*, edited by Charles C. Ragin and Howard S. Becker. New York: Cambridge University Press.

———. 1997. "On the Concept of Turning Point." *Comparative Social Research* 16:89–109.

———. 2001. *Time Matters: On Theory and Method*. Chicago: University of Chicago Press.

Adams, Paul C. 1996. "Protest and the Scale Politics of Communications." *Political Geography* 15(5):419–441.

Agnew, John A. 1987. *Place and Politics: The Geographical Mediation of State and Society*. Boston: Allen and Unwin.

Alexander, Jeffrey C. 2006. *The Civil Sphere*. New York: Oxford University Press.

Almeida, Paul. 2008. "The Sequencing of Success: Organizing Templates and Neoliberal Policy Outcomes." *Mobilization: An International Journal* 13(2):165–187.

Aminzade, Ronald R. 1992. "Historical Sociology and Time." *Sociological Methods & Research* 20(4):456–480.

Aminzade, Ronald R., Jack A. Goldstone, and Elizabeth J. Perry. 2001. "Leadership Dynamics and Dynamics of Contention." Pp. 126–153 in Aminzade et al., *Silence and Voice*.

Aminzade, Ronald R. and Doug McAdam. 2001. "Emotion and Contentious Politics." Pp. 14–50 in Aminzade et al., *Silence and Voice*.

Aminzade, Ronald R. and Elizabeth J. Perry. 2001. "The Sacred, Religious, and Secular in Contentious Politics: Blurring Boundaries." Pp. 155–178 in Aminzade et al., *Silence and Voice*.

Aminzade, Ronald R., Jack A. Goldstone, Doug McAdam, Elizabeth J. Perry, William H. Sewell Jr., Sidney Tarrow, and Charles Tilly, eds. 2001. *Silence and Voice in the Study of Contentious Politics*. New York: Cambridge University Press.

Anderson, Benedict. 1991. *Imagined Communities*. New York: Verso.

Andrews, Kenneth T. 1997. "The Impacts of Social Movements on the Political Process: The Civil Rights Movement and Black Electoral Politics in Mississippi." *American Sociological Review* 62(5):800–819.

Andrews, Kenneth T., Marshall Ganz, Mathew Baggetta, Hahrie Han, and Chaeyoon Lim. 2006. "Civic Associations That Work: The Contributions of Leadership to Organizational Effectiveness." Paper presented at the annual meeting of the American Sociological Association, Montreal.

Anspach, Renée R. 1993. *Deciding Who Lives: Fateful Choices in the Intensive-Care Nursery*. Berkeley: University of California Press.

Apetheker, Bettina F. 2006. *Intimate Politics: How I Grew Up Red, Fought for Free Speech, and Became a Feminist Rebel*. Emeryville, CA: Seal Press.

Appiah, Kwame Anthony. 2008. *Experiments in Ethics*. Cambridge, MA: Harvard University Press.

Armstrong, Elizabeth A. 2005. "From Struggle to Settlement: The Crystallization of a Field of Lesbian/Gay Organizations in San Francisco, 1969–1973." Pp. 161–188 in *Social Movements and Organization Theory*, edited by Gerald F. Davis, Doug McAdam, W. Richard Scott, and Mayer N. Zald. New York: Cambridge University Press.

Armstrong, Elizabeth A. and Mary Bernstein. 2008. "Culture, Power, and Institutions: A Multi-Institutional Politics Approach to Social Movements." *Sociological Theory* 26(1):74–99.

Armstrong, Elizabeth A. and Suzanna M. Crage. 2006. "Movements and Memory: The Making of the Stonewall Myth." *American Sociological Review* 71:724–751.

Assiter, Alison. 1996. *Enlightened Women: Modernist Feminism in a Postmodern Age*. New York: Routledge.

Atton, Chris. 2003. "Reshaping Social Movement Media for a New Millennium." *Social Movement Studies* 2(1):3–15.

Auyero, Javier. 2003. *Contentious Lives: Two Argentine Women, Two Protests, and the Quest for Recognition*. Durham, NC: Duke University Press.

Auyero, Javier and Débora Alejandra Swistun. 2009. *Flammable: Environmental Suffering in an Argentine Shantytown*. New York: Oxford University Press.

Bagguley, Paul. 2002. "Contemporary British Feminism: A Social Movement in Abeyance?" *Social Movement Studies* 1(2):169–185.

Balibar, Étienne. 2008. "Historical Dilemmas of Democracy and Their Contemporary Relevance." Unpublished lecture, Citizenship in the 21st Century: An International Colloquium, Pittsburgh, PA, March 18.

Balser, Deborah B. 1997. "The Impact of Environmental Factors on Factionalism and Schism in Social Movement Organizations." *Social Forces* 76(1):199–228.

Banaszak, Lee Ann, Karen Beckwith, and Dieter Rucht, eds. 2003. *Women's Movements Facing the Reconfigured State*. New York: Cambridge University Press.

Banaszak, Lee Ann, Karen Beckwith, and Dieter Rucht. 2003. "When Power Relocates: Interactive Changes in Women's Movements and States." Pp. 1–29 in Banaszak et al., *Women's Movements*.

Barker, Colin. 2001. "Fear, Laughter, and Collective Power: The Making of Solidarity at the Lenin Shipyard in Gdansk, Poland, August 1980." Pp. 175–194 in Goodwin et al., *Passionate Politics*.

Barnes, Barry and David Bloor. 1982. "Relativism, Rationalism and the Sociology of Knowledge." Pp. 21–47 in *Rationality and Relativism*, edited by Martin Hollis and Steven Lukes. Cambridge, MA: MIT Press.

Baron, James N., Michael T. Hannan, and M. Diane Burton. 1999. "Building the Iron Cage: Determinants of Managerial Intensity in the Early Years of Organization." *American Sociological Review* 64(4):527–547.

———. 2001. "Labor Pains: Change in Organizational Models and Employee Turnover in Young, High-Tech Firms." *American Journal of Sociology* 106(4):960–1012.

Baron, James N., Michael T. Hannan, Greta Hsu and Ozgecan Kocak. 2002. "Gender and the Organization-Building Process in Young, High-Tech Firms." Pp. 245–273 in *The New Economic Sociology: Developments in an Emerging Field*, edited by Mauro F. Guillén, Randall Collins, Paula England, and Marshall Meyer. New York: Russell Sage.

Baumeister, Roy, Kathleen D. Vohns, and David C. Funder. 2007. "Psychology as the Science of Self-Reports and Finger Movements." *Perspectives on Psychological Science* 2(4):396–403.

Bayazit, Mahmut and Elizabeth A. Mannix. 2003. "Should I Stay or Should I Go? Predicting Team Members' Intent to Remain in the Team." *Small Group Research* 34(3):290–321.

Becker, Howard S. 1960. "Notes on the Concept of Commitment." *American Journal of Sociology* 66(1):32–40.

———. 1995. "The Power of Inertia." *Qualitative Sociology* 18(3):301–309.

———. 1998. *Tricks of the Trade: How to Think about Your Research While You're Doing It.* Chicago: University of Chicago Press.

Beckwith, Karen. 2001. "Women's Movements at Century's End: Excavation and Advances in Political Science." *Annual Review of Political Science* 4:371–390.

Benford, Robert D. 2007. "An Insider's Critique of the Social Movement Framing Perspective." *Sociological Inquiry* 67(4):409–430.

Bernstein, Mary. 2002. "The Contradictions of Gay Ethnicity: Forging Identity in Vermont." Pp. 85–104 in Meyer et al., *Social Movements.*

Bernstein, Mary and James M. Jasper. 1996. "Interests and Credibility: Whistleblowers in Technological Conflicts." *Social Science Information* 35(3):565–589.

Bevington, Douglas and Chris Dixon. 2005. "Movement-Relevant Theory: Rethinking Social Movement Scholarship and Activism." *Social Movement Studies* 4(3):185–208.

Billings, Dwight B. and Kathleen M. Blee. 2000. *The Road to Poverty: The Making of Wealth and Hardship in Appalachia.* New York: Cambridge University Press.

Blee, Kathleen M. 1991. *Women of the Klan: Racism and Gender in the 1920s.* Berkeley: University of California Press.

———. 1998. "Managing Emotion in the Study of Right-Wing Extremism." *Qualitative Sociology* 21(4):381–399.

———. 2002. *Inside Organized Racism: Women in the Hate Movement.* Berkeley, CA: University of California Press.

———. 2005. "Racial Violence in the United States." *Ethnic and Racial Studies* 28(4):599–619.

———. 2007. "The Microdynamics of Hate Violence: Interpretive Analyses and Implications for Responses." *American Behavioral Scientist* 51(2):258–270.

———. 2011. "Trajectories of Ideologies and Action in U.S. Organized Racism." Pp. 239–255 in *Identity and Participation in Culturally Diverse Societies: A Multidisciplinary Perspective*, edited by Assaad E. Azzi, Xenia Chrssochoou, Bert Klandermans, Bernd Simon, and Jacquelien van Stekelenburg. London: Wiley-Blackwell.

Blee, Kathleen M. and Dwight Billings. 1996. "Reconstructing Daily Life in the Past: An Hermeneutical Approach to Ethnographic Data." *The Sociological Quarterly* 27(4):443–462.

Blee, Kathleen M. and Ashley Currier. 2005. "Character Building: The Dynamics of Emerging Social Movement Groups." *Mobilization: An International Journal* 10(1):129–144.

———. 2006. "How Local Social Movement Groups Handle a Presidential Election." *Qualitative Sociology* 29(3):261–280.

———. 2011. "Ethics Beyond the IRB: An Introductory Essay." *Qualitative Sociology* 34(3): 401–413.

Blee Kathleen M. and Lisa C. Huebner, with the assistance of John Nigro. 2008. "Three Rivers Community Foundation Funding Patterns, 2003–2005," unpublished document.

Blee, Kathleen M. and Amy McDowell. 2012. "Social Movement Audiences." *Sociological Forum* 27 (1), forthcoming.

Blee, Kathleen M. and Verta Taylor. 2002. "Semi-Structured Interviewing in Social Movement Research." Pp. 92–117 in *Methods of Social Movement Research*, edited by Bert Klandermans and Suzanne Staggenborg. Minneapolis: University of Minnesota Press.

Bodkin, Karen. 1998. *How Jews Became White Folks And What That Says about Race in America*. New Brunswick, NJ: Rutgers University Press.

Bourdieu, Pierre. 1984. *Distinction: A Social Critique of the Judgement of Taste*. Cambridge, MA: Harvard University Press.

Breines, Wini. 1982. *Community and Organization in the New Left, 1962–1968: The Great Refusal*. New York: Praeger.

Britt, Lory and David Heise. 2000. "From Shame to Pride in Identity Politics." Pp. 252–268 in Stryker et al., *Self, Identity and Social Movements*.

Bryant, Joseph M. and John A. Hall. 2005. "Theories and Methods Applied: Research Exemplars in Historical Social Science." Pp. vii–xi in *Historical Methods in the Social Sciences*, Vol. 4, edited by John A. Hall and Joseph M. Bryant. London: Sage.

Burns, Gene. 2005. *The Moral Veto: Framing Contraception, Abortion, and Cultural Pluralism in the United States*. New York: Cambridge University Press.

Butler, Judith. 1991. "Imitation and Gender Insubordination." Pp. 13–31 in *Inside/Out: Lesbian Theories, Gay Theories*, edited by Diana Fuss. New York: Routledge.

Calhoun, Craig. 2001. "Putting Emotions in Their Place." Pp. 48–57 in Goodwin et al., *Passionate Politics*.

Caniglia, Beth Schafer and JoAnn Carmin. 2005. "Scholarship on Social Movement Organizations: Classic Views and Emerging Trends." *Mobilization: An International Journal* 10(2):201–212.

Cantor, Norman F. 2002. *In the Wake of the Plague: Black Death and the World It Made*. New York: Perennial/HarperCollins.

Carey, Martha Ann and Mickey W. Smith. 1994. "Capturing the Group Effect in Focus Groups: A Special Concern in Analysis." *Qualitative Health Research* 4(1): 123–127.

Carmin, Joann and Deborah B. Balser. 2002. "Selecting Repertoires of Action in Environmental Movement Organizations: An Interpretive Approach." *Organization and Environment* 15(4):365–388.

Clemens, Elisabeth S. and Debra C. Minkoff. 2004. "Beyond the Iron Law: Rethinking the Place of Organizations in Social Movement Research." Pp. 155–170 in Snow et al., *Blackwell Companion*.

Collins, Patricia Hill. 1990. *Black Feminist Thought: Knowledge, Consciousness, and the Politics of Empowerment*. Boston: Unwin Hyman.

Collins, Randall. 2001. "Social Movements and the Focus of Emotional Attention." Pp. 27–44 in Goodwin et al., *Passionate Politics*.

———. 2004. *Interaction Ritual Chains*. Princeton, NJ: Princeton University Press.

Constable, Nicole. 2003. *Romance on a Global Stage: Pen Pals, Virtual Ethnography, and "Mail Order" Marriages*. Berkeley: University of California Press.

Creager, Angela N. H., Elizabeth Lunbeck, and M. Norton Wise, eds. 2007. *Science without Laws: Model Systems, Cases, Exemplary Narratives*. Durham, NC: Duke University Press.

Cresswell, Tim. 1996. *In Place/Out of Place: Geography, Ideology, and Transgression*. Minneapolis: University of Minnesota Press.

DeGloma, Thomas. 2007. "The Social Logic of 'False Memories': Symbolic Awakenings and Symbolic Worlds in Survivor and Retractor Narratives." *Symbolic Interaction* 30(4):543–565.

Della Porta, Donatella. 1995. *Social Movements, Political Violence, and the State: A Comparative Analysis of Italy and Germany.* New York: Cambridge University Press.

———. 2005. "Making the Polis: Social Forums and Democracy in the Global Justice Movement." *Mobilization: An International Journal* 10(1):73–94.

Della Porta, Donatella and Massimiliano Andretta. 2002. "Changing Forms of Environmentalism in Italy: The Protest Campaign on the High Speed Railway System," *Mobilization: An International Journal* 7 (1):59–77.

Della Porta, Donatella and Gianni Piazza. 2008. *Voices of the Valley, Voices of the Straits: How Protest Creates Communities.* New York: Berghahn Books.

Della Porta, Donatella and Dieter Rucht. 1995. "Left-Libertarian Movements in Context: A Comparison of Italy and West Germany, 1965–1990." Pp. 229-272 in *The Politics of Social Protest: Comparative Perspectives on States and Social Movements,* edited by J. Craig Jenkins and Bert Klandermans. Minneapolis: University of Minnesota Press.

Diani, Mario. 1995. *Green Networks: A Structural Analysis of the Italian Environmental Movement.* Edinburgh, Scotland: Edinburgh University Press.

Diehl, David and Daniel McFarland. 2010. "Toward a Historical Sociology of Social Situations." *American Journal of Sociology* 115(6):1713–1752.

Dobbie, David S. 2008. "More than the Sum of their Parts? Labor-Community Coalitions in the Rust Belt." Ph.D. dissertation, University of Michigan Department of Sociology.

Donaldson, Judith, Gloria Rudolf, and Cynthia Vanda. 2008. "Environmental Scan of Progressive Work in Southwestern Pennsylvania." Unpublished Report to the Three Rivers Community Foundation, Pittsburgh, PA.

Downing, Stephen. 2005. "The Social Construction of Entrepreneurship: Narrative and Dramatic Processes in the Coproduction of Organizations and Identities." *Entrepreneurship: Theory and Practice* 29(2):185–204.

Downton Jr., James and Paul Wehr. 1998. "Persistent Pacifism: How Activist Commitment Is Developed and Sustained." *Journal of Peace Research* 35(5):531–550.

Duchesne, Sophie and Florence Haegel. 2007. "Avoiding or Accepting Conflict in Public Talk." *British Journal of Political Science* 37(1):1–22.

Dugan, Kimberly and Jo Reger. 2006. "Voice and Agency in Social Movement Outcomes." *Qualitative Sociology* 29(4):467–484.

Durkheim, Emile. 1995 [1912]. *The Elementary Forms of Religious Life.* New York: Free Press.

Edwards, Bob. 1994. "Semi-Formal Organizational Structure among Social Movement Organizations: An Analysis of the U.S. Peace Movement." *Nonprofit and Voluntary Sector Quarterly* 23(4):309–333.

Edwards, Bob and Michael Foley. 2002. "Social Movement Organizations beyond the Beltway: Understanding the Diversity of One Social Movement Industry." *Mobilization: An International Journal* 8(1):87–107.

Edwards, Bob and John D. McCarthy. 2004. "Strategy Matters: The Contingent Value of Social Capital in the Survival of Local Social Movement Organizations." *Social Forces* 83(2):621–651.

Effler, Erika Summers. 2010. *Laughing Saints and Righteous Heroes: Emotional Rhythms in Social Movement Groups.* Chicago: University of Chicago Press.

Elder-Vass, Dave. 2007. "Reconciling Archer and Bourdieu in an Emergentist Theory of Action." *Sociological Theory* 25(4):325–346.

Eliasoph, Nina. 1998. *Avoiding Politics: How Americans Produce Apathy in Everyday Life*. New York: Cambridge University Press.

———. 2011. *Making Volunteers: Civic Life after Welfare's End*. Princeton, NJ: Princeton University Press.

Eliasoph, Nina and Paul Lichterman. 1999. "'We Begin with Our Favorite Theory . . .': Reconstructing the Extended Case Method." *Sociological Theory* 17(2):228–234.

———. 2003. "Culture in Interaction." *American Journal of Sociology* 108(4):735–794.

Emerson, Robert M., Rachel I. Fretz, and Linda L. Shaw. 1995. *Writing Ethnographic Fieldnotes*. Chicago: University of Chicago Press.

Emirbayer, Mustafa and Ann Mische. 1998. "What Is Agency?" *American Journal of Sociology* 103(4):962–1023.

Epstein, Barbara. 1991. *Political Protest and Cultural Revolution: Nonviolent Direct Action in the 1970s and 1980s*. Berkeley: University of California Press.

Epstein, Steven. 1995. "The Construction of Lay Expertise: AIDS Activism and the Forging of Credibility in the Reform of Clinical Trials," *Science, Technology & Human Values* 20 (October):408–437.

Ewick, Patricia and Susan S. Silbey. 2003. "Narrating Social Structure: Stories of Resistance to Legal Authority." *American Journal of Sociology* 108(6):1328–1372.

Ferguson, Neil. 2008. "Crossing the Rubicon: Deciding to Become a Paramilitary in Northern Ireland." *International Journal of Conflict and Violence* 2(1):130–137.

Ferree, Myra Marx. 1992. "The Political Context of Rationality: Rational Choice Theory and Resource Mobilization." Pp. 29–52 in Morris and Mueller, *Frontiers*.

———. 2002. "Soft Repression: Ridicule, Stigma, and Silencing in Gender-Based Movements." Paper presented at the Collective Behavior and Social Movement Section of the American Sociological Association workshop, Notre Dame, IN.

Fine, Gary Alan. 1995. "Public Narration and Group Culture: Discerning Discourse in Social Movements." Pp. 127–143 in Johnston and Klandermans, eds., *Social Movements and Culture*.

Fligstein, Neil and Doug McAdam. 2011. "Toward a General Theory of Strategic Action Fields." *Sociological Theory* 29(1):1–26

Foley, Michael W. and Bob Edwards. 2002. "How Do Members Count? Membership, Governance, and Advocacy in the Nonprofit World." In *Exploring Organizations and Advocacy: Governance and Accountability*, edited by Maria D. Montilla and Elizabeth J. Reid. Washington, DC: Urban Institute Press. Retrieved November 17, 2005 (http://www.uipress.org).

Foucault, Michel. 1976. *The History of Sexuality*. New York: Vintage.

Gamson, William A. 1990. *The Strategy of Social Protest*. Belmont, CA: Wadsworth.

———. 1991. "Commitment and Agency in Social Movements." *Sociological Forum* 6(1):27–50.

———. 1992. *Talking Politics*. New York: Cambridge University Press.

Ganz, Marshall. 2000. "Resources and Resourcefulness: Strategic Capacity in the Unionization of California Agriculture, 1959–1966." *American Journal of Sociology* 105(4):1003–1062.

———. 2004. "Why David Sometimes Wins: Strategic Capacity in Social Movements." Pp. 177–198 in Goodwin and Jasper, *Rethinking Social Movements*.

———. 2009. *Why David Sometimes Wins: Leadership, Organization, and Strategy in the California Farm Worker Movement*. New York: Oxford University Press.

Garfinkel, Harold. 2005. *Seeing Sociologically: The Routine Grounds of Social Action*. Boulder, CO: Paradigm.

Geertz, Clifford. 1973. *The Interpretation of Cultures*. New York: Basic Books.

Gersick, Connie J. G. 1988. "Time and Transition in Work Teams: Toward a New Model of Group Development." *Academy of Management Journal* 31(1):9–41.

Geuss, Raymond. 2010. *Politics and the Imagination*. Princeton, NJ: Princeton University Press.

Gibson, Cristina B. 2001. "From Knowledge Accumulation to Accommodation: Cycles of Collective Cognition in Work Groups." *Journal of Organizational Behavior* 22(2):121–134.

Gilmore, Ruth Wilson. 2007. *Golden Gulag: Prisons, Surplus, Crisis, and Opposition in Globalizing California*. Berkeley: University of California Press.

Ginzburg, Carlo. 2007. "Latitudes, Slaves, and the Bible: An Experiment in MicroHistory." Pp. 243–263 in Creager, *Science without Laws*.

Goldfarb, Jeffrey C. 2006. *The Politics of Small Things: The Power of the Powerless in Dark Times*. Chicago: University of Chicago Press.

Goodwin, Jeff. 1997. "The Libidinal Constitution of a High-Risk Social Movement: Affectual Ties and Solidarity in the Huk Rebellion, 1946 to 1954." *American Sociological Review* 62(1):53–69.

———. 2007. "'The Struggle Made Me a Nonracialist': Why There Was So Little Terrorism in the Antiapartheid Struggle." *Mobilization: An International Journal* 12(2):193–203.

Goodwin, Jeff and James M. Jasper, eds. 2004. *Rethinking Social Movements: Structure, Meaning, and Emotion*. Lanham, MD: Rowman & Littlefield.

Goodwin, Jeff, James M. Jasper, and Francesca Polletta, eds. 2001. *Passionate Politics: Emotions and Social Movements*. Chicago: University of Chicago Press.

Goodwin, Jeff, James M. Jasper, and Francesca Polletta. 2001. "Introduction: Why Emotions Matter," Pp. 1-24 in Goodwin et al., *Passionate Politics*.

Gould, Deborah B. 2009. *Moving Politics: Emotion and Act Up's Fight against AIDS*. Chicago: University of Chicago Press.

Guzzo, Richard A. and Marcus W. Dickson. 1996. "Teams in Organizations: Recent Research on Performance and Effectiveness." *Annual Review of Psychology* 47:307–338.

Hall, Jacquelyn Dowd. 2005. "The Long Civil Rights Movement and the Political Uses of the Past." *Journal of American History* 91(4):1233–1263.

Hannan, Michael T., M. Diane Burton, and James N. Baron. 1996. "Inertia and Change in the Early Years: Employment Relations in Young, High Technology Firms." *Industrial and Corporate Change* 5(2):503–536.

Harding, David J., Cybelle Fox, and Jal D. Mehta. 2002. "Studying Rare Events through Qualitative Case Studies: Lessons from a Study of Rampage School Shootings," *Sociological Methods and Research* 31 (2):174–217.

Hareven, Tamara K. and Kanji Masaoka. 1988. "Turning Points and Transitions: Perceptions of the Life Course." *Journal of Family History* 13(1):271–289.

Hart, Stephen. 2001. *Cultural Dilemmas of Progressive Politics: Styles of Engagement among Grassroots Activists*. Chicago: University of Chicago Press.

Haydu, Jeffrey. 1998. "Making Use of the Past: Time Periods as Cases to Compare and as Sequences of Problem Solving." *American Journal of Sociology* 104(2):339–371.

———. 2010. "Reversals of Fortune: Path Dependency, Problem Solving, and Temporal Cases." *Theory and Society* 39(1):25–48.

Heaney, Michael T. and Fabio Rojas. 2006. "The Place of Framing: Multiple Audiences and Antiwar Protests Near Fort Bragg." *Qualitative Sociology* 29(4):485–505.

Heimer, Carol A. 2001. "Cases and Biographies: An Essay on Routinization and the Nature of Comparison." *Annual Review of Sociology* 27:47–76.

Hirschman, Albert O. 1970. *Exit, Voice, and Loyalty: Responses to Decline in Firms, Organizations, and States.* Cambridge, MA: Harvard University Press.

Hitlin, Steven and Glen H. Elder Jr. 2007. "Time, Self, and the Curiously Abstract Concept of Agency." *Sociological Theory* 25(2):170–191.

Hoffman, Stefan-Ludwig. 2003. "Democracy and Associations in the Long Nineteenth Century: Toward a Transnational Perspective." *Journal of Modern History* 75: 269–299.

Hunt, Scott A. and Robert D. Benford. 2004. "Collective Identity, Solidarity, and Commitment." Pp. 433–458 in Snow et al., *Blackwell Companion.*

Ignatiev, Noel. 1996. *How the Irish Became White.* New Brunswick, NJ: Rutgers University Press.

Isaac, Rhys. 2005. "History Made from Stories Found: Seeking a Microhistory that Matters." *Common-Place* 6(1). Retrieved November 8, 2005 (www.common-place.org).

Jasper, James M. 1997. *The Art of Moral Protest: Culture, Biography, and Creativity in Social Movements.* Chicago: University of Chicago Press.

———. 2004. "A Strategic Approach to Collective Action: Looking for Agency in Social-Movement Choices." *Mobilization: An International Journal* 9(1):1–16.

———. 2006. *Getting Your Way: Strategic Dilemmas in the Real World.* Chicago: University of Chicago Press.

Johnson, Cathryn, Timothy J. Dowd, and Cecilia L. Ridgeway. 2006. "Legitimacy as a Social Process." *Annual Review of Sociology* 32:53–78.

Johnston, Hank and Bert Klandermans, eds. 2004. *Social Movements and Culture.* Minneapolis: University of Minnesota Press.

Kane, Anne. 2001. "Finding Emotion in Social Movement Processes: Irish Land Movement Metaphors and Narratives." Pp. 251–266 in Goodwin et al., *Passionate Politics.*

Kaplan, Temma. 2004. *Taking Back the Streets: Women, Youth, and Direct Democracy.* Berkeley: University of California Press.

Katz, Jack. 2001. "From How to Why: On Luminous Description and Causal Inference in Ethnography (Part 1)." *Ethnography* 2(4):443–473.

Katzenbach, John R. and Douglas K. Smith. 1993. "The Discipline of Teams." *Harvard Business Review* 71:111–120.

Katznelson, Ira. 1986. *Working-Class Formation: Nineteenth-Century Patterns in Western Europe and the United States.* Princeton, NJ: Princeton University Press.

Kelley, Robin D. G. 2002. "Finding the Strength to Love and Dream." *Chronicle of Higher Education* 48(39), June 7.

———. 2002. *Freedom Dreams: The Black Radical Imagination.* Boston, MA:Beacon Press.

Kerr, Norbert L. and R. Scott Tindale. 2004. "Group Performance and Decision Making." *Annual Review of Psychology* 55:623–655.

Kitzinger, Jenny and Clare Farquhar. 1999. "The Analytical Potential of 'Sensitive Moments' in Focus Group Discussions." Pp. 156–172 in *Developing Focus Group Research: Politics, Theory and Practice*, edited by Rosaline S. Barbour and Jenny Kitzinger. London, England: Sage.

Klandermans, Bert. 1988. "The Formation and Mobilization of Consensus." Pp. 173–196 in Klandermans et al., *International Social Movement Research.*

———. 1997. *The Social Psychology of Protest.* Cambridge, MA: Blackwell.

Klandermans, Bert, Hanspeter Kriesi, and Sidney Tarrow, eds. 1988. *International Social Movement Research, From Structure to Action: Comparing Social Movement Research across Cultures,* Vol. 1. Greenwich, CT: JAI Press.

Klandermans, Bert and Dirk Oegema. 1987. "Potentials, Networks, Motivations, and Barriers: Steps Towards Participation in Social Movements." *American Sociological Review* 52:519–531.

Klatch, Rebecca E. 1999. *A Generation Divided: The New Left, the New Right, and the 1960s.* Berkeley: University of California Press.

Kleinman, Sherryl. 1996. *Opposing Ambitions: Gender and Identity in an Alternative Organization.* Chicago: University of Chicago Press.

Klimoski, Richard and Susan Mohammed. 1994. "Team Mental Mode: Construct or Metaphor?" *Journal of Management* 20(2): 403–437.

Knoke, David and Nancy Wisely. 1990. "Social Movements." Pp. 57–84 in *Political Networks,* edited by David Knoke. New York: Cambridge University Press.

Koopmans, Ruud. 2005. "The Missing Link between Structure and Agency: Outline of an Evolutionary Approach to Social Movements." *Mobilization: An International Journal* 10(1):19–33.

Krugman, Paul. 1991. "History and Industry Location: The Case of the Manufacturing Belt." *American Economic Review* 81(2):80–83.

Kruse, Kevin M. 2005. *White Flight: Atlanta and the Making of Modern Conservatism.* Princeton, NJ: Princeton University Press.

Kurzman, Charles. 2004. *The Unthinkable Revolution in Iran.* Cambridge, MA: Harvard University Press.

Lamont, Michèle. 2000. *The Dignity of Working Men: Morality and the Boundaries of Race, Class, and Immigration.* Cambridge, MA: Harvard University Press.

Lamont, Michèle and Virág Molnár. 2002. "The Study of Boundaries in the Social Sciences." *Annual Review of Sociology* 28(1):167–195.

Larson, Magali Sarfatti and Silvia Sigal. 2001. "Does 'The Public' Think Politically? A Search for 'Deep Structures' in Everyday Political Thought." *Qualitative Sociology* 24(3):285–309.

Levi, Giovanni. 1991. "On Microhistory." Pp. 93–113 in *New Perspectives on Historical Writing,* edited by Peter Burke. University Park: Pennsylvania State University Press.

Lichterman, Paul. 1998. "What Do Movements Mean? The Value of Participant-Observation." *Qualitative Sociology* 21(4): 401–418.

———. 1999. "Talking Identity in the Public Sphere: Broad Visions and Small Spaces in Sexual Identity Politics." *Theory and Society* 28(1):101–141.

———. 2005. *Elusive Togetherness: Church Groups Trying to Bridge America's Divisions.* Princeton, NJ: Princeton University Press.

Mahoney, James. 2000. "Path Dependence in Historical Sociology." *Theory and Society* 29(4):507–548.

———. 2004. "Revisiting General Theory in Historical Sociology." *Social Forces* 83(2):459–489.

Mahoney, Joseph T. 2005. *Economic Foundations of Strategy.* Thousand Oaks, CA: Sage.

Mason, Jennifer. 2002. *Qualitative Researching.* Thousand Oaks, CA: Sage.

Massey, Doreen. 1991. "The Political Place of Locality Studies." *Environment and Planning* 23:267–281.

McAdam, Doug. 1986. "Recruitment to High-Risk Activism: The Case of Freedom Summer." *American Journal of Sociology* 92(1):64–90.

———. 1995. "'Initiator' and 'Spin-Off' Movements: Diffusion Processes in Protest Cycles." Pp. 217–239 in Traugott, *Repertoires.*

———. 2003. "Beyond Structural Analysis: Toward a More Dynamic Understanding of Social Movements." Pp. 281–298 in *Social Movements and Networks: Relational Approaches to Collective Action*, edited by Mario Diani and Doug McAdam. New York: Oxford University Press.

———. 2004. "Revisiting the U.S. Civil Rights Movement: Toward a More Synthetic Understanding of the Origins of Contention." Pp. 201–232 in Goodwin and Jasper, *Rethinking Social Movements*.

McAdam, Doug, Robert J. Sampson, Simon Weffer, and Heather MacIndoe. 2005. "'There Will Be Fighting in the Streets': The Distorting Lens of Social Movement Theory." *Mobilization: An International Journal* 10(1):1–18.

McAdam, Doug, Sidney Tarrow, and Charles Tilly. 2001. *Dynamics of Contention*. New York: Cambridge University Press.

McCarthy, John D., David W. Britt, and Mark Wolfson. 1991. "The Institutional Channeling of Social Movements by the State in the United States." Pp. 45–76 in *Research in Social Movements, Conflicts and Change: A Research Annual*, Vol. 13, edited by Louis Kriesberg and Metta Spencer. Greenwich, CT: JAI Press.

McCarthy, John D. and Mark Wolfson. 1997. "Resource Mobilization by Local Social Movement Organizations: Agency, Strategy, and Organization in the Movement against Drinking and Driving." *American Sociological Review* 61(6):1070–1088.

McFarland, Daniel A. 2004. "Resistance as a Social Drama: A Study of Change-Oriented Encounters." *American Journal of Sociology* 109(6):1249–1318.

McVeigh, Rory, Carl Neblett, and Sarah Shafiq. 2006. "Explaining Social Movement Outcomes: Multiorganizational Fields and Hate Crime Reporting." *Mobilization: An International Journal* 11(1):23–49.

Melucci, Alberto. 1995. "The Process of Collective Identity." Pp. 41–63 in Johnston and Klandermans, *Social Movements and Culture*.

———. 1996. *Challenging Codes: Collective Action in the Information Age*. New York: Cambridge University Press.

Meyer, David S. 2000. "Social Movements: Creating Communities of Change." Pp. 35–55 in *Feminist Approaches to Social Movements, Community, and Power: Conscious Acts and the Politics of Social Change*, Vol. 1, edited by Robin L. Teske and Mary Ann Tétreault. Columbia: University of South Carolina Press.

———. 2003. "Restating the Woman Question: Women's Movements and State Restructuring." Pp. 275–294 in Banaszak et al., *Women's Movements*.

———. 2004. "Protest and Political Opportunities." *Annual Review of Sociology* 30:125–145.

———. 2006. "Claiming Credit: Stories of Movement Influence as Outcomes." *Mobilization: An International Journal* 11(3):281–298.

Meyer, David S. and Douglas R. Imig. 1993. "Political Opportunity and the Rise and Decline of Interest Group Sectors." *Social Science Journal* 30(3):253–270.

Meyer, David S. and Debra C. Minkoff. 2004. "Conceptualizing Political Opportunity." *Social Forces* 82(4):1457–1492.

Meyer, David S., Nancy Whittier, and Belinda Robnett, eds. 2002. *Social Movements: Identity, Culture, and the State*. New York: Oxford University Press.

Meyer, Megan. 2004. "Organizational Identity, Political Contexts, and SMO Action: Explaining the Tactical Choices Made by Peace Organizations in Israel, Northern Ireland, and South Africa." *Social Movement Studies* 3(2):167–197.

Michels, Robert. 1966. *Political Parties*. New York: Free Press.

Miller, Byron A. 1992. "Collective Action and Rational Choice: Place, Community, and the Limits to Individual Self-Interest." *Economic Geography* 68(1):22–42.

————. 2000. *Geography and Social Movements: Comparing Antinuclear Activism in the Boston Area*. Minneapolis: University of Minnesota Press.

Minkoff, Debra C. 1999. "Bending with the Wind: Strategic Change and Adaptation by Women's and Racial Minority Organization." *American Journal of Sociology* 104(6):1666–1703.

Minkoff, Debra C. and John D. McCarthy. 2005. "Reinvigorating the Study of Organizational Processes in Social Movements." *Mobilization: An International Journal* 10(2):289–308.

Mische, Ann. 2009. *Partisan Publics: Communication and Contention across Brazilian Youth Activist Networks*. Princeton, NJ: Princeton University Press.

Molotch, Harvey, William Freudenburg, and Krista E. Paulsen. 2000. "History Repeats Itself, But How? City Character, Urban Tradition, and the Accomplishment of Place." *American Sociological Review* 65(6):791–823.

Moore, Barrington. 1966. *Social Origins of Dictatorship and Democracy: Lord and Peasant in the Making of the Modern World*. Boston: Beacon Press.

Moreland, Richard. 2009. "How Often Is Behavior Actually Measured by Social Psychologists Who Study Small Groups?" Presented at the Center for Interdisciplinary Research on Teams, Carnegie-Mellon University, February 27, 2009.

Morrill, Calvin, David A. Snow, and Cindy H. White. 2005. *Together Alone: Personal Relationships in Public Places*. Berkeley: University of California Press.

Morris, Aldon D. 1984. *The Origins of the Civil Rights Movement: Black Communities Organizing for Change*. New York: Free Press.

Morris, Aldon D. and Carol McClurg Mueller, eds. 1992. *Frontiers in Social Movement Theory*. New Haven, CT: Yale University Press.

Mueller, Carol McClurg and John D. McCarthy. 2003. "Cultural Continuity and Structural Change: The Logic of Adaptation by Radical, Liberal, and Socialist Feminists to State Reconfiguration." In Banaszak et al., *Women's Movements*, 219–241.

Mutz, Diana C. 2006. *Hearing the Other Side: Deliberative versus Participatory Democracy*. New York: Cambridge University Press.

Neiman, Susan. 2009. *Moral Clarity*. Princeton, NJ: Princeton University Press.

Nepstad, Sharon Erickson and Clifford Bob. 2006. "When Do Leaders Matter? Hypotheses on Leadership Dynamics in Social Movements." *Mobilization: An International Journal* 11(1):1–22.

North, Douglas C. 1990. *Institutions, Institutional Change and Economic Performance*. Cambridge, MA: Cambridge University Press.

O'Hearn, Denis. 2006. *Nothing but an Unfinished Song: Bobby Sands, the Irish Hunger Striker Who Ignited a Generation*. New York: Nation Books.

Oliver, Pamela E. and Hank Johnston. 2000. "What a Good Idea! Ideologies and Frames in Social Movement Research." *Mobilization: An International Journal* 5(1):37–54.

Orlikowski, Wanda J. 2005. "Material Knowing: The Scaffolding of Human Knowledge-ability." Unpublished paper. Retrieved October 19, 2010 (http://seeit.mit.edu/Publications/Orlikowski_OKLC_write-up_2006.pdf).

Paulsen, Krista E. 2004. "Making Character Concrete: Empirical Strategies for Studying Place Distinction." *City and Community* 3(3):243–262.

Pedriana, Nicholas. 2005. "Rational Choice, Structural Context, and Increasing Returns: A Strategy for Analytic Narrative in Historical Sociology." *Sociological Methods & Research* 33(3):349–382.

————. 2006. "From Protective to Equal Treatment: Legal Framing Processes and Transformation of the Women's Movement in the 1960s." *American Journal of Sociology* 111(6):1718–1761.

Perrin, Andrew J. 2006. *Citizen Speak: The Democratic Imagination in American Life.* Chicago: University of Chicago Press.

Perry, Elizabeth J. 2002. "Moving the Masses: Emotion Work in the Chinese Revolution." *Mobilization: An International Journal* 7(2):111–128.

Phillips, Mark Salber. 2003. "Histories, Micro- and Literary: Problems of Distance and Genre." *New Literary History* 34(2):211–229.

Pierson, Paul. 2000a. "Increasing Returns, Path Dependence, and the Study of Politics." *American Political Science Review* 94(2):251–267.

———. 2000b. "Not Just What, but *When*: Timing and Sequence in Political Processes." *Studies in American Political Development* 14:72–92.

Pile, Steve. 1997. "Introduction: Opposition, Political Identities, and Spaces of Resistance." Pp. 1–32 in *Geographies of Resistance*, edited by Steve Pile and Michael Keith. New York: Routledge.

Piven, Frances Fox and Richard A. Cloward. 1979. *Poor People's Movements: Why They Succeed, How They Fail.* New York: Vintage.

———. 1993. *Regulating the Poor: The Functions of Public Welfare.* Ann Arbor: University of Michigan.

Polletta, Francesca. 2002a. *Freedom Is an Endless Meeting: Democracy in American Social Movements.* Chicago: University of Chicago Press.

———. 2002b. "Plotting Protest: Mobilizing Stories in the 1960 Student Sit-Ins." Pp. 31–52 in *Stories of Change: Narrative and Social Movements*, edited by Joseph E. Davis. Albany: SUNY Press.

———. 2005. "How Participatory Democracy Became White: Culture and Organizational Choice." *Mobilization: An International Journal* 10(2):271–288.

———. 2006. *It Was Like a Fever: Storytelling in Protest and Politics.* Chicago: University of Chicago Press.

Polletta, Francesca and Edwin Amenta. 2001. "Conclusion: Second that Emotion? Lessons from Once-Novel Concepts in Social Movement Research." Pp. 303–316 in Goodwin et al., *Passionate Politics.*

Pred, Allan. 1981. "Of Paths and Projects: Individual Behavior and Its Societal Context." Pp. 231–255 in *Behavioral Problems in Geography Revisited*, edited by Kevin R. Cox and Reginald G. Golledge. New York: Methuen.

———. 1985. "Presidential Address: Interpenetrating Processes: Human Agency and the Becoming of Regional Spatial and Social Structures." *Papers in Regional Science* 57(1):7–17.

Putnam, Robert D. 2000. *Bowling Alone: The Collapse and Revival of American Community.* New York: Simon & Schuster.

Ragin, Charles and Howard S. Becker. 1992. *What Is a Case? Exploring the Foundations of Social Inquiry.* New York: Cambridge University Press.

Reed, Jean-Pierre and John Foran. 2002. "Political Cultures of Opposition: Exploring Idioms, Ideologies, and Revolutionary Agency in the Case of Nicaragua." *Critical Sociology* 28(3):335–370.

Revel, Jacques. 1995. "Microanalysis and the Construction of the Social." Pp. 492–502 in *Histories: French Constructions of the Past*, edited by Jacques Revel and Lynn Hunt. New York: New Press.

Reinke, Dana Colleen. 2006. "Assessing Place Character in Response to Wal-Mart." Ph.D. Dissertation, University of Pittsburgh Department of Sociology.

Rhomberg, Christopher. 2004. *No There There: Race, Class, and Political Community in Oakland.* Berkeley: University of California Press.

Ricoeur, Paul. 1973. "The Model of the Text: Meaningful Action Considered as Text." *New Literary History* 5(1):91–117.

Risman, Barbara J. 2004. "Gender as a Social Structure: Theory Wrestling with Activism." *Gender & Society* 18(4):429–450.

Robnett, Belinda. 1999. *How Long? How Long? African-American Women and the Struggle for Civil Rights*. New York: Oxford University Press.

Rosenthal, Anton. 2000. "Spectacle, Fear, and Protest: A Guide to the History of Urban Public Space in Latin America." *Social Science History* 24(1):33–73.

Roth, Silke. 2003. *Building Movement Bridges: The Coalition of Labor Union Women*. Westport, CT: Preager.

Routledge, Paul. 1996. "Critical Geopolitics and Terrains of Resistance." *Political Geography* 15(6–7):509–531.

Sampson, Robert J., Doug McAdam, Heather MacIndoe, and Simón Weffer-Elizondo. 2005. "Civil Society Reconsidered: The Durable Nature and Community Structure of Collective Civic Action." *American Journal of Sociology* 111(3):673–714.

Sanders, Lynn M. 1997. "Against Deliberation." *Political Theory* 25(3):347–376.

Scott, Joan Wallach. 2008. *Only Paradoxes to Offer: French Feminists and the Rights of Man*. Cambridge, MA: Harvard University Press.

Seidman, Steven. 1993. "Identity and Politics in a 'Postmodern' Gay Culture: Some Historical and Conceptual Notes." Pp. 105–142 in *Fear of a Queer Planet: Queer Politics and Social Theory*, edited by Michael Warner. Minneapolis: University of Minnesota Press.

Sewell, William H. Jr. 1992. "A Theory of Structure: Duality, Agency, and Transformation." *American Journal of Sociology* 98:1(July):1–29.

———. 1996. "Three Temporalities Towards an Eventful Sociology." Pp. 245–280 in *The Historic Turn in Human Sciences*, edited by Terrence J. McDonald. Ann Arbor: University of Michigan Press.

———. 2001. "Space in Contentious Politics." Pp. 51-88 in Aminzade et al., *Silence and Voice*.

Shank, J.B. 2008. "Crisis: A Useful Category of Post-Social Scientific Historical Analysis?" *American Historical Review* 113:1090–1099.

Shostak, Sara, Peter Conrad, and Allan V. Horowitz. "Sequencing and Its Consequences: Path Dependence and the Relations between Genetics and Medicalization." *American Journal of Sociology*. 114(1):287–316.

Small, Mario Luis. 2009. *Unanticipated Gains: Origins of Network Inequality in Everyday Life*. New York: Oxford University Press.

Smith Andrea. 2008. *Native Americans and the Christian Right: The Gendered Politics of Unlikely Alliances*. Durham, NC: Duke University Press.

Smith, Christian. 2003. *Moral, Believing Animals: Human Personhood and Culture*. New York: Oxford University Press.

Smith, Dorothy E. 1987. *The Everyday World as Problematic: A Feminist Sociology*. Boston: Northeastern University Press.

Snow, David A. 1992. "Master Frames and Cycles of Protest." Pp. 133–155 in Morris and Mueller, *Frontiers*.

Snow, David A. and Robert D. Benford. 1988. "Ideology, Frame Resonance, and Participant Mobilization." Pp. 197–217 in Klandermans et al., *International Social Movement Research*.

Snow, David A. and Doug McAdam. 2000. "Identity Work Processes in the Context of Social Movements: Clarifying the Identity/Movement Nexus." Pp. 41–67 in Stryker, *Self, Identity and Social Movements*.

Snow, David A., Sarah A. Soule, and Hanspeter Kriesi, eds. 2004. *Blackwell Companion to Social Movements*. Malden, MA: Blackwell.

Snow, David A., Louis A. Zurcher Jr., and Sheldon Ekland-Olson. 1980. "Social Networks and Social Movements: A Microstructural Approach to Differential Recruitment." *American Sociological Review* 45(5):787–801.

Spivak, Gayatri Chakravorty. 1988. "Can the Subaltern Speak?" Pp. 271–313 in *Marxism and the Interpretation of Culture*, edited by Cary Nelson and Lawrence Grossberg. Urbana: University of Illinois Press.

Steinberg, Marc W. 2002. "Toward a More Dialogic Analysis of Social Movement Culture." Pp. 208–225 in Meyer et al., *Social Movements*.

Steinmetz, George. 2004. "Odious Comparisons: Incommensurability, the Case Study, and 'Small N's' in Sociology." *Sociological Theory* 22(3):371–400.

Stoetzler, Marcel and Nira Yuval-Davis. 2002. "Standpoint Theory, Situated Knowledge and the Situated Imagination." *Feminist Theory* 3(3):315–333.

Stryker, Robin. 1996. "Beyond History versus Theory: Strategic Explanation and Sociological Explanation." *Sociological Methods & Research* 24(3):304–352.

Stryker, Sheldon, Timothy J. Owens, and Robert W. White. eds. 2000. *Self, Identity and Social Movements*. Minneapolis: University of Minnesota Press.

Tarrow, Sidney. 1995. "Cycles of Collective Action: Between Moments of Madness and the Repertoire of Contention." Pp. 89–116 in Traugott, *Repertoires and Cycles*.

———. 2001. "Silence and Voice in the Study of Contentious Politics: Introduction." Pp. 1–13 in Aminzade et al., *Silence and Voice*.

Taylor, Charles. 1979. "Interpretation and the Science of Man." Pp. 25–72 in *Interpretive Social Science: A Reader*, edited by Paul Rainbow and William Sullivan. Berkeley: University of California Press.

Taylor, Verta. 1989. "Social Movement Continuity: The Women's Movement in Abeyance." *American Sociological Review* 54(5):761–775.

———. 1995. "Watching for Vibes: Bringing Emotion into the Study of Feminist Organizations." Pp. 223–233 in *Feminist Organizations: Harvest of the New Women's Movement*, edited by Myra Marx Ferree and Patricia Yancey Martin. Philadelphia: Temple University Press.

———. 1996. *Rock-a-by Baby: Feminism, Self-Help, and Postpartum Depression*. New York: Routledge.

———. 2000. "Emotions and Identity in Women's Self-Help Movements." Pp. 271–299 in Stryker, *Self, Identity, and Social Movements*.

Taylor, Verta and Nancy Whittier. 1995. "Analytic Approaches to Social Movement Culture: The Culture of the Women's Movement." Pp. 163–187 in Johnston and Klandermans, *Social Movements and Culture*.

Tilly, Charles. 1984. *Big Structures, Large Processes, Huge Comparisons*. New York: Russell Sage Foundation.

———. 1988. "Future History." *Theory and Society* 17(5):703–712.

———. 1995. "Contentious Repertoires in Great Britain, 1758–1834." Pp.15–42 in Traugott, *Repertoires and Cycles*.

———. 1999. *Durable Inequality*. Berkeley: University of California Press.

———. 2006. *Why? What Happens When People Give Reasons . . . and Why*. Princeton: Princeton University Press.

Traugott, Mark, ed. 1995. *Repertoires and Cycles of Collective Action*. Durham, NC: Duke University Press.

Valocchi, Stephen. 2009. *Social Movements and Activism in the USA*. New York: Routledge.

Van Gunsteren, H. 1998. *A Theory of Citizenship: Organizing Plurality in Contemporary Democracies*. Boulder, CO: Westview.

Vaughan, Diane. 1986. *Uncoupling: Turning Points in Intimate Relationships*. New York: Oxford University Press.

———. 1996. *The Challenger Launch Decision: Risky Technology, Culture, and Deviance at NASA*. Chicago: University of Chicago Press.

Walsh, Katherine Cramer. 2004. *Talking about Politics: Informal Groups and Social Identity in American Life*. Chicago: University of Chicago Press.

Walsh, Katherine Cramer. 2007. *Talking about Race: Community Dialogues and the Politics of Difference*. Chicago: University of Chicago Press.

Watts, Duncan J. 2007. "Is Justin Timberlake a Product of Cumulative Advantage? The New Theory of the Hit Record." *New York Times Magazine*, April 25, 2007:22–25.

Weick, Karl E. and Karlene H. Roberts. 1993. "Collective Mind in Organizations: Heedful Interrelating on Flight Decks." *Administrative Science Quarterly* 38:357–381.

Weingart, Laurie R. 1997. "How Did They Do That? The Ways and Means of Studying Group Process." *Research in Organizational Behavior* 19:189–240.

West, Cornel. 2004. *Democracy Matters: Winning the Fight against Imperialism*. London: Penguin Press.

Whittier, Nancy. 1995. *Feminist Generations: The Persistence of the Radical Women's Movement*. Philadelphia, PA: Temple University Press.

Wood, Richard L. 2002. *Faith in Action: Religion, Race, and Democratic Organizing in America*. Chicago: University of Chicago Press.

Wooley, Anita William. 2009. "Collective Intelligence." Presented at the Center for Interdisciplinary Research on Teams, Carnegie Mellon University, Pittsburgh, PA February 27, 2009.

Young, Alford A. Jr. 2004. *The Minds of Marginalized Black Men: Making Sense of Mobility, Opportunity, and Future Life Chances*. Princeton, NJ: Princeton University Press.

Yuval-Davis, Nira. 2006. "Belonging and the Politics of Belonging." *Patterns of Prejudice* 40(3):197–214.

Zald, Mayer N. 2000. "Ideologically Structured Action: An Enlarged Agenda for Social Movement Research." *Mobilization: An International Journal* 5(1):1–16.

Zerilli, Linda M. G. 2008. "Toward a Feminist Theory of Judgment." *Signs: Journal of Women in Culture and Society* 34(2):295–317.

Zerubavel, Eviatar. 2006. *The Elephant in the Room: Silence and Denial in Everyday Life*. New York: Oxford University Press.

Zhao, Dingxin. 1998 "Ecologies of Social Movement: Social Mobilization during the 1989 Prodemocracy Movement in Beijing." *American Journal of Sociology* 103(6):1493–1529.

INDEX

Abu-Jamal, Mumia, 19, 105
activism
    as cultural project, 31
    as democracy, 4
    as secondary to democracy, 4
    birth of, 16–17
    cultural blueprint of, 166–167n18
    defined, 164–165n9
    fluidity of, 11
    social imagination, 3, 163n2
activist groups
    as different from social movement
        organizations (SMOs), 6
    case comparison, advantages and
        problems of, 14–15
    categories and names, 12–15
        problems with labels, 13
    collapse, 7, 126
    decision making of, 7–8
    democracy eroded, 4, 135,
        163–164n3
    described, 4–8
    emergent, 6–7
    events by type, 10, Table 1.1
    excluded from study, 164–165n9
    funding, 5, 15–16, 171n44
    identification of, 5–6
    joining as sorting principle, 110
    membership, 65–58
    origins of, 6–7, 165–166n15
    racial dynamics of, 58–61
    See also research methodology
    self-definition, 7–8, 53–54, 166n17,
        171n43, 179n4
        as exclusionary, 54, 179n7
        as spatial, 55

    as temporal, 55
    See also belonging
    skewed sampling of, 7–8
    study of, 8–11
agency, 134
    life course, 176–177n40
    limitations of, 186n3
    pragmatic, 176–177n40
    theory of individuals, 38, 177n42
    turning points
        time as key, 37–38, 175–176n35,
            176–177n40
Alexander, Jeffrey, 82
allies
    as local individuals, 15
    changing definitions of, 42, 47
    for conservative groups, 16
ALLIES 2007
    anti-violence activist group, 23–26, 136
    scope of problem, 85–86
    talk about family, 24–25
    talk about race, 24
Aminzade, Ron, 65
Animal Liberation League (ALL)
    as trajectory and turning point case
        study, 41–51
        issue, 42–44
        mood, 46–49
        tactics, 44–46
        time orientation, 50
    foie gras campaign, 42–43
    leadership, 130–131
    recruitment, 71–73
Appiah, Kwame Anthony
    moral perception, 91
    shadow of the past, 41

Balibar, Étienne, 4
Becker, Howard
   cases shape scholarship, 5
   congealed social agreements, 35
   life trajectories, 40
   social worlds, 5
Beckwith, Karen, 118–119
belonging
   as action, 57–61
   boundaries of, 63–65
      emotional, 64, 180n14
      social, 64–65
      tactical, 63
   case comparisons, 75–79
   described, 56–57
      case example, 57
   disputes about, 61–63
   expediency and mission logics,
      62–63, 179n11
   self-definitions, 53
Black Antiwar Pittsburgh (BAP)
   kinds of members, 53
   mission logic, 61–62
   talk of internal dynamics, 118
boundaries
   See belonging
Burns, Gene, 7
Bush, George W., 52, 93
   impact on activism, 15, 20

Calhoun, Craig, 111
case comparison
   ideological character, 104–107
   interpersonal character, 128–131
   organizational character, 75–79
Center for Progressive Values (CPV), 16,
   92, 93
civic engagement
   avoidance in political life, 3,
      163n1
   limitations of, 134
cognitive centrality, 101–103, 139,
   187n18
cognitive integration, 82
collective identity, 6
   foundation of, 181n3
   interpersonal ties, 183n4
collective intelligence (CI), 30,
   108, 137
   foundation of, 171–172n1

collective learning, 99–100, 182–183n19
   phased out, 100–104
   See also Lichterman, Paul
CONSERVE
   recruitment, 70
   scope of problem, 84
context
   as important, 169–170n39
   organizational field, 170n42
   place-based politics, 15–16, 42
   social movement family, 15,
      171n43
credibility
   as self-reinforcing sequence, 128
   bestowed, 118–123, 185n13
      through rules, 121
   by action, 119
   by connection, 120
   status inequities, 121, 124, 132,
      185n17, 18
culture
   cultural blueprint, 8
   cultural dynamics, 11
   described, 31–32
      as property of social groups,
         172n2
   idioculture, 31–32

della Porta, Donatella, 15
democracy
   as action, 4
   defined, 3–4
   definitional problems, 4
   democratizing qualities of activist
      groups, 134
   how eroded, 135
   implications for making
      democracy, 138–140
   non-democratic aspects, 121,
      134
   in conversation, 186n1
Democratic Party
   Pittsburgh, 5
doxa, 169n32
Duchesne, Sophie, 88, 124
dynamics
   cultural, 11
   interactions, 11, 168n28
   internal, 9
   preserved in study, 8, 10

eco-terrorism, 41
Ecology Now (EN)
  kinds of members, 52
  leadership, 124
Eliasoph, Nina, 83
Eliminating Police Violence Together
    (EPTV)
  debates over who belongs, 57–59
  problem, classification of, 104–105
  racial dynamics, 58
  storytelling, 106
Emirbayer, Mustafa
  agency, 38
  process models, 40
emotion
  affective cohesion, 184n5
    positive style, 129–130
    unfriendly style, 130
  Animal Liberation League (ALL)
    mood of, 46–49
  boundaries, 64, 180n14
  interpersonal character, 111–112,
    131–132
  membership, 69
  negative interactions, 111
  positive interactions, 110, 115–117
End the War and Occupation
    Committee (EWOC)
  leadership, 78
  membership, 77
environmentalist group
  scope of problem, 87–88
  talk of internal dynamics, 118
ethics
  in assessments of opportunities, 90
  in research, 140

faith groups, 92–93
Fine, Gary Alan
  idioculture, 31–32
  talk in activism, 112
frames, 5
  as different from defining the
    problem, 82
  as instrumental, 82
  internal dynamics, 8, 167n19
  of opportunity/need, 6

gender
  diverse group, 128

inequities, 121
Gilmore, Ruth Wilson, 135, 140
GLBT, 54, 63, 81, 121
  scope of problem, 86–87
grassroots activism
  See activist groups
Greenview Against Drugs (GAD)
  as task team, 30
  categories and names, 29
  mission logic, 62

Haegel, Florence, 88, 124
Heimer, Carol, 94
hermeneutics
  first-order and second order
    interpretations, 40
Hirschman, Alberto O., 66

ideological character
  case comparison, 104–107
  creation of, 82–83, 85, 107–108,
    181n6
  evoked, 87
  See also problem, definition of
interpersonal character
  as established by rules, 127, 131,
    186n21
  case comparison, 128–131
  of activist groups, 110, 111, 131–132,
    183n3

Jasper, James, 39
Johnston, Hank, 83

Kelley, Robin D. G., 3
Kleinman, Sheryl, 120
Kurzman, Charles, 39

leadership
  Animal Liberation League (ALL),
    130–131
  as problematic, 125–126
  as unacknowledged, 124–125
  cognitive centrality, 101–103, 139,
    187n18
  disavowed, 124–126
  End the War and Occupation
    Committee (EWOC), 78
  focused mission, 19–20
  See credibility

leadership (*continued*)
  status inequities, 124
  structural rigidity, 20–22
  turning points, 126–128
Lichterman, Paul
  idea of a forum, 99
  implicit meanings, 12
  learning, 100
  talk, 83

Marx, Karl, 32
Massey, Doreen, 15
McAdam, Doug
  activism as a collaborative cultural
    project, 31
  membership, 65
Mead, George Herbert, 38
media
  absence, 24
  group performance, 61
  group possibilities, 36
  publicity of activist event, 23
  relationship to, 182n16
  stories adapted from, 105
  tactics to attract, 43, 105
meetings
  difficult to find, 29
  easy to find, 27
  moral paths of, 92
  no agenda, 28
  rules, informal and official, 127,
    186n21
Melucci, Alberto, 31
membership
  as action, 68–69
  as emotional, 69
  as gradual process, 67
  case comparisons, 75–79
  heterogeneous, 7
  meaning of, 65–68, 180n21
  newcomers, 73–75
  ordinary, 11
  overlap among activist groups, 68–69
  size and kinds of, 22, 45, 52, 53
Mische, Ann
  agency, 38
  process models, 40
Moloch, Harvey
  cause and effect, 35
  comparative study of Ventura and

    Santa Barbara, 33
  rolling inertia, 34
  See also sequences, path-dependent
moral
  paths, 92–93
  principles, 90
    indirect, 91, 182n15
  See also Smith, Christian
  status of problem, 90–92
MoveOn, 20
  New Army of Revolution (NAR)
    membership overlap with, 64

National Rifle Association (NRA), 19,
  59, 105
  See Stop Gun Violence (SGA)
New Army of Revolution (NAR)
  case example of trajectories, 20–22
  MoveOn, membership overlap, 64
newcomers, 73–75
  as disruptive, 73
  emotional dynamics, 130
  not welcomed, 74–75
  welcomed, 65
No War Committee (NWC)
  newcomers, 74
  recruitment, 72
  talk about efforts, 116
  talk about scope, 88–89

Oliver, Pam, 83
organizational character
  case comparison, 75–79
  defined, 53–55
  lingering effects, 79
  organizational field, 170n42

Patriot Act, 76, 77
Pierson, Paul, 36
Pittsburgh Antiwar Network (PAN)
  problem, classification of, 96–99
  problem, scope of, 87
  problematic attendance, 71
Pittsburgh, PA
  economy, 5, 27
  income, 164n8
  party politics, 5
  racial politics, 5
Planet Protection Society (PPS), 128–131
  affective cohesion, 129

political imagination, 85–88
    external discussion as expanded, 86
    internal discussion as limited, 86
    narrowed, 85–86, 108, 134
        by capacities, 186n3
political opportunity, 12, 50
    ethical criteria, 90
    studies of, 182n12
Polletta, Francesca, 106
Pred, Allan, 32
problem, classification of, 93–94
    case comparison, 104–105
    representative knowledge, 94–96
    unique knowledge, 96–99
problem, definition of
    as different from movement frames, 82
    collective identity, 7–8, 166n17, 181n3
    ideological character, 82, 107–108
    moral paths, 92–93
    moral status, 90–92
    See also political imagination
    settled, 87
    shapes action, 107
    through political talk, 88–90
publicity
    Animal Liberation League (ALL)
        events, 45
    Center for Progressive Values (CPV), 16
    of activist groups, 5–6

race
    dynamics of activist groups, 58–61
    group belonging, 28–29
    inequities, 121
    politics, 5
Radical Cheerleaders, 16
Raging Grannies, 16
REBORN
    group rules, 126–127
    membership and action, 68
    self-definition, 54
recruitment, 35
    as activist continuity, 70
    case comparison, 75–79
    interpersonal character of activist
        groups, 110–111, 183–184n4
    of audience, 29
    of new members, 72–73
    off the agenda, 72
    problematic attendance, 71

Republican Party
    Pittsburgh, 5
research methodology
    activist groups
        excluded from study, 164–165n9
        included in study, 6–7
    case comparison, 75–78, 104–107,
        128–131
    coding
        of emotions, 180n23
        of leadership, 125
        of time, 49–50
    comparative and longitudinal data,
        8–9, 135
    described, 8–15
    documents, 11–12
    ethics, 140
    ethnographic observations, 9–10
    group processes, 10, 11, 88, 168n26,
        174n23, 186n9
    limitations of study, 187n13
    question, 7
    semi-structured interviews, 11
    skewed-sampling, 7–8, 135
    studying activist groups, 8–12
Ricouer, Paul, 89
RISE, 70
    change in dynamics, 127
Rucht, Dieter, 15
rules, informal and official, 126, 127,
        131, 186n21
    as ways to relate, 25, 111

Sanders, Lynn M., 121
SECURE
    disputes over belonging, 61–63
    talk avoided, 114
sequences, path-dependent
    agency, 37–38, 175–176n35
        time as key, 176–177n40
    as revealed by comparative data, 135
    as revealed by longitudinal data,
        137–138
    cause and effect, 35
    constrained, 34, 36, 174–175n26
    democracy eroded, 135
    described, 32–33
        in geography, 173n7
    in time, 34–37, 39, 41, 174n22,
        176–177n40

sequences, path-dependent (*continued*)
  patterns studied, 174n23
  properties of, 33–35
  self-reinforcing, 35, 49, 110, 114,
    128, 174n24
  theory of, 32–33
  Tilly, Charles, 34
  turning points
    described, 37–39
    in time, 39–41, 50, 79, 176–
      177n40
    incidental action, 41, 136–137
    talk of internal dynamics, 117–118
  unclear, 15
Sewell, William, 33
Smith, Christian, 40
  communities of believers, 53
  human reflection, 11
  intentionality, 136
  moral criteria, 55
social movement
  as analytic concept, 169n37
  family, 15–16, 171n43
  progressive family, 16
social movement organizations (SMOs)
  as different from activist groups, 6
  as focus of scholarship, 6
  meaning of membership, 180n21
  skewed sampling, 7–8
social structure
  influence of, 36, 175n30
  Marx, Karl, 32
  See also agency
Spivak, Gayatri, 82
status inequities
  See credibility
Steinberg, Mark, 3
Stoetzler, Marcel, 85
Stop Gun Violence (SGA)
  absence of talk, 112–113
  National Rifle Association, protest
    against, 105
  problem, classification of, 104–105
  racial dynamics, 59–61
Stop the Killing (StK)
  membership, 66
  problem, classification of, 94–96
  storytelling, 105
storytelling
  collective narration, 168–169n29

drug addiction, 28
  influence of media, 105
  of activist cooperation, 116–117
  problem, classification of
    case comparison, 105–106
Street Medics Action Group (SMAG)
  cognitive centrality, 103–104
  leadership, 124
structuration theory, 34

tactics
  affective cohesion, 130
  as group distinction, 63
  End the War and Occupation
    Committee (EWOC)
    recruitment, 78
  positive interactions, source of,
    115–116
talk
  absence of, 12, 112–113
    commonsense, 169n32
    shapes action, 135
  avoided, 10, 168n27
    about inequities, 118, 124
    as self-reinforcing sequence, 114,
      118
    turn to action, 115–117
  observed, 11, 168–169n29
  private and public, 132
  rules, informal and official, 126, 127,
    186n21
  See credibility
  turning points, 117–118
  vulnerability of, 126
task teams, 30
  culture, 31
Taylor, Verta, 17
Tilly, Charles
  collective action scholarship, 41
  sequences, path-dependent, 34
time
  agency, 30, 37–38, 175–176n35,
    176–177n40
  cultural blueprint, 8, 166–167n18
  origins of social movements, 6–7, 14,
    165–166n15
  See also dynamics
  See also sequences, path-dependent
  sequences of action, 10, 35–37,
    168n26, 174n22

turning points, 30, 38
    location of, 176–177n40
turning points
    agency, 37–39
    Animal Liberation League (ALL)
      case study, 41–51
    consequences of problem solving, 39,
      176n36
    GAYVOTE, 82
    in and over time, 30, 38, 39–40
    leadership, 126–128
    Marriage Now (MN), 81
    permissible talk, 117–118,
      132

problem, classification of, 98
Women against War (WAW), 81

Walsh, Katherine
    group processes, 11
    voluntary groups, 109
Women against War (WAW)
    deciding the issue, 81
    who belongs, 62

Yuval-Davis, Nira
    imagination, 85
    membership as emotional, 69
    politics of belonging, 56, 63

Lightning Source UK Ltd.
Milton Keynes UK
UKOW03f1918231216
290780UK00003B/48/P